THE MYTH
OF WOMEN'S
MASOCHISM

Also by Paula J. Caplan

BETWEEN WOMEN: LOWERING THE BARRIERS

THE MYTH
OF WOMEN'S
MASOCHISM

PAULA J. CAPLAN, Ph.D.

E. P. DUTTON ◇ NEW YORK

*For Kathryn Pauly Morgan and Frances M. Newman,
with love, respect, and appreciation*

*Portions of this book were originally published in part or
in somewhat different form as follows:*
Caplan, Paula J. *"The Myth of Women's Masochism,"*
American Psychologist 39 (2), 130–39. *Copyright 1984 by the
American Psychological Association. Used by permission of the publisher.*
"Sex-based Manipulation in the Clinical Psychologist's Workplace,"
International Journal of Women's Studies 8 (1985), 175–82.
With Ian Hall-McCorquodale:
"Mother-blaming in Major Clinical Journals,"
American Journal of Orthopsychiatry, *July 1985;*
and "The Scapegoating of Mothers: A Call for Change,"
American Journal of Orthopsychiatry, *October 1985.*
Copyright 1985 by the American Orthopsychiatric Association, Inc.

*Published in the United States by
E. P. Dutton, a division of New American Library,
2 Park Avenue, New York, N.Y. 10016*

Library of Congress Cataloging in Publication Data

Caplan, Paula J.
The myth of women's masochism.
Bibliography: p.
Includes index.
*1. Women—United States—Psychology. 2. Masochism.
3. Self-denial. 4. Mothers—United States—Psychology.
I. Title.*
HQ1206.C265   1985   155.6'33   85-10216

ISBN: 0-525-24361-5

*Published simultaneously in Canada by
Fitzhenry & Whiteside, Ltd., Ontario*

DESIGNED BY MARK O'CONNOR

COBE
10 9 8 7 6 5 4 3

Contents

Acknowledgments

I wish to acknowledge with love and thanks the support, patience, and ideas given to me as I wrote this book by my parents, Theda Ann Karchmer Caplan and Jerome Arnold Caplan, and my children, Emily Julia and Jeremy Benjamin.

My agent, Connie Clausen, and her assistant, Guy Kettelhack, were also warmly supportive and encouraging, and my editor, Jennifer Josephy, has been a rich source of thought and patience. Debbie Kay of the Ontario Institute for Studies in Education Library kindly carried out the computer search through the literature for me, and Isabelle Gibb of the same library helped locate many important materials.

I also wish to express my gratitude to the following, who in their various ways provided warmth, assistance, inspiration, and/or ideas: Sandra Bem, Graham Berman, Anne Braus, Joan M. Caplan, Jennifer Chambers, Phyllis Chesler, Ellen Cohen, the Cornell University Women's Studies Program, Ronnie deSousa, Family and Children's Services of Ithaca, New York, Gina Feldberg, Frieda Forman, the Gannett Health Center Psychological Services at Cornell University, Dan Goleman, Sherwood Gorbach, Margi Gorski-Sermer, Esther Greenglass, Beth Gutcheon, Amy Hanen, Elizabeth Harris, Tom Hopkins, Chaviva Hosek, Tazim Jadavji, Mary Kiely, Daria Love, Gael MacPherson, Maria Matias, John Murtagh, Joann O'Mara, David A. E. Pelteret, Susan Sanford Schumaker, Rachel Josefowitz Siegel, Efim Svirski, Patricia Tobin, Mary Roth Walsh, Georgina White, and Jeri Wine.

The fear that we cannot grow beyond whatever distortions we may find within ourselves keeps us docile and loyal and obedient, externally defined, and leads us to accept many facets of our oppression as women. . . .

. . . as we begin to recognize our deepest feelings, we begin to give up, of necessity, being satisfied with suffering and self-negation, and with the numbness which so often seems like their only alternative in our society.

—AUDRE LORDE

CHAPTER 1

Why Do You Do This to Yourself?

The powerless are regarded as bringing it on themselves.
—FAMILY THERAPIST MICHELE BOGRAD

When the man in my life hurts my feelings, or when I've put on weight, or when I'm frustrated about my children or my job, people sometimes ask me, "Why do you *do* this to yourself?," suggesting that I set out to put myself in unhappy situations. Such words are the most common expression of the myth of women's masochism, the myth that is responsible for profound and far-reaching emotional and physical harm to women and girls. "Masochism" means the need to derive pleasure from pain, and that is what usually comes to mind when we hear the word spoken. In the *Random House Dictionary of the English Language,* "masochism" is defined first as sexual masochism—"the condition in which sexual gratification depends on suffering, physical pain, and humiliation''—and second as "gratification gained from pain, deprivation, etc., inflicted or imposed on oneself, either as a result of one's own actions or the actions of others, esp. the tendency to seek this form of gratification.'' If my ten-year-old daughter were to hear women described as masochists, and if she went to the dictionary to see what that word meant, she would learn that women enjoy their suffering.

Often women's behavior is used as evidence of our innate masochism, our sickness, while men's similar behavior is used as evidence that they are real men and good providers. Thus, in 1974 Andrea Blanch wrote in the *Cornell Journal of Social Relations*:

> There is nothing essentially more masochistic about a housewife running herself ragged waiting on her husband hand and foot than there is about a businessman driving himself to a heart attack to further pad an already solid bank account. The only difference lies in the social value attributed to each activity.

The businessman's behavior is admired, but the housewife's is considered masochistic.

The recognition in recent years of women's second-class status has sparked the reassessment of such assumptions about women. When a theory causes serious harm, it is time to ask, "Are there other, reasonable ways to explain the behavior in question?" As we shall see, the behavior in women that has been called masochistic actually has other explanations, all of which reflect a healthier view of women, justify optimism about women's potential for happiness, and point the way to changes that will improve women's lives.

The belief that females seek out pain and suffering, that we have an innate *need* for misery, poisons every aspect of women's lives. Often, we are not even aware when the myth comes into play, since it is such a familar part of our culture that stories like the ones that follow are the rule rather than the exception.

◇ When Louise's husband insults her she may briefly feel angry at him, but quickly she says to herself, "I guess I brought this on myself. After all, I *did* choose to marry him." She recalls the many times she has heard it said, "Women's lot is to suffer. They really enjoy it, you know. Women aren't happy unless they are being martyrs." Her thinking all too often stops there. She does not go on to consider that before they married her husband did not insult her and that his insults have little or no relationship to her behavior toward him but (as some of his comments make clear) are expressions of his frustrations at work.

◇ Elizabeth is one of those Superwomen we hear so much about. She has three children and a full-time job as a teacher. When her children are making more than their usual demands on her, and it's an especially busy time at school, she becomes tired and frazzled. When she mentions this to her friends, some of them smile knowingly and say, unsympathetically, "You really are a masochist!" They do not consider that Elizabeth must work to feed her three children and that even if she didn't, she—like many women—relishes living life to the fullest, enjoying both motherhood and employment. Men have not taken on this "masochistic" double role, because they have been taught that primary responsibility for child care is beneath them and unmasculine. Men rarely have had the opportunity to take full advantage of what life has to offer in terms of personal *and* professional fulfillment, but the motives of women who fill dual roles are considered suspect and sick.

◇ Maria was a successful journalist before her son was born and she now stays home to care for him. Usually she takes great pleasure in the time she spends with him, but sometimes, when he has colicky and fretful spells, or when he goes for weeks without sleeping more than three hours in a row, she becomes irritated and exhausted. At those times, she thinks to herself, "It was my decision to stay home with him, so I brought this suffering on myself. Subconsciously, I must have *wanted* to suffer." Maria has been exposed to just enough personality theory through the media to learn popular explanations for her feelings. She does not take into account the fact that few things in life bring us only happiness and that it is simply part of maturity to make choices that, on balance, bring joy but often entail difficulties as well.

◇ Joanie wonders why she feels more attracted to men who act superior and cold toward her than to men who treat her well. It is because, like most women raised in this culture, she has severe problems with self-esteem. When a man is nice to her, she feels that he is a fool, that she has put one over on him by convincing him that she is terrific. When a man acts superior, however, any attention or approval she gets from him greatly enhances her self-esteem, since this is obviously a man who does not give praise lightly.

◇ Stephen was a friend of both Jane and Marshall, a married couple who were having serious conflicts in their relationship. On the one hand Stephen genuinely wanted to help them resolve their difficulties, but on the other hand he enjoyed feeling powerful and he found Jane very attractive. To his credit, he often had lunch with either Jane or Marshall, trying to help them work out their marital problems. One day he had lunch with Jane in a crowded French restaurant. Jane told him that Marshall had become furious and accused her of calling him a terrible father when, in fact, she had only asked him to listen to their children describe their first day at school. Irritated because Jane had not stood up to Marshall, Stephen shouted at her, "No wonder he treats you badly! You're such a weak, sniveling little thing!" Jane was cut to the quick, but so totally uncalled-for was Stephen's behavior that even in her unhappy state she saw that it had less to do with her than with some personal problem of Stephen's. After his outburst, Stephen sat back, looked at her, and grinned broadly. "You loved that, didn't you?" he said. "You felt like I had just fucked you!" Jane burst out laughing, so ludicrous to her was the idea of equating a vicious attack with lovemaking. But it was clear that Stephen, like many other men, believed that women want to suffer and even derive sexual pleasure from it.

In the world of work, similar things happen. Recently I had dinner with a woman who had majored in history thirty years before at Radcliffe College. Now in her mid-fifties, she was sad and depressed because her husband had left her for another woman. She had never worked outside the home and did not know what to do with all the empty hours in her day. She explained that after receiving her bachelor's degree she had refused the Harvard history department's offer of a place in their Ph.D. program. When I asked why, she said, "Women with Ph.D.s in history had no chance of getting decent teaching jobs at the college level then, and that was what I wanted to do. To get my degree would have meant setting out on a road to certain disappointment." She now wishes that she had gotten the Ph.D., because at least she would have some advanced academic credentials to her name. Even today it is difficult for women to receive tenured academic appointments, and thirty years ago it was nearly impossible. I thought that she had fully answered my question, but in her next breath she said, "I guess it was just my own need to fail." Already feeling old, unattractive, and unlovable because of the circumstances surrounding her divorce, somewhere she had also learned to berate herself as though she had made a masochistic choice. This woman had made a reasonable decision in light of the facts about the job market for women at the time, a decision that would help her to *avoid* frustration and disappointment. But she had been taught to believe that she had made the decision because she craved disappointment and humiliation. Most women have thought this way not only about themselves but also about other women. This is a common pattern for women: blaming themselves rather than other people or the larger society, because that is the "feminine" thing to do.

This book has grown out of my frustration and sadness over the time, energy, and love wasted by so many women and girls because of the myth. Like the concept of Original Sin, the concept of women's innate masochism limits the definition of who we are and what we can become and makes us feel ashamed and self-blaming. Only by understanding how the myth grew and what perpetuates it now, only by learning to recognize the numerous forms it takes in our lives, can we demolish the myth and open wide the possibilities for women freely to be and do what they want.

Once we realize that women's masochism is a myth, we shall see more clearly the real causes of women's unhappiness—those events that come from external sources, which can be changed. But it is not enough for us simply to believe that women are not masochistic. To protect ourselves and others from destructive self-blame and unnecessary acceptance of a harmful status quo, we need to recognize the various guises that the myth takes in our society.

I have spent many years attending case conferences at various mental hospitals and clinics in the United States and Canada, first as an undergraduate at Harvard University, as a graduate student at Duke University, as a clinical and research psychologist, and later as a teacher of psychology. It was that series of professional experiences that first drew my attention to the myth of women's masochism. Over and over I heard and accepted with only a flicker of discomfort other clinicians' claims that female patients needed to suffer. At first my reaction was embarrassment that patients of my sex could be so "sick," so despicable. What, I thought, could be more bizarre than seeking out pain or chasing after unhappiness? Pain is, by definition, unpleasant. What a twisted creature must the person be who actively seeks it!

I did not question these interpretations of women's behavior, because the people who voiced them spoke with the authority of Freud and decades of psychoanalytic history behind them. As Barbara Ehrenreich and Deirdre English wrote in their book, *For Her Own Good: 150 Years of the Experts' Advice to Women,* the psychoanalysts' view that women are inherently masochistic has, since the 1930s, "found mounting acceptance" both in the culture at large and among therapists in particular.

Being a graduate student in psychology is similar in many ways to being a medical student. You feel overwhelmed by the responsibility of trying to help others, and you feel that you are supposed to know more about other people than they know about themselves. Because of the feelings of inadequacy these expectations raise, you are vulnerable to the confidently stated claims that your clinical teachers make. Only later did I question these assertions. I was able to do this because of my increasing confidence that my own interpretations of people's behavior might sometimes have as much validity as those made by other clinicians, and because I came to recognize how extensively some of my colleagues' interpretations of patients' behavior was colored by their own needs.

I began seriously to question some traditional clinical beliefs when I worked at a clinic where most of the patients were young delinquents. Some had gotten into fights, some had stolen or destroyed other people's property, some were abusing alcohol or illegal drugs. It was never pleasant to trudge down to the detention home and talk to these unhappy, incarcerated youths, but one day, as I was talking with Frances Newman, a psychology intern at the clinic, she and I discovered that there was one kind of delinquent who upset us more than the others—the juvenile female prostitutes. These girls were often 13 or 14 years old, and after talking with any of them for an hour or two at the detention home Frances and I each experienced a kind of emptiness and depression that we rarely felt with the other delinquents. This led us to do some reading and research about these girls, and on the basis of that work we wrote a paper. Although clinicians often labeled juvenile female prostitutes "masochistic," we could find no signs that they enjoyed pain or humiliation, and we set out to see what was really going on. Some of our colleagues had written that such girls sought out degradation because they craved suffering and shame, but the girls told us that they loved the money they made, the power they had over their clients, and the admiration that they sometimes received for their bodies or their sexual skills. Some of them actually said, "I like everything about this life except the men I have to sleep with." When the men treated them badly they did not like it.

All of these girls came from severely emotionally deprived backgrounds. Most of their fathers had left home by the time the girls reached puberty, and many of their mothers were immature or emotionally disturbed. Thus, the girls had never had much in the way of love and attention. For them the money, power, and admiration they received as prostitutes were better than anything they had known before. The point was not that they sought the misery of such a life but that they had no reason to believe they could ever improve their situations. When Frances and I talked with these girls, the reason we felt so profoundly empty and depressed afterward was that the girls themselves felt empty and had devastatingly low self-esteem as a result of their early emotional deprivation. This low self-esteem and their impoverished backgrounds made it almost impossible for them to imagine having a better life.

After I presented our findings to a group composed mostly of male psychiatrists, one of them approached me in the hallway. Looking down at me from his height of more than six feet, he said patronizingly, "Well, Paula, that was a very interesting paper. From what you said it certainly sounded as though those girls are not consciously masochistic." But he went on to add, "However, no doubt they were *un*consciously masochistic."

According to this traditional view of female behavior, if girls say they love to suffer, that is taken as proof that females are masochists, but if they say they do not love to suffer or prefer not to suffer, that is proof that their masochism is unconscious. Because of no-win theories like this, I became interested in understanding and dispelling the myth of women's masochism.

Throughout history women have frequently had to endure some suffering to get what they enjoyed, but that is worlds away from *wanting* to suffer. They have often been in situations that did not make them happy but they had no way to move into better ones without taking a big chance that they would end up even worse off. For such women to stay in their original, less than happy situation is also a far cry from hungering after pain and sorrow. None of this has kept psychiatrists, psychologists, and social workers from developing intricate theories designed to prove that women are naturally masochistic.

In the course of my work, I realized what a denial of women's dignity it is when mental health professionals spend years working with a patient, helping her to understand the many ways she "needs to" bring her misery on herself. These same professionals, in case conferences and supervision of therapists in training, transmit the message that it is somehow unprofessional or inappropriate to tell patients what strengths and other good characteristics they see in them. Even many therapists who would not call such praise inappropriate never offer it to their own patients. Their students, using them as models, do not learn to do so either. The myth that women are natural masochists contributes to a difference in attitude toward suffering women and men, so that the focus of many therapists tends to be on discovering how women supposedly bring suffering on themselves but on encouraging males to be "real men" and to refuse to put up with whatever gets in the way of their happiness.

A misogynist society has created a myriad of situations that make women unhappy. And then that same society uses the myth of women's masochism to blame the women themselves for their misery. Women are far more likely than men to be held responsible if anything goes wrong in their relationships or if harm befalls their children. In the work place women are underpaid and subjected to sexual harassment or other mistreatment because of their sex. And at every newsstand and on television females see degrading, humiliating, pornographic depictions of women and young girls. As a psychologist, a mother, a daughter, and a friend, I have never met a woman who sought out these unequal responsibilities, frustrations, and degradations. I have never spoken to a woman who would not gladly have waved a magic wand, if she could, to banish the painful aspects of her life. But such common aphorisms as "Women *like* to suffer," Jewish mother jokes, pornographers' depictions of smiling women in bondage, and—appallingly—mental health workers' confident assumptions that their women patients are masochists show that the myth of women's masochism still thrives.

The myth serves two purposes: It leads both women and men to believe that women are deeply, inevitably pathological—for is it not sick to enjoy misery?—and it is a powerful block against social action that could help women. Because of the myth, women's problems can be attributed to our deep-seated psychological needs, not to the social institutions that really are the primary causes of the trouble.

Women have been placed in a tragic, Catch-22 situation. We are told in a thousand different ways that "real women don't blame others," whether the "others" are individuals close to us or larger, impersonal social institutions. *Real women* are patient, selfless, and able to give whatever it takes to make a relationship or job successful. Women who do not behave in those ways usually face a painful fate. Developing a sense of their identity and self-worth is difficult, for a woman who does not take the blame for her troubles is not "feminine," and femininity traditionally constitutes a significant portion of a woman's identity.

Once we see where our problems come from, part of a healthy response is anger, often leading us to protest against our situation. But anger is neither womanly nor feminine. Harvard University psychologist Carol Gilligan and Wellesley College psychiatrist Jean Baker Miller have pointed out that a guiding principle of women's lives is the importance of establishing and maintaining close personal relationships. Anger and blame tend to drive people away—even if only temporarily—and this is a devastating consequence; for we have learned to take much pleasure from our relationships and to believe that "real women" maintain closeness with others, regardless of the cost to themselves. A real woman nurtures, a real woman never stops giving, a real woman does not get angry (except, occasionally, in defense of her children or her man) or blame others for her problems. She suffers in silence.

One still hears comments such as, "If women would just stay home where they belong, our unemployment problems would be solved" or, "Women's liberation is making men impotent." As social scientists like Gordon Allport have been warning for decades, oppressed groups are likely to be blamed for their society's problems. Indeed, women have been blamed both for life's inevitable unhappiness—no relationship or job is always easy—and for the troubles that result from women's second-class status in society. It is no accident that our society tends to blame women for their own troubles as well as for those of men and children. These tendencies are the defining characteristics of scapegoating. Scapegoating a group forces its members to spend a lot of energy defending themselves against charges that they are hurting *other* people. In this way a group's resources for protecting its own members and maintaining its dignity are seriously depleted. This is particularly true for women, since asserting and defending oneself is not perceived as womanly. We have been taught that men will defend and protect us, that we should value the tradition of chivalry. But when chivalry primarily amounts to having doors opened and coats held for us and not to genuine sharing of the burdens of child care or to comprehensive implementation of equal pay legislation, then chivalry is a cover-up. We are left without men to defend us, yet feeling uncomfortable about defending ourselves.

The myth of women's masochism has helped to justify the view of women as appropriate targets of mockery and of sexual objectification and depersonalization, as the appropriate people to carry out society's low-status work of housekeeping and child rearing, and as the objects of verbal degradation and physical abuse for men who feel frustrated or insecure. All such treatment is part of the same view of women, and no female escapes. How many of us have avoided rape, sexual abuse by a man (usually a family member), physical beatings by a male, sexual harassment, or emotional abuse? On September 27, 1984, actress Farrah Fawcett told a television audience that, in preparation for her film about wife abuse, *The Burning Bed,* she watched videotapes of wife batterers, and a typical comment from one man was, "What am I supposed to do when she nags me?" Sadly, we are not surprised to hear such words. We know that many men feel that way, that society supports the notions that women who are beaten have asked for it (because they are nags and because they need to suffer). The power of that pervasive attitude becomes clearer if we imagine how different it would sound for a *woman* to say, "Sure, I beat him up. What am I supposed to do when he nags me?" In a study that psychology doctoral student Nicole Walton-Allen and I did last year, well-educated, middle-class adults of both sexes said they thought that abused husbands were highly unlikely to stay with their abusive wives, but abused wives were likely to stay with the men who beat them—often because they were masochistic! Our discovery was particularly shocking in view of the large number of media stories in recent years that have publicized the *real* reasons battered women stay with their abusers, such as economic necessity, fear of hurting the children by depriving them of their father, or terror that people will think that they have failed in their wifely duty. Our research makes it clear how deeply the myth of women's masochism is entrenched in our society, how resistant it is, even in the face of evidence that disproves it.

As long as the myth that women have an innate need to

suffer is maintained, millions of women will be needlessly unhappy. They will be afraid to stand up for themselves, believing themselves unfeminine if they do so, and—what is more destructive—believing that they have no power to change, that the evil, the masochism, is within them.

In the face of widespread support of the myth of women's masochism, there has been an occasional voice of reason. Psychiatrist Robert Robertiello, as long ago as 1970, wrote: "In my opinion, masochism can never be considered part of normal development. . . . And it is hardly the exclusive province of women." In 1981 Martin Silverman wrote in the *Journal of the American Psychoanalytic Association* that masochism in women is not a normal, inevitable trait. But few have listened to these voices, and books, newspapers, magazines, and television programs continue to be forums for professionals who give women "expert" advice about their masochistic propensities. In addition, the millions of people who at some time in their lives seek psychotherapy are also exposed to mental health workers who believe the myth. Often, therapists fail to explore nonmasochistic reasons for women's behavior and simply set out to discover what form the masochism that they know is there takes in a particular client. We do not have to be told explicitly that women are masochists; we learn it by osmosis when the mental health professionals around us do not question the belief but instead put their talents and training into identifying its various alleged forms.

There are occasional reports in the mental health literature of extreme cases of "masochism." For example, one seventy-nine-year-old man apparently sought sexual stimulation by wiring his penis to a radio transmitter and rheostat so that he could give himself 12-volt electrical shocks. In fact, most of these extreme cases are men. Furthermore, many of them are plagued by guilt—about sex or about other matters—and the pain serves to ease that guilt. Thus, it is unclear how many of these people legitimately qualify for the label of one who enjoys pain for its own sake. However, these extreme cases are not the subject of this book. This book is about what happens to most women in their daily lives, to many healthy women who are mislabeled masochistic, and to many women who are called disturbed, either on the grounds that they are masochistic or that they are not willing to suffer enough.

In fact, most of the behavior in women that has been called masochistic is actually one of the following:

◇ The ability to delay gratification, wait for rewards and pleasure, or attempt to earn happiness through effort;

◇ The capacity to put other people's needs ahead of one's own;

◇ The belief, based on past experience, that what one has is about all one can expect to get; or

◇ The effort to *avoid* punishment, rejection, or guilt.

Even the last of these has been mislabeled as the need to suffer. Women's efforts to avoid pain have been twisted into "proof" that they eagerly seek it out. The most grotesque case of this distortion is the battered wife who stays with her husband because she has good reason to believe that, if she leaves, he will find and kill both her and her children. Such women have often been accused of staying because they enjoy pain and fear.

A new understanding of women's behavior and motives will not come all at once. My patients often feel embarrassed to discover that the source of the problem in some agonizing experience was the same old conflict or mistaken assumption that we had identified months before, this time in a slightly different form or with a different person. Of course, there is no need for them to be embarrassed; this is what happens to us all when we try to understand the previously unquestioned feelings and beliefs that control our lives. The myth of women's masochism is one of these beliefs—a web, woven of countless, almost imperceptible threads that depend on each other for their stability. Once we begin to untangle the threads, we begin to weaken the web that enmeshes us in passivity and self-blame.

CHAPTER 2

What the "Experts" Have Said

Eve, the first human being who chose to disobey authority, was brought low; from the day she disobeyed, her right to choose was severely restricted. —ELIZABETH WAITES

When authorities tell us that women are naturally masochistic, we don't have to accept their word as gospel even though by refusing to believe their claims we risk being brought low, like Eve. We wouldn't buy an appliance without knowing something about how it works and what it was designed to do, and the same rule should apply for all of us as "consumers" of personality theory. Like all salespeople, personality "experts" can be intimidating because of their aura of mystery, because they want us to think that they have some special knowledge. We are often left feeling we couldn't possibly understand the subtleties of what they know, so we satisfy ourselves with relying on their expertise. There is nothing very special or complicated about what the "experts" have said about women and masochism, but in order to know how to rid ourselves of the myth, we need to understand what has been said and why the myth has been allowed to stand largely unchallenged.

The first theorists to propose that women are naturally, inevitably masochistic were psychoanalysts who believed with Freud that "biology is destiny" and that our bodies dictate what happens in our minds and feelings. In women's bodies, they felt, were the seeds of their biologically determined masochism. Freud was, of course, the most influential of the early theorists. Largely because of his gurulike aura, the people who worked most closely with him rarely challenged his basic ideas. If they did, they were usually forced out of his inner circle. And the occasional person who did put forth a challenge was likely to be dismissed as a kind of outlaw or nut. Therefore, Freud's theoretical assumptions were rarely subjected to outside analysis. It is important to understand the vacuum in which Freud worked, because he and his followers had such an overwhelming impact on our culture, and his assumptions have only been widely and effectively challenged in the past ten or fifteen years, largely as a result of the feminist movement.

Helene Deutsch, who was first a psychoanalytic patient of Freud's and later one of his most loyal disciples, became famous (and more recently, infamous) for her statement that women are *naturally* masochistic, narcissistic, and passive. Those, she said, were the three fundamental feminine traits. (Considering the strict limits the nineteenth-century Viennese placed on their women's behavior, Deutsch's conclusion is not surprising.) Deutsch suggested that a girl becomes masochistic when she discovers that her clitoris is an "inadequate organ" for the release of her sexual excitement and transfers her sexual pleasure to the "passive" vagina. This process leads to masochism because in order to feel sexual excitement in her vagina she needs to be overpowered by a male, according to Deutsch. Related to this is Freud's notion that the girl is biologically destined to turn her aggression inward, a process which is helped by her resolution of her sexual desire for her father. When she learns that she will be punished for her desires, she attempts to renounce them, in part by becoming passive rather than by actively pursuing her aim. Freud called this a major component of female "masochism," although he himself explained this pattern not as a fundamental enjoyment of passivity and pain but largely as a consequence of the girl's fear of punishment by her mother and need to keep her mother's love.

The most hilariously extreme form of the notion that woman's body leads her to masochism was written by analyst Marie Bonaparte, who trained with Freud and was an ardent admirer and follower of his. She wrote: "In coitus, the woman, in effect, is subjected to a sort of beating by the man's penis. She receives its blows and often, even, loves their violence." Bonaparte said that the moment of conception embodied the foundation of women's natural masochism: ". . . the fecundation of the female cell is initiated by a kind of wound; in its way, the female cell is primordially masochistic." She would have us believe that heterosexual intercourse is a beating and that the ovum itself—a single, unconscious cell—is masochistic.

It was sex expert Dr. Richard von Krafft-Ebing who, in his classic tome *Psychopathia Sexualis* at the turn of the century, coined the term "masochism" and defined it as "the wish to suffer pain and be subjected to force." He had derived the term "masochism" from the name of the author of *Venus in Furs*, Leopold von Sacher-Masoch, who had created a caricature of a dominant/submissive heterosexual relationship. Interestingly, in that story it was the male character who would now be called the masochist, because he was subservient to his mistress's whims and desires. But as Clea Elfi Kore pointed out in her Stanford University doctoral dissertation in 1983 on von Sacher-Masoch, the "Masochian" woman is the construct of a male imagination and acts in accordance with some men's fantasies; such men wish for women who would suffer for them. The female masochist, then, is a creation based not on accurate observations of most women's behavior but rather on the wishes of some men to be dominant and domineering.

Once Krafft-Ebing had coined the word, it was not long before Freud began to inquire into its causes. Although Freud wrote about masochism in both sexes, he explicitly said many times that masochism *is* feminine. Even masochistic behavior in a man was labeled feminine by Freud, so that masochism, which was not considered normal or typical in a man, was thought to be both in a woman. The belief that masochism is always feminine gained such widespread acceptance among psychotherapists that, as authors Barbara Ehrenreich and Deirdre English observed, "The idea that women were masochistic seemed to solve everything" and therapists who were treating women who wanted to stop doing menial labor or to refuse to submit to sexual humiliation believed that the women were rejecting their femininity and behaving unnaturally. They cite Dr. Hendrik Ruitenbeek's claim in *Psychoanalysis and Female Sexuality* in 1966 that there were too many women who "want to do or to get something for themselves rather than merely to reflect the achievement of their husbands." These women were regarded as fighting against their masochistic feminine nature, and that struggle was the cause of their unhappiness.

Having said that women were masochistic, Freud began to explain *why* they were that way. He wrote different things at different times on this subject and made little or no attempt to reconcile his various theories. But of all the things he wrote, only one part of one of his theories is really about masochism, and that is part of what is called his "death instinct" theory. In order to understand the theory, it is important to know how Freud became interested in masochism. He had taken note in his patients of what he called the "masochistic repetition compulsion," that is, the tendency to fall into the same type of situation or to become involved with the same type of person who always brings one unhappiness. He wondered what might cause this repetition. The explanation he

proposed was as follows: People are born with two basic instincts—Eros and Thanatos, or the life and death instincts. Eros
includes the energy that drives humans to struggle to survive
and reproduce; Thanatos is the drive to return to the previous
inanimate state, the state we are in before we are born. Any
behavior that seemed to be creative or positive was said to be
a manifestation of Eros, and any behavior that seemed self-
defeating or self-destructive was said to be a manifestation of
Thanatos, a drive—in a sense—toward death. Freud suggested that when people continually put themselves in situations that bring them sorrow and pain, their death instinct is
at work. However, that does not really tell us much; in fact,
it doesn't explain anything. Freud never *proved* there was a
death instinct; he only suggested that there was one. After all,
we don't conclude that because people drive cars there must
be an automobile-driving instinct. Perhaps Freud's description of the death instinct is not much more than a way of saying that when we see people getting into unhappy situations
we should not be surprised, because self-harm is natural. If
we believe that, it might leave us feeling pretty hopeless about
trying to avoid behaving in ways that make us unhappy.

Interestingly, Freud's Thanatos theory is the only theory
I have found that really *is* about the seeking out of pain and
suffering. Every other theory that is supposedly about "masochism" is instead about other things.

Let us look at a few examples of theories about women
and "masochism" that are not really about masochism at all.
First, we turn to back to Freud. In the same book, *Beyond
the Pleasure Principle,* in which he wrote that Thanatos gives
rise to repetition compulsion, Freud also said that repetition
compulsion comes from Eros, the survival/creativity instinct!
He never reconciled these two very different explanations, but
here is his Eros explanation, which is probably a very accurate account of the motivation of such compulsions: The
"masochistic" repetition compulsion arises because the person has had a horribly upsetting experience and tries to relive
that kind of experience in order to be better prepared and less

devastated if it should happen again. In other words, his Eros explanation of so-called masochistic behavior is actually a description of the attempt to *avoid* pain.

In a separate paper on masochism published four years after *Beyond the Pleasure Principle,* Freud proposed yet another explanation of masochism. He said that masochists seek pain in order to expiate some guilt that troubles them. This is similar to punishing a child for wrongdoing. Often, a child who is not punished for some transgression will suffer longer and more intensely than one who is punished. Once the parent has punished the child, the child often feels great relief and can get on with living. Since feeling guilty is unpleasant, it makes no sense to label masochistic a person who wants to be punished or hurt *so that the guilt will go away.* Such behavior would properly be called a wish to *end* the discomfort of guilt, not the seeking out and enjoyment of pain for its own sake.

In still another paper, " 'A Child is Being Beaten': A Contribution to the Study of the Origin of Sexual Perversions,'' Freud proposed a quite different explanation of masochism, beginning with the observation that a number of his patients who "obsessively" masturbated had reported being aroused by the fantasy of a child being beaten. It was crucial for the beating to occur only in fantasy and seem not to do a serious injury. Witnessing an actual beating was not pleasurable for Freud's patients, nor was imagining serious harm to the child who was being hit. Freud believed that these fantasies were pleasurable because they were the products of the fantasizer's rivalry with her or his siblings for their father's affection. As these patients grew up, the nature of their fantasies changed; at first, they imagined another child being beaten, but later they imagined themselves as the object of the blows. Freud called the later fantasy masochistic and suggested that this change was the patients' self-punishment for their forbidden Oedipal feelings—their love or sexual longing—for their father. (It was that longing that had led to the sibling rivalry, which gave rise to the initial fantasy.) Thus,

Freud concluded, "masochism is not the manifestation of a primary instinct" but a turning toward the self of the anger at the sibling. This theory, then, is not so much about the need to suffer as about the attempt to conceal from oneself one's forbidden—and punishable—feelings.

Psychiatrist Wilhelm Reich, like Freud in the theory just described, concentrated his discussion on sexuality, identifying masochism as the wish to be beaten in order to be sexually aroused. But he explained sexual masochism by saying that for both males and females sex often seems dangerous or guilt-laden, and for such people sexual arousal becomes difficult until they have been punished, after which they feel that the danger has passed. He suggested that for males the sense of danger comes from the fear that they will be castrated as punishment for their sexual desires. For females, sex has long been laden with guilt, because women were not supposed to have strong sexual needs, so women have often feared their sexual feelings. Reich wrote that when a person

> senses the mounting of the pleasure as a danger of melting or bursting but naturally longs for the pleasurable release, he [sic] develops the attitude of expecting and beseeching others to help him achieve release, i.e., to help him to burst, a sensation which he simultaneously fears and wards off.

Almost any girl who has passed through adolescence in North America has known the temptation of getting drunk or convincing herself that she is deeply in love, in order to "justify" her sexual activity; she seeks any excuse to feel absolved of the guilt she has been taught to feel about sexual activity. This is very close to Reich's explanation of what he misnamed "masochistic" behavior. Both for Reich's patients and for our high school girls, it is inaccurate and confusing to observe what Reich called "striving toward the pleasurable goal which lies behind" the pain or unpleasantness and call it "masochistic striving" as Reich did. This mislabeling can even be damaging, since it leads us to regard as "sick" some behavior that is actually not such a bad way to cope with a difficult dilemma.

Let us look at one more theory that is supposedly about masochism, this time a contemporary one from Toronto psychoanalyst Alan Parkin's article in 1980 about women's masochism in the *International Journal of Psychoanalysis*. In that article, Parkin recounts only one case history, and here is what he offers as the sum total of evidence that his patient, whom he calls "Miss C," is a masochist:

> There were also some indications that she felt herself to be abused and exploited by those with whom she had business or professional relationships: her physician who had prescribed a birth control pill was blamed for causing a malignant growth which was discovered in her breast, the mechanics who repaired her car defrauded her in ways to which she passively acquiesced, and merchants sold her goods which she frequently felt were not as represented. Occasionally, she sought legal opinion about her rights but rarely proceeded to litigation.

In that little story I found no signs that "Miss C" enjoyed her upsetting experiences. Furthermore, Miss C's experience with the physician, the birth control pill, and the tumor is presented with the implication that (1) she had *sought out* such suffering, and (2) that she perhaps knew that if she took the pill she might develop a malignant growth, though Parkin does not suggest that the doctor ought to have warned her of the possible side effects. Although it is possible that the pill did not cause the tumor, the important point is that Parkin suggests neither that possibility nor that the physician ought to have warned her of the risk of a malignancy. Instead, he focuses on presenting her response as though it were a sign of masochism.

In addition, for a woman to be defrauded by automobile mechanics is a depressingly common occurrence, and in the face of such treatment, unless a woman is unusually well informed about car repair, there is little recourse. Finally, many people of both sexes have been sold goods that were not what the sellers claimed they were. However, all of this is Parkin's "evidence" that his patient is masochistic. Coming at the end, as though it were the final, convincing flourish, is Parkin's statement that Miss C rarely proceeded to litigation. One implication of this is that if you are not masochistic you seek legal redress and proceed to litigation, but that of course is just not true. In fact, knowing what we do about how many psychoanalysts interpret women's behavior, it is likely that if Miss C *had* regularly proceeded to litigation, she would have been diagnosed as hysterical, castrating, or something equally distasteful or contemptuous. Furthermore, although Parkin offers Miss C's behavior as proof that she is a masochist, he does not suggest that the people who mistreated her might have been sadistic or otherwise disturbed. Although this book is not about sadism—the enjoyment of causing pain to others—it is worth taking note here of the fact that in clinical practice men's aggressiveness and cruelty are less likely to be called sadistic than women's passivity and patience are to be called masochistic, and although there has long been a large body of theory about women's supposedly innate masochism, men's learned aggressiveness and belligerence—reflected in the nuclear arms race, for example—have only recently come under close, serious scrutiny as signs of sadism. Thus, Parkin was operating within the contemporary tradition of studying women's "masochism" while failing to regard, for example, the possibly hostile, greedy auto mechanics as power-hungry, money-grubbing, and sadistic.

After presenting Miss C's case history, Parkin proposes an explanation of why women seek pain. As do so many psychoanalysts when trying to explain any kind of emotional problem, Parkin blames the mother. He says that a masochist is a person filled with rage and hate, and this hate is "a reaction to the hate or at least the withholding of love of an emotionally disturbed mother." His theory is multilayered, but at the deepest level Parkin says that the masochistic daughter has a mother who is "hugely aggressive" with "prominent . . . phallic characteristics." Analysts typically use this last term to describe women who are assertive and achievement-oriented. The daughter, says Parkin, behaves in as hateful, contemptuous, or withholding a way as her mother did toward her. He writes that the "masochistic" daughter's behavior is a way of saying, "I am just as hateful and contemptuous as my mother—whom I love—so you should love me." Even if we believed this description of mother-daughter dynamics, how could we call pain-seeking behavior the daughter's *efforts to be loved*?

Even more recently, New York psychoanalyst Natalie Shainess wrote in 1984 about women and masochism in her book, *Sweet Suffering: Woman as Victim.* The title itself can only strengthen the prejudiced view of many readers that women find suffering sweet. Shainess states initially that women's masochism is not innate; however, she then spends most of her book relating stories about "masochistic" women that do not lead the reader to feel much compassion for them or to believe that women can do much to stop being masochistic. Rather, the reader is overwhelmed by the weight of Shainess's evidence that women seek out their suffering. For example, she writes about a "masochist" called Lucille, who worked in a public relations firm. According to Shainess, when Lucille was asked to justify to a client the program that her firm was proposing, she did well "until suddenly the client asked a rather technical question about some radio spots that were planned." Shainess says that Lucille replied: "I don't know. . . . I'm sorry, but it just never occurred to me that this was important. I guess I wasn't as thorough as I should have been. I'm sorry. . . ." A few weeks later, according to Shainess, "when an executive was named for this account, Lucille was passed over and another woman, whose contribution to the project had been far less substantial, was designated. Lucille's response to this was to tell me that while she was unhappy, she was also relieved. 'I don't think I have the drive or the personality for an executive position,' she said.'' Shainess's implication is that Lucille's reply to the client's question was aimed to ensure that she would lose the account. However, this story is instead typical of many women, as well as men, who have little self-confidence. When asked a question they cannot answer, they feel instantly ashamed, afraid that they will be regarded as hopelessly incompetent, believing that their inferiority has now been revealed. Instead of saying calmly, "I hadn't yet considered that, but I can get the information for you in a few minutes (or tomorrow)," they apologize for their presumed incompetence. For such people, taking positions of increasing responsibility can be terrifying, since they live in constant fear that they will fail—*not* constant *need* to fail, but constant *fear* of failure.

In another of Shainess's examples of "masochistic" women, we read about Anne, whose husband had many extramarital affairs, each time returning to Anne, contrite and promising to reform. Sometimes, he slapped her, "once punching her so hard that she had to have a dentist repair the damage to her teeth." When Anne turned to her mother in her time of need, her mother "reminded Anne of her marriage contract—for better or worse—and she cautioned her about separating as that would throw Anne into a world where she had little status and only a limited ability to support herself." It seems to me that Shainess has demonstrated not that Anne was a masochist but that she was willing to put up with mistreatment because of the double fears of being regarded as a bad wife (she said, "Part of my job as a wife is to help him through difficult times") and of being thrust into an even more terrifying situation. These two fears were more frightening than the painful situation she was already enduring. Shainess herself goes on to point out that yet another fear—the fear of hurting her children by depriving them of their father through divorce—also kept her from leaving her husband.

It is not surprising that Shainess has misinterpreted women's behavior in this unflattering, pessimistic light, for she does not appear to have much faith in women. Indeed, she remarks that she has never met a "truly expansive woman" but has met many expansive men; this comment is particularly puzzling, since "expansive" means "having a generous spirit," a traditional feature of feminine behavior.

How have past and contemporary personality theorists gotten away with making such claims, with so grossly distorting and misinterpreting women's behavior that we are still regarded as innately pain-seeking? Worse still, how does this happen despite such voices of reason as that of psychiatrist Harold Blum, editor of the book *Female Psychology: Contemporary Psychoanalytic Views,* who wrote in 1977 that "there is no evidence that the human female has a greater endowment to derive pleasure from pain" than the human male and that he "would not regard masochism as an essential or organizing attribute of mature femininity." And Elizabeth Waites wrote in 1982 in the *Journal of the American Psychoanalytic Association* that men who need to regard women as passive, pliable, and stereotypic have a deep need to devalue women and then to deny that devaluation, a practice she calls a fetish. Even this insight into the less than admirable motives of the "experts" did not dampen the experts' enthusiasm for the belief that women are innately masochistic.

The professionals have been able to perpetuate the myth partly because of the powerful influence of a paper written by Sigmund Freud called "Negation." The paper is supremely important, because once Freud's "negation" premise is accepted, all of human behavior can be interpreted as support for Freudian theory. If a certain kind of behavior seems to support Freud's theories, we should be satisfied; if it seems to be the opposite of what those theories would lead us to expect, we can interpret the behavior as a "reaction formation" to the "real truth," since "reaction formation" was Freud's term for behaving in a way that is the *opposite* of what one feels; and if the behavior we observe does not seem in any way related to the theory, we can interpret it as a denial of the relevant feelings. So, if we "learn" from Freud, Deutsch, and Bonaparte that women are indubitably masochistic, when we see a woman in an unhappy situation, we have found "proof" of her masochism; when we see a woman who appears happy, she is no doubt denying her masochism or displaying a reaction formation against it, trying desperately not to show it; and when we see a woman who is neither unhappy nor happy, she must be avoiding dealing with her masochism.

This theory is not some artifact of only historical interest from the nineteenth century, for contemporary male Freudian analysts are taken terribly seriously. For example, consider Kurt Eissler, who has lately been in the news because of his objections to analyst Jeffrey Masson's questioning of the purity of Sigmund Freud's motives in constructing one aspect of his theory. Eissler, a guardian of the Freud Archives, wrote in 1977 in *The Psychoanalytic Study of the Child*: "The concept of feminine masochism is basic and necessary to a psychoanalysis of femininity even though the defenses against that masochism are 'the spirit of the present decade.' " Thus, anyone who says that women are not masochistic is simply being defensive. No doubt Eissler would consider this book one grand defensive maneuver.

Not only the psychoanalytic community but also society at large has helped to foster the myth. There is a continuing pervasive and powerful belief that it is important for women to stay "in their place," to take what is offered to them, and not to make a fuss. As my friend and colleague Karen Howe says, "Nagging is what it's called when a woman asks for something."

Recently, I began to wonder why people who are not mental health workers—and who, therefore, are not under pressure from their professional colleagues to agree that women are naturally masochistic—have been so willing, even eager, to adopt this theory. Many other aspects of traditional psychological or psychoanalytic theory have been discredited in recent years by lay people.

The masochism myth has been embraced so widely because, as we have seen, it helps to justify the continuing subjugation of women. At the turn of the century, when the theory was first formally proposed, women led lives that were so constricted and repressed that one way to rationalize their unequal status was to assume that they must enjoy suffering. Furthermore, espousing the theory that women "enjoy" pain makes the espouser feel important. Why? Because it is unlike much personality theory, which seems intuitively obvious, such as "Kids get depressed if their parents don't show that they love them." The claim that women enjoy what is by definition *not* enjoyable makes the speaker appear to have deeper psychological understanding than the rest of us.

Belief in the myth also allows people to feel superior to masochists. Precisely because it sounds so sick to enjoy and seek out pain and suffering, the person who believes that women do this feels far superior to, and greatly distanced from, these women and their unhappiness.

Furthermore, since "pleasure in pain" sounds so disturbed and since "masochism" has sexual connotations, the myth evokes kinky images. Someone who believes that women are masochistic becomes a voyeur; for such a person, looking at women and "understanding" their allegedly sick motives is like looking at animals in the zoo.

One other factor that has made it easy for people to accept the myth has been that proponents of theories about women's masochism have generally grounded their theory in women's physical characteristics. They observed many of the things about women—menstruation, sexual intercourse, childbirth, the possibility of rape, less muscular bodies than men—and noted that because all but the last of these are often accompanied by pain, and the last is a sign of weakness, suffering in women must somehow be natural. Connecting women's presumed masochism with these common physical experiences has seemed to some people to prove that the theory is true. If you are saying to yourself, "But no one *enjoys* that pain," then your thinking is freer and more advanced than the thinking of many of the so-called experts.

Sociobiologists like E. O. Wilson of Harvard are contemporary theorists who seek biological explanations for trends in human behavior, and many of them, like Alexander Pope, tend to think that "Whatever is, is right." In their view a current behavior pattern exists because it helped the human species to survive for millions of years. Some social theorists have gone from this claim to the warning that we should not attempt to make major changes in social arrangements, because if we do we risk interfering with human survival. By extension, this attitude implies that women are biologically predestined to suffer and that women's lot is to bleed and to feel pain, because if they did not, the species would die out. The sociobiologists are contemporary advocates of the early psychoanalytic notion that anatomy is destiny. There is a great deal wrong with this line of reasoning, and it is worth thinking about each of the physiologically based points in turn. First, the fact that women experience menstruation and childbirth may mean that they go through some pain and shedding of blood, but it does not follow that women seek out pain. Menstruation is not an option for women; it is part of our physical nature. And what women seek through pregnancy is children, not the pain of childbirth.

Heterosexual intercourse has been thought to give rise to masochism because it was assumed—at least for the sake of theory-construction—that for biological reasons intercourse has to take place with the woman underneath the man. However, it has been shown that women are not more likely to conceive in the missionary position than in other sexual positions, so the argument that women must "suffer" sexually in this way for the sake of species survival is not valid. It is also wrong, of course, to assume that the missionary position is painful and to assume that the main thing most women crave in sexual situations is penile penetration. For most women this is not the essence and totality of sexuality, an assumption that *The Hite Report: A Nationwide Study of Female Sexuality* finally should have laid to rest. For many women, the moment of penetration by a penis is not the crux of their experience of sexuality, and since women have various means of achiev-

ing sexual pleasure, the focus on penetration as the cornerstone of a woman's personality, leading her to become generally masochistic, seems completely misguided. It is also
incorrect to assume that woman's role in heterosexual intercourse is necessarily passive. Psychiatrist Ruth Moulton has
written, "*Receptive aims do not imply inertness:* the truly receptive vagina is grasping, secreting, and pleasure-giving
through its own functions rather than just through the eroti-
zation of pain." Moulton thus reminds us that even in the
missionary position one can move and experience pleasure,
not simply lie there passively and helplessly; one does not have
to find pleasure in intercourse through distorting real pain and
total passivity into eroticism.

That women can be raped does not mean women enjoy
pain any more than that men—who can be stabbed, murdered, or sodomized—enjoy pain. Finally, the fact that men
are often physically stronger than women might tend to make
some women feel physically inferior, but that is worlds away
from leading them to want to suffer.

A number of brave theorists, beginning with analyst Karen
Horney in Freud's time, have asserted that women are *not*
natural masochists. Freud is reputed to have been so irritated
by her criticism of him that he called her "the Danish cow."
Horney said that women's biology did not make them inevitably masochistic but did prepare them to accept silently society's imposition of unhappy conditions on their lives. Many
recent feminist theorists have said that society, by teaching
women to deny our own needs, makes us behave in ways that
can be misconstrued as a wish to suffer.

Psychoanalyst Clara Thompson wrote, for example, that
women's "masochism also often proves to be a form of adaptation to an unsatisfactory and circumscribed life."
Thompson pointed out that women have been forced to deny
their sexuality and that denial has been interpreted as evidence of their "natural masochism." In a related vein, soci-
ologist Jessie Bernard in 1981 pointed out that sociologists
have demonstrated that considerable social pressure is placed

on women to behave in altruistic ways and that they have often been punished for deviating from such behavior. As we shall see, this is the form of learned behavior that is most frequently taken to be a sign of women's "natural masochism." In 1976 feminist psychiatrist Jean Baker Miller echoed Bernard's point as she described the way society shapes females to become thoroughly absorbed in meeting their men's and their children's needs, and in *The Reproduction of Mothering: Psychoanalysis and the Sociology of Gender* published in 1978, Nancy Chodorow drew the same conclusions in regard to the meeting of children's needs.

Despite detailed descriptions by feminist theorists of the social forces that keep women in unhappy, self-denying roles, the myth of women's natural masochism persists. This is partly because even the feminist theorists have continued to misuse the word "masochism," unwittingly perpetuating the belief that, even if their masochism is learned, women *are* masochistic. It is possible, however, to demonstrate that what has been called women's *learned* masochism is not really masochism but one of the healthy motives mentioned in Chapter 1.

As Frances Newman and I wrote in our article about young female prostitutes, there is a tremendous and meaningful difference between nonmasochistic motives and the real seeking of pain or sorrow. It is important to be aware of the enormous range of behavior that has been labeled "masochistic." Consider, for example, the following descriptions, each of which illustrates a type of behavior that has been called masochistic.

◇ A 13-year-old girl was raised by a young, single mother who came from a problem-ridden family and was not able to offer her daughter much in the way of love and emotional support. The girl's father left her mother when he learned that his child was a girl, and his involvement with her was limited to sending her a Christmas card about every third year. When the girl reached puberty, she began working as a prostitute. Her pimp told her that she was his best girl and that he planned to set her up in a special apartment with him "very soon." She continued to believe his promises—although they were not kept— for eight months, when a new pimp took her away by making a similar promise.

◇ "A series of photos with text in *Chic* magazine [is] called 'Columbine Cuts Up.' Here, Columbine is shown stabbing herself in the vagina with a large butcher knife and cutting her labia with scissors. She is smeared with blood and on her face is a fixed smile. In a purported interview with this 'panting mime' *Chic* has Columbine say, 'I would much rather masturbate with a knife than a dildo. I guess, because I've always had an inferiority complex, I think of myself as deserving to be stabbed and killed.' "

The girl in the first description is typical of the girls in our study of young prostitutes. She does not seek out pain but tries to make do with what she has and to endure unpleasantness in the hope that if she does, she will have a better future. The second example comes much closer to what might be legitimately considered the pursuit, although not the enjoyment, of pain—if it had not been created by magazine writers. The example is taken from an article on pornography that appeared in a recent issue of a large women's magazine. The essential point here is that the kinds of behavior in both instances have been given the same label.

Not only is a wide spectrum of women's behavior called masochistic, but behavior motivated by the delay of gratification, limited availability of alternatives, or the need to avoid pain is rarely called masochism when it is seen in men. Whether or not behavior is called masochistic depends almost entirely on the sex of the person being studied. In regard to this, Frances Newman and I wrote:

If one were to apply the label of "masochist" to any individual—male or female—who pursues a painful and

dangerous occupation that holds little in the way of secure future rewards, one might discover that professional football players (virtually all of whom are male)
would fall within this diagnostic category. Picture the
adolescent male athlete who . . . spends many hours
being brutally assaulted in the cold, the mud, and the rain.
He can count on frequent and serious injuries to his body
in exchange for admiration and applause for his physical
strength and willingness to experience pain and injury so
that others may enjoy themselves. . . .

We do not, however, focus on the pain and injury
inherent in the footballer's occupation as the primary
motivation in his choice of career and label him a masochist. . . . What is regarded as secondary to the motivation of males is focused on as primary and pathological in the motivation of females. This distorted thinking,
then, permits society's critics to overlook the brutal consequences of certain activities to females—exploitation
by pimps, assault by rapists, and wife-beaters—because
these are considered to be simply what the woman wants.

Once people begin calling women's behavior masochistic and the same or similar behavior in men something less
sick, less disturbed, they think that they have found a trait
that needs to be explained, namely, *why* women are so masochistic. Complex theoretical structures have been created to
"explain" women's masochism. It certainly is true that if a
phenomenon is widespread, some explanation is needed as to
how it came to exist. The problem is that we are "explaining" something that does *not* exist.

What, then, is the behavior that in women has led to their
being called masochistic? Much of it is in fact *learned* behavior, the very essence of femininity in Western culture. Girls
and women are supposed to be nurturant, selfless (even self-
denying), and endlessly patient. What often goes hand in hand
with these traits is low self-esteem. Since no one with decent
self-respect would be endlessly nurturant and consider it unnatural to want something for herself, society must train women

to believe that without their nurturant behavior, without what they can give to another person, they are nothing. This leads to what social psychologists J. W. Thibaut and H. H. Kelley have called a "low comparison level of alternatives," the situation of feeling that one can expect nothing better if one tries to make a change.

Once females have been trained in this way, and act nurturant, charitable, and compassionate, this behavior is then labeled masochistic. What is ignored is that women have been intensively rewarded for behaving in this way and that a strong association has been formed between such behavior and the *pleasure* of the reward (usually someone's approval or an increased sense of their own identity as "feminine" or "womanly").

An important variation on the mislabeling as masochism of women's search for pleasure is the mislabeling as masochistic of women's efforts to exercise power. In writing about the development of the young girl's masochism, Helene Deutsch asserted that the father squelches her aggression, so she turns it inward, toward herself. Although I would not call that innate, inevitable masochism—since the turning inward is her attempt to win her father's approval for her feminine behavior—Deutsch has accurately described what happens to little girls' assertion of both aggression and power: it is suppressed, even repressed. Elaborating on the way that not only within the family but also at the societal level women are made to suppress the human need to feel powerful, Jean Baker Miller says that women "have been led by the culture to believe that their own, self-determined action is wrong and evil [and] . . . must be destructive." Thus, philosopher Kathryn Morgan writes, women wishing to exercise power are reduced to doing so in a manipulative way, and, "It is generally agreed that the most effective way to exercise manipulative power is by simulating a position of weakness and vulnerability." That simulation of weakness and vulnerability is then used as proof of masochism.

Not only is women's so-called masochistic behavior often

directed toward bringing pleasure, but also, as one of my psychology doctoral students, Lynne Dennis, has pointed out, some of it is aimed at *avoiding pain*. When the "masochist" label is applied, it is usually forgotten that women have been frightened by the threat of being considered unfeminine, unattractive, and unnatural if they do *not* behave selflessly. It goes unremarked that in developmental psychology textbooks one sign of maturity is said to be the ability to delay gratification for a greater good or a greater reward and that what women do is learn to delay their own gratification, hoping to be loved or appreciated at some later time. This is what Harvard psychologist David McClelland has called the Persephone complex in women.

Persephone was the mythical figure who was snatched away from her mother and taken to live in the underworld. Since her mother was the goddess Ceres, she was able to negotiate with the god of the underworld to let her have her daughter back for six months of the year. This was the ancient Greeks' explanation for the changing seasons. When Persephone came home to her mother, Ceres rejoiced, and the fields bloomed. But Persephone had to suffer for six months in order to reap her reward. A major part of the feminine condition has long been the understanding that, for women, life is to be lived like that, and one is admired for being as patient as Persephone, or as her sister-in-spirit Penelope, who waited for Ulysses for so many years, hoping if she was good enough that happiness would come to her eventually. Thus, women have denied their own needs in part or altogether for the sake of meeting the needs of others: their children, their husbands, their parents, their friends. If people were told of someone who behaves in the way just described, they would probably think, "What a fine, generous person that is!" But if that person were then placed in a psychological clinic or on a psychoanalyst's couch and were female, many therapists and many lay people would interpret the person's behavior as indubitably masochistic.

As noted, the word "masochism" originally meant

something very specific, namely, the enjoyment of pain. This word with a highly specific meaning, however, has come to be applied to a host of other types of behavior—usually with respect to women—and although the categories of behavior it is used to describe have broadened dramatically, the word has kept its connotations of psychopathology and extremity. As feminist historian Gertrud Lenzer wrote in 1975, even within Freud's lifetime ". . . it was surprising that the term 'masochism' had spread so widely in so short a time, that it had been applied to different kinds of phenomena which were never before thought to have any relation to what had come to be understood as masochism.''

Why should the misuse of one word be considered a serious problem? Because a major function of language is to help us understand our world, to help us to categorize the wealth of our experience, and because the use and misuse of words affect the way people think. If no one had ever suggested that women are naturally and inevitably masochistic, we would be freer to find other explanations for women's suffering. We do not currently have such freedom, however. As Mary Jane and William G. Herron wrote in 1982 in *Psychological Reports,* the word ''masochism'' has ''negative connotations of behavioral extremes,'' so whenever it is used ''there is a strong possibility of a hostile response'' to the word and to ''the people so labeled.'' Related to the Herrons' point is the fact that many people think of sadism and masochism as intimately connected and believe that a masochist can turn sadistic without warning. Thus, calling a woman masochistic also raises the specter of her as a potential sadist. Indeed, I have been asked why, when I lecture about the myth of women's masochism, I hardly mention sadism. The reason is that I am not talking about masochism but about what is misnamed masochism.

A similar instance of words and their relation to how we perceive women helps to clarify the point, I think. For years, some people have objected to the use of the generic ''he'' to mean ''he or she'' as in the sentence, ''If a child wants to, he can become a teacher.'' There have always been some people who said that such objections were absurd, because "everyone knows that when we say 'he' we really mean 'he or she,' and when we say 'Man invented language' we're using 'man' as a shorthand for 'men and women.' '' Research has shown, however, that the words we use *do* shape our thinking. In studies reported by Casey Miller and Kate Swift in their book *Words and Women,* the relationship of language and thought was systematically tested on both schoolchildren and adults. The studies followed this pattern: An adult announced that a textbook was being prepared and that help was needed in finding pictures from magazines to illustrate the chapter titles. Some of the people were given chapter titles like "Man and Culture" and others were given titles like "Human Culture." People of both sexes who were given titles that included the word "man" overwhelmingly chose pictures that only, or primarily, included men. Both males and females who were given the other titles chose pictures that included far larger numbers of women. Furthermore, the pictures chosen by the former group were more likely to include warlike or conflict-filled scenes than the pictures chosen by the latter group. There can be no doubt that language affects our thinking, as language is a large part of *how* we think.

When questioned closely, some mental health workers and other people will say, "Oh, well, we don't really mean exactly that women enjoy the pain. We are using the word loosely." But that is not good enough. When someone says "masochism," we certainly tend to think of something approximating the dictionary definition. The following incident illustrates the damaging consequences of the loose, everyday use of the word.

An extremely intelligent feminist graduate student who had read a great deal about the theories of masochism in women commented to me, "But it is true—women *do* behave masochistically and that has to be explained." When I asked to what behavior she was referring, she said, "Women are often very nurturant, self-denying, giving people." Like many of the theorists, this student had applied the term incorrectly to nonmasochistic, even prosocial, mature, loving behavior. If that behavior is called masochistic, then indeed one would misconstrue it as a sign of disturbance and would feel a need to try to understand how women became so disturbed.

If, however, the term "masochistic" is not applied to such behavior but instead the behavior is described for what it really is, then the reasons women behave that way become clear: because they have been told that they are good girls for behaving in a way that society wants them to behave and that society takes great pains to enforce.

Now, the tall psychiatrist might say, "Even if everything you say is true, it is *still* the case that women are also motivated by *un*conscious masochism." My answer would be: Part of the frustration in attempting to chart the unconscious is that it is nearly, if not totally, impossible to prove or disprove that particular bits of content or particular motives really exist. However, it is not my purpose to prove that there is no such thing as unconscious masochism. My purpose is to demonstrate two things. First, the notion that women are unconsciously, naturally masochistic is entirely unnecessary, because all of the behavior that needs to be explained can be explained satisfactorily and fully by other means (attempts to avoid guilt or punishment, putting the needs of others first, delaying gratification, or having few or no alternatives or, because of poor self-esteem, believing erroneously that one has no alternatives). Second, the notion that women are unconsciously, naturally masochistic tends, by and large, to do women a profound disservice. It often leads people to take what is most admirable and important about women and to distort those traits into evidence of sickness.

We must demand a halt to the labeling of woman as naturally, inevitably masochistic. We can start by refusing to let the moment pass when someone describes other women—or ourselves—as masochistic or as needing to fail. We will, of course, be accused once again of being humorless, just as when we took a deep breath and refused, for the first time, to let a racist, anti-Semitic, or antifemale comment go by. But putting up with such accusations is a small price to pay for the respect that we shall gain when the myth of our masochism is chiseled away. If enough of us strive to raise people's awareness, it will be harder for the "experts" to "bring us low," like lonely Eve.

CHAPTER 3

Mothers

. . . historically and theoretically, the domain of mothering and reproductive labor has been seen, at best, as a deficient and devalued moral domain. . . .

—PHILOSOPHER KATHRYN MORGAN

The myth of women's masochism seriously impedes women's attempts to function competently and happily in nearly every aspect of their lives. Since women's worth is largely gauged by their success as mothers, the harm done by the myth to women as mothers is particularly devastating.

As explained in Chapter 2, from the psychoanalysts came the theory that, since pregnancy and childbirth can be painful but are essential to our species' survival, it is natural for women to suffer. It is interesting that the theory of woman's innate need to suffer was developed long before most of the current methods of birth control were in use, so that in fact pregnancy then was far more often unplanned than now. Thus, in one respect the theory of women's masochism was less necessary when it was first developed, since pregnancy simply happened rather than being planned. Now that women are better able to choose whether or not to conceive, the danger is that the theory has become more "useful" in explaining why—if they *can* avoid pregnancy—so many women do not avoid it. Also, as discussed in Chapter 2, the mislabeling of much of mothers' selfless, compassionate behavior as "masochistic" further fuels the myth. We see this in unfortunately common images like that of the so-called Jewish mother, giving rise to such "masochistic-mother" jokes as: "How many Jewish mothers does it take to change a light bulb? Answer: None. 'It's all right. I'll sit in the dark.' "

Society teaches women that they ought to become mothers and ought to *want* to become mothers but then shows us through bombardment with images of impossibly beautiful, endlessly patient Supermothers in advertisements, television sitcoms, and sentimental songs, that a good mother behaves according to unattainable standards. Society also teaches that mothers are virtually single-handedly responsible for their children's upbringing and that if anything bad happens to their children, the mothers will almost inevitably be blamed. Naturally, mothers often become frightened and depressed because of this overwhelming responsibility for their children's welfare, and as a result they sometimes come to believe that women, including themselves, are unhappy because they are natural masochists, that by having children they went looking for sorrow. Furthermore, Barbara Ehrenreich and Deirdre English have documented how mental health professionals give mothers confusing messages, saying that they should expect no joy or reward from their children and mustn't be ambitious for themselves but may channel their "masculine" ambitions through their sons. Then, however, they have been instructed, in Helene Deutsch's words, not "to strive to achieve any other goals through [a] child than those of its own existence."

In effect, mothers have nearly all the work and receive nearly all the blame. What is even more discouraging is that, since activities associated with women have over the years come to be regarded as low-status and even degrading, when women have had some success in the work of mothering, they have rarely been given any credit (except on Mother's Day, when even strong men grow tearful, thinking, briefly, of what their mothers have done for them). Women have been raised to feel they should want to be mothers, having been encouraged to play with dolls, take care of younger sisters and brothers, help with the housework, and learn to cook. However, rather than being esteemed for providing the love and nurturance that make life both possible and pleasurable, they are likely to be trivialized. Women are seen as always *fussing* about diapers and recipes rather than as taking the lion's share of the responsibility for rearing children and providing nourishing and attractive food. Still worse, the mother-housewife's work is not regarded as requiring real effort and energy. Kathryn Morgan says in "Women and Moral Madness" that "women are encouraged to describe [mothering] as 'doing nothing' while exhausting themselves in the process of trying to prove that they are . . . 'real women.' " Despite society's trivialization of the work that mothers do, for most women their sense of identity comes to depend on how well they fill the roles of mother and wife. For this reason, deviating from those roles can be terrifying, because it can mean losing social approval and losing love and economic support from one's husband or parents.

Countless women have thus been subjected to anxiety, shame, and fear in their mothering roles and have felt that there is nowhere to turn and no one to blame but themselves.

◇ As Anna and I stood on the school steps one afternoon, waiting to walk our kindergarten children home at 3:30, we talked about how we had felt one year earlier, during our daughters' first week of nursery school. Both of our daughters had cried when we left them. Anna said she had felt deeply embarrassed by her daughter's tears. "I thought, 'Why me, God, why me? Why do I have to be shamed in front of the other mothers by having a child who can't handle it when I leave her?' '' Our neighborhood includes some very reserved, stiff-upper-lip people, and I could well imagine that they might believe that children who cry at major separations simply need to be toughened up. Hoping to help Anna feel less ashamed of her daughter's normal behavior, I suggested that if her daughter had not cared about her at all, the separation would not have bothered her, and in my view that would have been *real* cause for concern. Completely ignoring what I said, Anna replied sharply that she knew she had no right to complain, since she had "brought it on" herself by allowing her daughter to get "too close" to her emotionally.

What had happened to Anna was that two traditional lines of advice to mothers had clashed in her head. On the one hand, we mothers hear the advice-givers who say that children should be loved and nurtured, that it is not possible to spoil a child with too much love, and that the child will signal us clearly when she or he feels ready for a major separation. On the other hand, we hear the advice-givers who claim that a primary responsibility of mothers is to teach our children to separate and become independent of us as soon as possible. Caught in the crossfire between the two conflicting philosophies of child rearing, and watching perfect "Brady Bunch" and "Bill Cosby Show" television mothers who always know how to strike the correct balance between too much and too little closeness, many of us have felt—like Anna—that whatever we do must be inadequate or wrong. Having been taught that real women do not get angry and have an instinct for doing the right thing in rearing their children, we are less likely to take the advice-givers to task for confusing us and the media for setting up impossible standards than we are to blame ourselves for not being successful women. Then, haunted by the myth of women's masochism, we think, "I have no right to complain. I should have known to follow the advice of Expert X rather than Expert Y. I brought this on myself." No one tells us that we are not to blame and that we deserve better than this isolating, self-blaming agony.

◇ Kay is a mother of three, who works on an assembly line in a textile factory so that she and her husband can keep up the mortgage payments on their modest home. She feels guilty that she does not have time to bake chocolate chip cookies for her children to take to school on their birthdays as the "nonworking" mothers of other children do. She tries telling herself—and other people—that what makes one a good parent is the quality of time, not the quantity, spent with children. Her time at home, however, is mostly spent doing laundry, cooking, cleaning, and saying things like "Do your homework and brush your teeth and go to bed." She feels, accordingly, that she doesn't even spend "quality" time with her children. She has heard it said that women need to suffer, and she guesses that she probably needs to feel guilty. She does not see that her worries come from her love for her children. She wants to be the ideal mother for them, and so she is very susceptible to the impossibly high standards set for mothers. The problem is not her "enjoyment" of guilt but rather a society that created the Supermother image and told women that their worth depends primarily on mothering and that almost anything a mother does can "mess up" her child.

◇ Naomi is a single mother of one child, Zachary. Naomi left Zachary's father after he had a series of affairs with other women, which he used to humiliate Naomi and make her feel inadequate and unlovable. She has read that it is important for boys to have their fathers living with them as role models, and so she worries that she alone can't give Zachary a "normal, healthy" upbringing. If she had remained married, she would have continued to feel unwanted, hurt, and depressed. Now a single mother, she is often anxious and unhappy, because of her worries about her son. Neither of her two alternatives was easy, but these days when she feels the burdens of raising Zachary alone, her best friend tells her, "You made your choice!" and this makes Naomi feel that she somehow chose to be unhappy. It is clear that Naomi chose the more bearable of her two alternatives. In a better world, single parents would be less isolated, but in today's world single parenting is a hard choice. What Naomi needs to keep in mind is that her reasons for making her choice were healthy, reasonable, non-masochistic ones.

What no one tells young girls, and what they all too often learn only when they become mothers, is that mothers in our society are often terribly isolated and are forced to bear more child-care responsibility on their own than in other societies. When I was raising an infant, a toddler, and two school-aged children, I used to wake up many mornings wondering, with panic in the pit of my stomach, how I would get through the day. Having recently moved to a new city, I had not yet made any friends. I called a woman who had two school-aged children and asked if she had any suggestions about how to keep children entertained and happy during an entire day. One or more of them always seemed to need something and I never had a moment to myself or even a moment to relax my vigilance, lest a child run out into the street or fall down the stairs. To my amazement, the woman laughed and said she was amused by my question. "That's so like you, Paula," she said, "trying to get information about how to handle a situation." I didn't understand what she thought was so amusing about that until she said, "No one ever tells you how to be a good or a competent mother. You just have to figure out your own way."

I used to sit on the front step and look longingly at other mothers on the street, wishing I had the nerve to ask them how they coped but feeling far too shy. After all, if no one else asked such questions, I would look foolish or—far worse—like a bad mother if I asked them. This was in the mid-1970s, years after Betty Friedan had described in *The Feminine Mystique* the isolation of the mother-housewife, but things had hardly changed.

What has further increased women's sense of incompetence as mothers has been the prevalent belief that women's physiology and hormones—unlike men's—make them naturally suited to take care of children. When a baby is born, our natural instincts are supposed to transform us into serene, competent mothers. Simone de Beauvoir has observed that mothering is presented not only as "natural" but even as divinely ordained: "Given that one can hardly tell women that washing up saucepans is their divine mission, they are told that bringing up children is their divine mission." But the fact is, as Elizabeth Badinter pointed out in her 1981 book, *Mother Love: Myth and Reality,* good mothering does not necessarily happen automatically. Even at the moment of birth, some mothers describe feeling joyful and loving toward the infant, but others describe feeling frightened, strange, and not particularly close to the baby. Some new mothers find it much easier than others to interpret their babies' cries, to know how to play with babies, and when to start teaching their toddlers rules. As social psychologist Ronna Kabatznick wrote in a 1984 review of research on this subject, fathers are as good—and as bad—as mothers at caring for infants and children when they are given the opportunity and the confidence to do so. Perhaps the most remarkable point about the "motherhood comes naturally" theory is that its proponents have never been challenged to explain how, if women come by child-rearing skills instinctively, they manage to create all the emotional disturbances in their children for which they are blamed.

If you read the "Community Bulletin Board" sections of local newspapers these days, you will likely find announcements of mothers' support groups. I am filled with envy as I read these notices, wishing I had been part of such a group when my children were younger, when I, like so many moth-

ers, felt the fault was mine for not feeling relaxed and confident about being a mother. Despite the increasing number of
such support groups, as well as the increasing acceptability
for mothers to ask for help, as I travel around North America
giving lectures these days, my briefest mention of the isolation that mothers face and the sense of being overwhelmed by
responsibility is enough to elicit vigorous, nearly universal head
nodding. When question and discussion periods follow, I hear
outpourings of the anxiety and loneliness that mothers still feel.

Why shouldn't mothers feel anxious? After all, mother-
blaming still thrives. Working with psychology master's student Ian Hall-McCorquodale, I have found through extensive
research that mental health professionals continue to attribute
children's problems to their mothers. So, in asking women to
bear children, our society is saying to them, in essence, "We're
offering you a job, but if anything at all ever goes wrong,
even if it's forty or fifty years later, *you* will be held totally
responsible for it." If anyone offered you a job on those terms,
you'd tell them to keep it. But that is the position in which
mothers are placed. It is no wonder that they often come to
mothering filled with fear, guilt, and anxiety. Then they are
called masochistic for suffering in that role, and when they
try to avoid causing problems for their children by meeting
the children's needs and neglecting or denying their own, they
are called masochistic for their self-neglect. It is an impossible choice that women are given: If you don't become a self-
sacrificing mother (or a mother at all), you seriously risk being
punished and considered unnatural. If, partly to *avoid* such
punishment, you become a mother, then you are punished by
being given enormous responsibility, little appreciation, and
a great deal of actual or potential blame. Researcher Stella
Chess in the 1982 *International Journal of Mental Health*
quoted a letter from a school guidance counselor that is, unfortunately, not atypical: "To meet Johnny's mother is to understand his problem." Nowhere was Johnny's father mentioned. Mother-blaming is in large part a reflection of society's
general tendency to degrade or undervalue women, and Letty

Cottin Pogrebin has traced this tendency in everyday life and language: "A nasty woman is a 'bitch,' but a nasty man isn't nasty in his own right: he's a '*son* of a bitch' or a 'bastard,' both words reflecting badly on his mother."

Nancy Chodorow has described how, during the 1940s, the "overprotective mother" became a focus of concern:

> These mothers were rearing children when the new psychology was emphasizing maternal responsibility for children's development, when women were putting more time into child care even as there were fewer children to care for, when family mobility and the beginnings of suburbanization were removing women from daily contact with female kin. Women were expected to mother under precisely those conditions which, according to cross-cultural research, make it hardest to care for children and feel unambivalently affectionate toward them: as full-time mothers, with exclusive responsibility for children, in isolated homes.

These mothers were told that good mothering meant constant preoccupation with their children, although eventually this behavior was labeled "overprotective" or "overanxious" mothering. Thus, mothers were thought either to provide "too much" care or to be cold and rejecting. Whatever they did, mothers lost. Consistently, they were made to feel ashamed of their mothering ability; no one alleviated the shame by pointing out that all varieties of mothering behavior have been given pejorative labels.

The women's movement has had profound effects on our society and women have an easier time in many ways than they used to. But in some significant areas of women's lives very little has changed. Mothers are still being blamed by mental health professionals, among others, for most of their children's emotional problems. Ian Hall-McCorquodale and I set out to examine what the clinicians were really saying about mothers and whether the resurgence of the women's movement in the late 1960s might have reduced the frequency of mother-blaming.

We read every article from nine major mental health journals during 1972, 1977, and 1982 that included some mention of the cause of a patient's (or a prisoner's, a high school student's, or some other person's) emotional problem. (We chose these three years because articles conceived and written during the latest wave of the feminist movement were published by 1972, the study was done in 1983, and so 1982 was the last full publication year, and 1977 was the halfway point.) The results were so extreme that they came as a depressing surprise. In the 125 articles that we read and classified, mothers were blamed for an astounding array of problems in their children—72 different kinds of problems in all. These included anorexia nervosa, arson, chronic vomiting, bedwetting, poor bowel control, inability to deal with color blindness, male children's fear of penile shrinkage and death, minimal brain damage, a need to be anally penetrated, poor language development, schizophrenia, self-induced television epilepsy, homicidal transsexualism, and ulcerative colitis, to name just a few.

We identified 63 practices by psychologists and other mental health professionals that could lead to mother-blaming, and we grouped those into five major types:

(1) Methods of information gathering, such as whether the history of the child's problem was taken only from the mother or only from the father;
(2) Attribution of blame, including whether or not the clinician/writer said the mother's pathological behavior— or the father's—affected the family;
(3) Treatment-related items, such as whether the clinician involved only the mother—or only the father—in therapy with the child;
(4) Items related to previously published writings about mother-blaming, such as whether previous literature in which mothers are blamed was simply cited as "evidence," without being critically considered; and

(5) Miscellaneous issues, such as the number of words used to describe the mother, compared to the number used to describe the father.

Our results showed that for 52 of the 63 items a highly statistically significant tendency existed for clinicians to blame mothers more than fathers. The clinician-writers frequently did not even mention the fathers. They used more than two and one-half times as many words to describe the mothers as the fathers and used the child-mother interaction far more often than the child-father interaction to illustrate how the child had become disturbed. This last practice was found even when the authors claimed that the "parents," not specifically the mother, had emotionally harmed the child. But when it came to giving concrete examples, the mother was much more likely to be cited than the father. In many articles in which the father was mentioned, the only thing said about him was that he was dead or absent. Research was much more likely to be done on the mothers than on the fathers of therapy patients, and the mothers were more likely to be required to participate in their children's therapy than were the fathers. In these ways, mothers were more subject to the professionals' scrutiny than were fathers. Chances are that if any parent is observed interacting with his or her child, a mental health professional will be able to find something to criticize. And even though mothers were more likely than fathers to participate in therapy related to their children's problems, it was the fathers who were more likely to be given credit for having "done well" in treatment.

Various kinds of activity by mothers—such as alcohol abuse, paying "too much" attention to the child, or behaving in "too strong" a way—were likely to be regarded as harming their children. In contrast, activities by the fathers—including alcohol abuse and using illegal drugs in front of the child—were not described as harmful.

The year in which the article was written did not affect the degree of mother-blaming, which highlights the sad truth that, for many mental health professionals, it is as though the women's movement never happened. Furthermore, the mother-blaming appeared regardless of whether the article was written by a man or a woman and regardless of the journal in which the article was published, although for a few items the psychoanalytic and family therapy writers were even more likely to blame mothers than were writers in the general psychiatric and psychological journals. For example, writers in the former were more likely to attribute even the *parents'* problems to their mothers, to say that the mother's pathology was intractable, to use judgmental terms about the mother, to make the child's treatment the mother's responsibility, and to make both theoretical statements and statements about particular patients that "revealed" the mother-child relationship as the source of the problem. The reasons for these differences among journals are probably complex, but a primary reason was also reflected in our data: The psychoanalytic and family therapy writers were more likely than the others to take a very traditional view of sex roles and parenting roles. That is, they were more likely to say that a traditional division of labor (woman doing the child care, man bringing home the paycheck) and a traditional division of roles (woman as expressive, man as reserved) are healthy and normal, and to rely on the theoretical writings of earlier authors about what is necessary for a child's healthy emotional development. Since it is only within the last ten years that social science researchers and clinicians have given much attention to the father's actual and potential role in the child's development (beyond the claim that boys need "male role models"), writers who base their thinking on traditional theories and research are naturally more likely to blame mothers.

Those are some of the quantitative results of the study, and although they are revealing, what is even more informative, I think, is the *quality,* the specifics, of some of these patterns. For example, the other side of woman-blaming is man-idealizing, and this pattern often appeared in the articles in our study. In many, the only references to the father relate to his occupational status or to the fact that he is absent or dead or, in several cases, compliment him, by saying, for example, that "he helped the child and was upset that his wife had trouble with the child and asked him to 'bail her out.'" In another article, the authors wrote: "The mother was nurturant and overprotective. The boy's relationship with his father appears to have been ideal in virtually every respect." In no article was a mother's relationship with her child described as ideal or even as simply healthy, nor was she ever described only in positive terms.

In another article, the following description was given about the parents of twin homosexual men who had an incestuous relationship with each other and could not form emotional attachments with other people: "Their father, a carpenter, was 33 years old when they were born. He was described as patient and easygoing. Their mother was 31 years old at the time of their births and she was described as wearing the pants and hardheaded." That is all that is said about the parents of these men, leaving readers who might wish to understand the childhood origins of the twins' disturbances with the impression that the mother's assertive behavior had led to the young men's problems, since no other information is given that betrays any hint of abnormality.

In still another article, at the beginning of the case history, the following is noted: "The father, a brick layer, was 35 yr old when the patient was born. He is healthy. The mother was 33 yr old when the patient was born; she is 'nervous.'" Later in that article, the authors write that the father hit the child and was very dominating and that the patient cried every time he talked about his father and feared that his father did not love him. We can only guess why, if the father treated his disturbed son in this way, the father is described at the start of the case history in terms of his occupation and his physical health, whereas the mother is described only as "nervous." This article is about emotional disturbance in children who have Klinefelter's syndrome, which is a chromosomal disorder. After relating three case histories—the most vivid by far being the one just described—the authors reach the following conclusion: "Mothers of patients with Kline-felter's syndrome are often overprotective or anxious. . . . The behavior disturbance [of the children] may start at the age of 4–5 if their mothers do not protect them or take care of them. . . ." (It is worth noting that, whereas some mothers are taken to task for being overprotective, here mothers are implicitly blamed for not being protective enough.) How do clinicians reach such a conclusion, especially when the mothers in the case histories are not described as overprotective or anxious, and the only really serious problem noted for any parent is in the father just described?

In reporting a case of school phobia, the authors of one article wrote: "It was evident that Billy's mother was allowing reinforcement of his school avoidance behaviors by permitting him to watch television during the day and to stay up all night." This is the same case in which the father was described as having an ideal relationship with his son. The father was a farmer and presumably worked near home during the day and did not work at night. One might wonder where he was when his wife was said to be permitting their son to watch television all day and to stay up all night. However, the authors of that article did not raise that question.

Even in those few articles in which the mother is not blamed, the father's possible contribution to the problem is never considered. In one study of women prisoners who violated the prison's rules, four characteristics of the rule violators, in contrast to the obedient prisoners, were related to their perceptions of their mothers and two characteristics to their perceptions of their fathers, but only those related to mothers are described as having done any harm. Similarly, in a study of fire-setters, the only significant relationship between an item of family history and the offspring's arson was the father's drinking—but it is entirely omitted from the discussion section, in which the authors are supposed to explain the meaning and importance of what they have found.

The article in which the author had to reach the furthest

to blame the mothers was one about the offspring of men who had served in the armed forces and been kept in prisoner-of-war camps for 44 months. Some of the children of these men were found to have emotional problems, and the author explains this as follows: The men go off to work full of anxiety, pain, and a sense of depletion because of their wartime experiences. When they are at home, their lack of involvement with the family is striking. All of this upsets the wives, so that their performance of their mothering functions is disturbed, and *that* is what upsets the children!

Recent social changes are not even taken into account much of the time, so determined are many clinicians to hold mothers to blame. For example, since fewer mothers are doing all of the child care and staying at home the entire day than formerly, we might expect that clinicians would take more care in making certain kinds of interpretations. For example, school phobia has traditionally been blamed on overprotective, dependent, immature mothers who want to keep their children at home with them to meet their needs and keep them company. Since fewer mothers are home during school hours nowadays, surely that fact should be taken into consideration; but in many recent articles on school phobia this change has simply been ignored. Thus, child rearing is still primarily considered the mother's responsibility, and even explanations of children's problems that have depended on full-time mothering have not been abandoned. This state of affairs has been exacerbated by the increasing number of single mothers—in some cases the result of separation or divorce and in others the result of the decision by single mothers—both teenagers and older, working women—to have babies and raise them by themselves. This means that, above all, the mothers are *there* for professionals who assess and treat their children to study and question. They are also there for the general public to observe, rearing their children. They, more than the absent fathers, are easy targets for blame, simply because they are around. It is easier to attribute a child's problems to the behavior of a parent who is present than to attribute them to the imagined or suspected behavior of a now-absent parent or to that very absence.

This stress on mother-blaming has also been fueled by theories like the one about the importance of "bonding" between mother and infant, the claim that what happens between mother and infant during the first hour of the infant's life has a profound effect on the infant's emotional, intellectual, and even physical development. These theories have led mothers who give birth under so-called abnormal conditions, such as by Caesarean section or under some anesthesia, to feel guilty for the rest of their days for not having seen their baby— or perhaps seen but not held it—until a few hours after its birth. In fact, at least one psychiatrist has made a name for himself by claiming that a mother's thoughts and feelings while she is pregnant can deeply wound her child psychologically. While there is no doubt that drug and alcohol abuse, and perhaps prolonged, intense anxiety and tension, can have harmful effects on the fetus, the stridency of the before-birth alarmists has caused countless mothers to feel needlessly guilty and frightened. And how is a mother to know whether her feelings have hurt her baby? The theorists don't tell us. At a parents' meeting at a synagogue, though, I once heard a psychiatrist blithely announce that Sudden Infant Death Syndrome—or crib death—is caused by the parents' failure to love their children enough. He made this claim on the basis of not one shred of evidence, and my heart went out to parents in the audience who might have had a baby who died from crib death. Some therapists say that *they* can tell, from their work with psychotherapy patients, when the behavior or feelings of the patient's mother while the patient was *in utero* hurt the patient. How can they tell? We are asked to believe that their sensitive, highly trained clinical powers somehow make it possible for them to know when such things have happened and when the patient is just imagining it. In fact, carefully monitored research during the growing-up years of large numbers of patients has shown that the range of ongoing relationships the growing infant and child has is what makes the greatest difference in a child's development, not the moment-of-birth experience or single, before-birth traumas that come from the mother's feelings and thoughts. This is not to say that a horrible, extreme experience cannot have damaging effects, such as when an infant is severely deprived of oxygen at birth or suffers brain damage in the course of a difficult delivery, but these problems are related to physical damage. This is quite different from the theory that makes a mother feel that she has only moments in which to establish a powerfully positive emotional bond with her child and that even before the child's birth she can doom it to lasting mental agony.

Mother-blaming is not done only by professionals; it is also done by mothers themselves. Sometimes, as in the following letter to Ann Landers, it acquires added force from misguided religious guilt:

> I never thought I'd be writing to you, but the letter from "Los Angeles Grief" needs an answer. Her mother convinced her that God had given her a handicapped child as a punishment for some terrible thing she had done. My mother had the same cruel philosophy.
>
> I was married only two years when I came down with polio. We had a beautiful 10-month-old daughter at the time.
>
> Within a few months I was partially paralyzed. Several weeks into my therapy I suffered a terrible setback. Our child died from sudden crib death. Against doctor's orders, I became pregnant again. I had a miscarriage in the sixth month.
>
> During those terrible days my mother's early preaching ("You must have done something awful to deserve this") continued to haunt me.

In an attempt to reduce the frequency of thoughtless, groundless mother-blaming, Ian Hall-McCorquodale and I have put together four recommendations that we feel everyone, and especially those in the helping professions, should follow in thinking about the causes of a child's problems.

First, whenever possible, emphasis on *mother*-infant and *mother*-child interaction should be changed to interaction between *parent* and infant or child. Unless the data clearly warrant an emphasis on the mother's role, and possible effects of the father's or other caretaker's behavior—or absence—have been ruled out, emphasis on the mother is unjustified and unfair. Ruling out the influence of other adults' behavior or absence is exceedingly difficult to justify, but only rarely in the articles we examined were such attempts even made.

Second, the effects of the child's own innate and developing characteristics must be taken into account before mothers are blamed for what goes wrong. Some children are more difficult than others to handle, right from birth, and it is not the fault of the person who takes care of that child. The caretaker may begin to behave in certain ways, such as setting firmer limits than she or he would with a different child. This behavior may be misinterpreted as excessive strictness and a cause of the child's problems when, in fact, the strictness is a response to the child's need for firmer limits. Something similar can happen to a parent whose infant, from birth, is easily made anxious; a parent who responds by holding such a child a great deal is likely to be called overprotective and accused of spoiling the baby and making it anxious by being "afraid" to let it cry itself to sleep, for example.

Third, our recommendation is to keep in mind that social practices—strongly encouraged by clinicians, as we have seen—that classify the responsibility for child rearing solely as the mother's can *only* perpetuate mother-blaming. While these practices continue, fathers' absences or actions will not tend to be interpreted as causes of children's problems. Such interpretations strengthen the notion that the problems are the mother's fault, and the vicious cycle continues. If it is usually the mother who is there to do the child rearing, or at least to see that it gets done, and to provide the history for the mental health worker and who thereby becomes a subject of study for that professional, then all material on which to base theories about children's emotional disturbances will come from their mothers' lives. Fathers are generally more reluctant than mothers to participate in such interviews. Therefore, what the father did or did not do or might have done if things had been different to prevent, reduce, intensify, or create his child's problems will not be known and will rarely be considered.

Fourth, as long as mothers are held to be primarily responsible for their children's emotional adjustment, a dangerous source of intense anxiety, self-deprecation, and fear will be brought to the relationships many mothers have with their infants and children. For these women, the pervasiveness of mother-blaming means that when they give birth to or adopt a baby, they will almost surely be accused if anything goes wrong. There are very few jobs in which one individual is blamed for everything that goes wrong, and there is probably no other job in which what can go wrong (and the feeling that follows when one is blamed for it) can be so disastrous.

People who think it is clever or amusing to call mothers masochists because mothering involves some stress or pain have ignored the joy that comes with the work, a joy that can be so intense that it makes the difficult times well worth enduring. These people rarely call a business executive masochistic as a result of the stress under which he works, because the money, power, and opportunity to be creative are assumed to be worth enduring the stress. Why is our society so quick to take note of the benefits of being an executive and so slow to appreciate the pleasures of motherhood? I think there are at least two main reasons. One is that mothering is a low-status occupation in our society. Feminist social psychologist Jeri Wine has shown that traits and behavior associated with males tend to be given names that embody respect and high status. For example, "assertiveness" has been considered primarily a characteristic of males and to be high status; but according to Wine, what the research actually shows is that men are more often rude, belligerent, and unresponsive than women. Because social psychologists have called such behavior "assertive" it has appeared that men are the more assertive sex. In fact, Wine reports, studies of the ability to state one's opinion straightforwardly and to stick to it—true assertiveness—show that this is more characteristic of women than of men. By contrast, "dependency" is the often contemptuous, infantilizing term applied by researchers and clinicians to what is frequently warm, caring behavior in females. With regard to mother-blaming, since mothering has been classified as low status, the pleasures and sense of accomplishment that mothers can experience are often overlooked, for it seems strange that such a low-status job *could* be enjoyable.

The other main reason that business executives' job satisfaction but not mothers' job satisfaction is respected is that, since motherhood is limited to females, the myth of women's masochism is easily hauled into play. Any endeavor that is primarily or entirely female is susceptible to being characterized as masochistic. If we believe women are masochistic, then when we find something that is done mostly by women and is not perfectly pleasurable (and what is?), then we assume that it must attract masochists.

Sometimes, looking at another culture or subculture helps us to understand our own more clearly. Anthropologist Carole Browner has written about Latinas in San Francisco, who—as mothers—behave in traditionally feminine ways, appearing passive and not openly seeking pleasure and personal gratification. This pattern of behavior has been called "Marianismo" because of its relationship to the qualities of the Virgin Mary and as a counterpart to "machismo" or "macho" behavior. A "Marian" woman feels that no personal sacrifice for her husband and children is excessive and "she responds to their needs with passivity and patience, with limitless, enduring self-denial." In return, she receives their love. Browner points out that such behavior has been called masochistic but, in fact, it is the opposite. Since these women often have few or no economic resources and would be ostracized if they sought paid employment and no longer were perfect stay-at-home mothers, their only "appropriate" avenue of self-expression and eventual economic security is through devotion to their children, who will then support them out of gratitude and loyalty. Writes Browner: "The dream of upward mobility gives mothers the hope that a stable source of financial support will grow directly from these emotional bonds." The women's need to ensure their children's loyalty is intensified, according to Browner, by the fear that their husbands will abandon them and by their frequent loss of women friends because of the high degree of social mobility that leads to frequent changes of residence. Browner says: "Given the difficulties involved in establishing permanent affiliative ties with both men and women, children appear to be a secure source of continuous emotional gratification, and most importantly, one over which women may exercise control." Thus, these Latinas stand to reap both economic rewards from their children in the future and emotional rewards in the present through their allegedly masochistic behavior, which is actually goal-oriented, pragmatic, self-enhancing behavior. Browner calls such behavior "an adaptive mechanism, part of a strategy for dealing with the mediated, indirect quality of women's relationships to essential resources."

Everywhere in North America single mothers are trapped by the masochism myth as it works in combination with prevalent beliefs about the impossibility of rearing well-adjusted children in a one-parent home. Since the number of single mothers is growing rapidly, it is particularly crucial that their lives not be made more difficult than they are. The moralistic attitude that divorce is wrong and that only the traditional, two-parent family is normal has given rise to the prevailing "wisdom" that one-parent homes are unnatural and incomplete and the children of divorce grow up seriously disturbed. Despite important research by such respected psychologists as Mavis Hetherington and her colleagues showing that many postseparation and postdivorce problems are merely temporary, much attention has been focused on uncovering major problems in these families. Hetherington reported that

many postseparation problems are not lasting because they have
more to do with the family's attempt to adjust to changed
economic circumstances (which, for single-mother families,
often puts them below the poverty line), to redefine itself, and
to settle into new routines, than they have to do with permanent emotional damage or disturbance. This being the case,
it may be incorrect—and is certainly damaging and frightening to the single mother—to classify all of her concerns and
her children's difficult behavior as symptoms of psychopathology. This can only add further to her guilt, anxiety, and
hopelessness, rather than allowing her to channel her energy
into helping her children to adapt. As with Zachary's mother,
Naomi, who was described earlier in this chapter, many women
are single mothers through no fault of their own or because
divorce was the lesser of two evils. Single parenting packs a
cruel double whammy if we unjustifiably claim that a single-
mother home cannot produce normal children and also that
women bring their suffering on themselves. Furthermore, although single parenting is not easy for a parent of either sex,
social work professor Geoffrey Greif has found that single
fathers receive more moral support, sympathy, and admiration than single mothers, and that single mothers are more
likely than single fathers both to lose their jobs and—when
they do have jobs—to be paid little more than half as much
as single fathers.

The situation has perhaps been worst for single mothers
with sons, as I saw one afternoon when I took my children to
a production of the play, *You're a Good Man, Charlie Brown*.
My daughter Emily was four years old and my son Jeremy
was six at the time. During intermission and after the play
my daughter struck up a friendly conversation with an en-
chanting little boy her age. I began to talk with his mother
and after a while suggested that we consider getting the children together to play, since they seemed so compatible. The
woman's face went white and she explained that that was impossible. "You see," she told me, "I am divorced, and I don't
want my son to play with little girls. Psychologists say that
since there's no man in our house, my son is in grave danger

of growing up to be less than a real man. Playing with little girls is out!''

This woman had been made to feel that, because there were no male genitalia in her home, she probably could not raise a normal child. As a divorced mother myself, I knew that there was enough to worry about as a single parent without having to exclude half of all children as your child's playmates. It saddened me to think how fragile that woman must think her son is that she has to be so vigilant and protective of him. A valuable antidote to the fears of single mothers raising sons is a recent book by Joann Ellison Rodgers and Michael F. Cataldo called *Raising Sons: Practical Strategies for Single Mothers,* in which the authors debunk the myth that single mothers cannot raise psychologically healthy sons.

What is the effect on children, particularly boys, of having no adult male in the household? Clinicians and researchers have often said that the most problematic pairing in a postseparation family is that of the single mother and son. This theory has been based on reports that boys have more behavior problems than girls after a divorce. The traditional explanation for this difference has been that the little boy lacks a same-sex role model in the home, that he is overburdened with trying to be the man of the house (which his mother is said to force him to be), that his mother scapegoats him because she is now angry at all males, or some combination of these factors. But this entire line of reasoning needs to be reexamined.

To begin with, it is by no means clear that the single mother and son pair is the most problematic parent-child relationship. What *is* known is that when children are under stress, boys are more likely than girls to react in ways that attract the notice of others and to be labeled ''disturbed.'' This is because boys tend to behave disruptively or aggressively under stress, whereas little girls tend to withdraw or try harder to be nice and win acceptance. Therefore, it is simplistic to assume that divorce upsets boys more than girls just because boys show their distress in more noticeable ways.

The question of whether actual harm is caused by the

absence of an adult male also needs to be examined. Most child development theorists postulate that a child needs a same-sex role model in the household in order to achieve a healthy psychological adjustment. But, in fact, an adult's sex is far less important than people used to assume it was when they believed that most behavior was the exclusive province of one sex or the other. The more we believe that only women can be nurturant and only men aggressive, the more we might believe that girls need to have nurturant mothers and boys aggressive fathers in order to develop properly. But once we realize that healthy children of both sexes need to be able to behave in both nurturant and aggressive ways, then does it matter from whom they learn this? We can go back one step further. Common sense, clinical experience, and research teach us that a child develops characteristics that are similar to parents of *both* sexes, although many people seem to forget this in their concern over fatherless households. In addition, even the most traditional psychotherapist knows that a little boy learns much about what it means to be a boy from the way the parent of the other sex treats him, not simply from the same-sex parent.

The acceptance of mistaken ideas about single mothers has led many of these women, especially those with sons, to bring fear, anxiety, and guilt to their interactions with their children. Since the quickest way to upset a child is to fill a relationship with these emotions, the labeling of the single-parent family as abnormal becomes a self-fulfilling prophecy. Women need to speak out against such gloomy predictions as "Your daughter will have trouble when she starts dating, having grown up with no man in the house" or "Your son will certainly suffer from the lack of a male adult at home." We can all learn from the young child from a single-parent family who said, "My home is not broken, it works."

Since problems appear from time to time in any human relationship, why should we focus exclusively on them, ignoring the delights of mothering, when we try to understand the reasons women choose to mother? Furthermore, we must reject harmful and erroneous beliefs about mothering (including single mothering), particularly the belief that all child-care responsibility should be relegated to the individual mother and the belief that the mother is to blame for whatever goes wrong. Mothers are not innately masochistic, but our society's misguided attitudes do make mothers' tasks more onerous than they need be. A change in these attitudes would make mothers' lives easier and happier and thus would make it harder to impute masochistic motives to them.

CHAPTER 4

The Child's Growth Toward "Masochism": "Expert" Opinion and Reality

I was learning that I would be damned by self-expression or passivity—in one case, with the loss of love, in the other, with the loss of self. —ROSEMARY DANIELL

In William Styron's novel, *Sophie's Choice,* we learn gradually that Sophie's father was a steely-cold, rejecting, vicious man both in the way he dealt with the world in general and in the way he treated his daughter. Styron writes: "Her subservience to her father . . . was complete, as complete as in any neopaleolithic pigmy culture of the rain forest, demanding utter fealty from the helpless offspring." Styron describes further "her virtually menial submission, the 'Yes, Papa's' and 'No, thank you, Papa's' she was compelled to say daily, the favors and attentions she had to pay, the ritual respect, the enforced obsequiousness she shared with her mother." Throughout the book, we are presented with horrifying examples of the degree to which Sophie's father mocked and rejected her. Then we are told, "She may have been, she admitted, truly masochistic." After reading about her father's overwhelming, unquestioned power and his capacity to punish and humiliate her, it is shocking to be told that Sophie obeyed him because she enjoyed the suffering, rather than to avoid further pain, as we, too, would have done. If we are to combat the myth of women's masochism we need to understand what the growing girl is thought by the experts to experience—and what she in fact experiences—that might make her seem, or believe herself to be, masochistic, like the fictional character Sophie.

A growing daughter has unlimited occasion to observe her mother in the predicament described in the previous chapter. It is hard for a child to take note of her mother's no-win situation with respect to a "masochistic" role and then make a rational decision to avoid falling into the same trap. She is still subject to most of the same pressures that have weighed on her mother—fear of being thought unfeminine and unnatural if she doesn't embrace a mothering role herself and learn to be self-denying without uttering a word of complaint. The words of Rosemary Daniell, cited at the beginning of this chapter, illustrate the young girl's dilemma of choosing between loss of love and loss of self; in such a situation, most children choose to keep the love. The traditional demand on growing girls to make this choice has meant that they, like their mothers, have been given two undesirable options and then, in choosing the less self-serving of the two, have been called natural masochists. As Jeanette Nichols, Darlene Pagano, and Margaret Rossoff recently wrote in the book *Against Sadomasochism: A Radical Feminist Analysis*: "The concept of 'free choice' is often a smokescreen for socially determined behavior"; that is, when behavior is socially imposed, the people who have imposed it often claim that the behavior was freely chosen.

Suppose someone gave you the following advice: Teach your child that she won't be loved and accepted by you or by other people unless she does X, and teach her that X is the most important thing about her, that she's not a real female unless she does X. Much later, society will teach her that X is despicable, that it has an awful name, that she was fated from birth to do X, and that this despicable tendency is rooted deep within her. This is what happens with little girls. Mothers are made to feel they are failures as mothers if they have not taught their daughters to be self-sacrificing, self-denying, and willing to put other people's needs first. Then, as girls grow up they hear more and more that although such behavior is "feminine," it is also a sign of "sickness"; indeed, they often learn that femininity and womanhood themselves are low-status, laughable, even despicable. They learn that women are born masochists and that masochism is sick. If mothers could see all this coming from the start, they would be in a better position to decide what to teach their daughters.

One theory that has been used to reinforce the view that growing girls' natural style is a passive, patient one rather than a self-assertive, self-defining one is psychoanalyst Erik Erikson's theory of females' "inner space." Erikson is probably best known for his development of the concept of the "identity crisis," and much of his theory is characterized by thoughtfulness and sensitivity to the dilemmas involved in growing up. As a product of his time, however, he claimed that because the female has an inner space—a womb—a woman cannot have a sense of her identity until she knows, literally, "who will fill her inner space." Erikson's physiology is a bit hazy, though, as there simply is no such inner space. The uterus looks like a folded flapjack except when it is filled with a growing fetus, and the vaginal walls touch each other except during brief episodes of sexual activity and when something separates them. In addition to the mistaken physiology that is the basis for this theory, Erikson points to a research project he carried out several decades ago, in which he claims to have shown that females' inner space is so important that it leads them to "perceive and organize space" differently from boys.

In his research, Erikson asked children aged 11, 12, and

13 to take some toys and create an exciting scene from an imaginary motion picture. He then took note of the types of structures they built and claimed that the male type of structure was the tower and the female type of structure was the enclosure. Further, he claimed that boys' phalluses lead them to build tall, phallic structures, and that girls' wombs lead them to arrange toys in enclosure shapes, or "inner spaces." He has used these "findings" as proof of the importance to females of the inner space that passively waits to be filled.

When I first read Erikson's original article about the children's play constructions, I was astonished. In the first place, nearly every child had built an enclosure. Only a very few children had built towers, and of those slightly more were built by boys than by girls. The data clearly did not justify calling the tower the "male" structure, because both boys and girls built overwhelmingly more enclosures than towers; the enclosure was the typical structure built by children of both sexes. Second, it occurred to me that since Erikson presented blocks, doll furniture, and moving objects like toy cars to some prepubescent and pubescent children—children just at the age when one sees the greatest amount of concern about behaving "appropriately" for one's sex—he could hardly have expected the girls to choose toy cars or blocks and the boys to choose doll furniture! And once you have chosen doll furniture, it probably won't occur to you to build a tower; toy chairs and cradles are not very stackable. If you are a boy, though, you are more likely to choose blocks than furniture, and children learn early that blocks are great for building towers. I wondered what would have happened if Erikson had first asked the children to construct a scene but had given them *only* blocks, then asked them to do a scene using *only* toys, and so on. That is just what I did in my study, using my son's nursery school classmates (Jeremy, my son, was the only child who refused to participate in the study). I also chose nursery school children, because if Erikson's theory is correct and it is simply the presence of a womb in one's body that predestines one to preoccupation with enclosures, domesticity, and passivity, then those traits should be present from birth. Furthermore, once a child has had 11, 12, or 13 years in which to hear about what boys and girls are supposed to do, it is impossible to know whether their behavior is a product of that learning or whether it comes from their possession of a penis as opposed to a uterus.

In my son's class, I found no sex differences whatsoever in tower building and enclosure building. Not even the small difference Erikson had found for tower building was evident. In fact, among the children in my experiment who built towers, the girls were likely to build slightly *higher* ones than the boys. My one study was not enough, of course, to convince the many psychoanalysts who believe with Erikson that females' identity comes from knowing who will fill their inner space. Sadly, the whole tradition of belief in females' natural passivity and concern with home life to the exclusion of self-assertion and achievement is alive and thriving. It often includes not only a belief about how things *are*—females are naturally passive—but also an attitude about how things *ought to be*, a moral attitude—it is right and good for females to be passive. These beliefs do a great deal to block the way for girls who want to avoid the role of passive recipient of whatever unhappiness life brings their way.

Psychiatrist Harold Blum has said there is a distinction that is crucial to understanding the growing girl's situation. He writes: "It is important to distinguish between masochistic suffering as a goal in itself, and tolerance for discomfort or deprivation in the service of the ego or ego ideal." What does it mean to say something is tolerated in the service of the ego or ego ideal? Freud called the ego the "reality principle," which takes note of the real consequences of a person's behavior. For a young girl to tolerate discomfort or deprivation in the service of the *ego* means that she tolerates it in order to protect herself, because she knows that she will be punished (called unfeminine) if she refuses to tolerate it. Tolerance in the service of the *ego ideal* is a little different. Our ego ideal is our ideal self, what we would like to be.

Little girls learn early that if they are "real girls," they must tolerate discomfort or deprivation. Here again we see the familiar pattern: Daughters are threatened with rejection and contempt if they do *not* put up with unhappiness and pain, and then are said to have sought that unhappiness and pain because of their masochism, their inborn need to do so.

Boys rarely face this dilemma. I would never argue that it is easy to grow up male, but a major difference between girls and boys is that, for boys, *being self-serving and self-developing tends to bring them love and admiration,* because it is consistent with the male role. Asserting one's own needs and rights is what males are supposed to do; denying one's needs and rights is quintessentially "feminine."

What do the personality theorists believe are some of the steps that little girls take that lead them, inexorably, toward masochism? Most of the theorists' work is characterized by the claim that females are born with a tendency to deal in masochistic ways with certain life situations that all females encounter. Different theorists have different ideas about which of these life situations are the most important to the full emergence of the growing girl's masochism. Examining this second type of theory, we are not surprised to discover that nearly every modern theorist claims that the mother is to blame for the unfolding of the daughter's inborn masochism. A brief look at some of these theories will illustrate the pattern and show us what we are up against. I'll start with the mother-blaming ones and then describe the single example in which mothers are not blamed.

Three of a mother's characteristics are blamed for her daughter's growing masochism—inadequacy, aggression, and an unloving nature.

We shall look first at the *inadequacy* theories, which are heavily based on Freud's original work. Psychiatrist Robert Robertiello describes what he believes to be the crux of masochism, which he does not regard as part of normal development: a child becomes angry at her mother because the mother does not care enough about her, but since the child is dependent on her mother she cannot express rage directly at her mother (who is presumed to deserve it), so she turns her rage against herself. To his credit, he says that masochism is *not* part of a woman's normal development, but his mother-blaming theory of why some women do become masochists is so close to Freud's that it is used by those who *do* believe female masochism is innate.

In their professional training, virtually all psychotherapists are required to read Freud's work, and since our social climate is hospitable to mother-blaming, many therapists eagerly accept what Freud wrote. Freud said that females *constitutionally* suppress their aggression. That is, from birth they are destined to suppress their aggression, and society helps that process along. This, he writes, is masochism—destructiveness turned inward. According to Freud, what speeds this turning inward is the Oedipal conflict. At about the age of four, the young girl begins to wish for her father's love (and lust) but realizes that she cannot fully have it. At approximately the same time, Freud writes, the girl "discovers" what he calls her "castration," that she has no penis. Freud assumes that the normal and desirable body has a penis and presumes that all little girls see it that way, too. Before we accept Freud's concept of "penis envy"—the idea that all girls wish that they had penises—we need to bear in mind that some girls (and even boys) feel "penis pity"; when they first see a penis they think it is funny-looking or silly and are glad they don't have to worry about having an appendage that doesn't seem very easy to control. But Freud ignored any negative feelings girls might have about penises and wrote that not only were little girls disappointed to discover that they themselves had no penis, but they also felt disappointed and even contemptuous toward their mothers when they discovered that they, too, lacked this glorious organ. The little girl, he thought, blamed herself and her mother for her own lack of a penis and wondered whether her father's lack of love for her might be related to this "inferiority." Freud didn't say why the little girl might not blame her father, rather than her mother, for not having given her a penis. But, in any case, Freud felt that these disappointments in herself and in her mother led the little girl to "need to accept her feelings of bodily and personal inferiority," according to Harold Blum. This acceptance was considered to be predetermined by her congenital masochism (which was assumed to exist because of the inevitable physical pain in women's lives, as discussed in Chapter 2).

Psychoanalyst Isidor Bernstein in the *Journal of the American Psychoanalytic Association* in 1983 suggested that a mother who is loving and "feminine enough" will not make her daughter feel that she has a "defect," that is, that she was castrated. This is another example of the "inadequate mother" category of theories, because if all females have the defect of masochism, which some analysts attribute to the girl's recognition that she is "castrated" (has no penis), the implication is that their mothers were not loving and feminine enough.

Thinking about these theories in much detail can be like falling into a black hole. If you dwell on what such writers mean by being "feminine," you realize that they want mothers to be traditionally passive and accepting of whatever comes their way. But if mothers act that way, they are accused of being masochists and of providing masochistic role models for their daughters! The potential for holding mothers to blame for whatever happens to their daughters is seemingly limitless.

We learn something important about females' alleged masochism, though, if we look at the case study that Isidor Bernstein offers us to support his theory. He describes a girl who had a young, overburdened mother. The daughter felt that she was an additional burden to her mother, according to Bernstein, and her father and brothers always told her that females are inferior. She developed into a quiet, undemanding, self-sacrificing, and nurturant child in her attempt to be unlike her mother and to prove that females are not inferior. It seems to me that, given an overworked mother and a rejecting father and set of brothers, about all a girl *could* do in order to survive and perhaps win a little appreciation would be to do what she did. If she had become more assertive in such a traditional family she would have risked further mockery and rejection. She chose to try to gain some self-esteem by becoming something that families always accept—an unselfish workhorse. Like the Latinas described by Carole Browner, this daughter chose an adaptive survival mechanism, a way of getting something positive, some approval, if not love. But Bernstein calls her behavior "masochism," ignoring the strength and reasonableness of her behavior in favor of interpreting it as sick and self-defeating.

In another type of mother-blaming theory a mother's *aggression* is held responsible for her daughter's developing masochism. Psychoanalyst Arthur Valenstein, in the *Journal of the American Psychoanalytic Association,* described in 1981 a female child who had an "overwhelming widowed mother who often was aggressive toward her." He claims that her mother's influence combined with the "innate primary masochistic drive" to make the child even more masochistic than normal. The implication is that the daughter treated herself the way her mother treated her, both of them directing aggression toward the daughter in a variation on the familiar theory of masochism being aggression turned inward.

In regard to this theory, too, the "masochism" explanation is both unnecessary and puzzling, in view of the psychological facts of the case. Valenstein says that this daughter's relationship with her mother was "symbiotic," or excessively close. Symbiotic relationships are characterized by a great deal of mutual love and a great deal of mutual dependence. The excessive dependence ultimately leads to difficulty in achieving a healthy separation and that difficulty is often expressed through hostility and aggressiveness. Therefore, we can assume that the daughter in this symbiotic relationship received some love from her mother. If her mother was also aggressive toward her, then the daughter's self-esteem was probably damaged. This girl, then, would be accustomed to some love and affection but would have poor self-esteem. People with poor self-esteem are usually hesitant to take risks in relationships, reluctant to give up whatever they have, because they believe they do not deserve any better. It is *not* that they *want* to suffer; it is that they have good reason to feel that a change is likely to lead to something still worse. This, then, is another case study that has been interpreted only as a sign of female masochism but which could justifiably be interpreted as another instance of a female doing her best, given the circumstances, to find some happiness.

Valenstein does not explain *why* a mother's aggressiveness might lead to her daughter's masochism. Perhaps we find the answer in Robert Bak's suggestion that "masochism endangers the self in order to preserve the (valued) object"; in other words, if you are a child, you are dependent on your mother, and so you need to believe that she is good and dependable. If she does something "bad" to you, it is more frightening if you believe *she* is bad—and, therefore, that you can't count on her to meet any of your needs—than if you believe that your own badness led her to treat you as she did.

The last category of mother-blaming theories about a daughter's masochism is that of the *unloving* mother. An example of this is psychoanalyst Rudolph Loewenstein's claim that masochistic behavior is the child's attempt to "force the mother into manifestations of love," a claim that does not reflect much faith in mothers' willingness to act lovingly toward their children. For example, a child may refuse all rewards that are offered until a parent at last shows concern by saying, "Oh, honey, *do* eat something! I don't want you to go hungry!"

The one type of theory that is not mother-blaming is exemplified by psychoanalyst Robert D. Stolorow, who in 1975 wrote in the *International Journal of Psychoanalysis* about what he calls "the narcissistic function of masochism." According to Stolorow, masochists stunt their own development in order to protect their image of their parent as all-good. This is similar to Robert Bak's suggestion that children behave masochistically because of their need to believe in the goodness of the parent on whom they depend. Stolorow, refreshingly, does not specifically mention the mother as opposed to the father in this connection. Even in Stolorow's theory, though, it makes no sense to call this behavior masochistic. A more appropriate explanation would be that it is the willingness to take blame upon oneself as a way to deny the frightening thought that one is dependent on a parent who is not dependable or good.

In the face of all these mother-blaming theories, we might well ask the ancient, plaintive question, "What's a mother to do?" The first, most important step is to be aware, as we raise our daughters, of the danger to which society subjects both them and us, by teaching girls to behave passively and selflessly and then calling that behavior masochistic and sick. New mothers need to see far enough into the future to realize that the "feminine" behavior they are instructed to teach to their daughters will later make them likely to be *called* sick and disturbed and also to *be* too self-denying for their own good. We can begin to explore ways to enhance our daughters' self-respect other than by teaching them to be traditionally feminine or to lose touch with their own deepest feelings and wishes. We can help them to focus on their developing strengths and sense of justifiable pride rather than encouraging them to stake all their self-esteem on their sense of traditional femininity, which is called "masochism." In this way we can help to protect our daughters from being shaped or beaten into submission and then told that the seeds of their self-defeat were in them from birth; we can prevent them from being unjustly blamed for their own unhappiness, as Sophie was blamed for hers.

CHAPTER 5

Women in Relationships with Men

CHLOE   Why are you so against [my husband] Oliver?
MARJORIE Because I'm hungry and the waiter's being bloody.
         And because he makes you unhappy.
CHLOE   No he doesn't. Men don't make women unhappy.
         Women make themselves unhappy.
MARJORIE Who says so? Oliver?
CHLOE   Yes.   —FAY WELDON, *Female Friends*

Do certain women become involved with certain men because they need to suffer, and do they stay involved *because* the men bring them pain? A character in John Updike's novel, *The Witches of Eastwick,* thinks so: "She needed pain to remind her she was a woman. She needed to get down on her knees and drink some horrible man's nice cold come. She needed to be beaten." I do not think that women seek suffering in their relationships with men, but I do think that we need to examine these relationships very closely in order to understand what gives rise to that mistaken impression. You may have heard the saying, "It takes two to make a bad marriage or relationship." That is not always true. Sometimes it takes one disturbed or self-centered person and one person who has been taught that the best way to be a "good woman" is to remain in her relationship with her man—not in order to suffer but in order to improve it. The effort to improve a relationship with a man rather than simply ending it is particularly understandable in view of the fact that in 1980 there were 123 single women for every 100 single men.

I want to tell you the story of Sheila, whose relationship with Lyndon shows how much of what passes for masochism in women in their relationships with men is worthy of our understanding and admiration rather than our scorn. Although this story is about a young couple, its themes characterize most female-male relationships of all ages and social classes.

Sheila is an intelligent, reasonably self-aware young woman. At age 20, she met Lyndon, a bright, interesting man three years her senior. It was clear from the beginning that Lyndon found Sheila attractive but that he had some fears of emotional closeness. Sheila and Lyndon lived in different cities, about 1,000 miles apart, and could not see each other very often. Sometimes they had great fun together, dancing, spending time with mutual friends, or discussing common interests. When Sheila told Lyndon that his blue eyes looked particularly lovely when he wore a blue shirt, he narrowed those blue eyes suspiciously and asked her, "What do you want from me?" At such times, Sheila said to herself, "I know he's afraid of anyone getting too close to him and he's told me he doesn't like dependent women. *I* know I didn't compliment him because of my dependence on him, but I need to find a way to make that clear to him." She tried her best, but he didn't seem to understand.

Lyndon did show Sheila that he cared about her. When they were apart, he sent her long, loving letters and he spoke affectionately and longingly when he telephoned her. When they were together, he occasionally made some abrupt comment, such as, "I might marry you. . . . Now let's go cook dinner." When he made these remarks, Sheila saw that he loved her but had to overcome some fear in order to show

how he felt. Once he had said what was on his mind he had to change the subject quickly.

They continued to see each other during Sheila's junior and senior years. Sheila applied to graduate schools in San Francisco, because she loved the city, and also in the small town where Lyndon attended graduate school, in case he wanted her to live with him. In February of Sheila's senior year, Lyndon proposed marriage. Sheila was not in any hurry to marry, but she realized that this was a big step for Lyndon to take. After talking it over with him and giving the matter some thought, she decided to marry him, since she loved him, believed he loved her, and felt they had a great deal in common—their religious and socioeconomic backgrounds, their intellectual orientation, and a number of similar interests such as dancing and traveling.

At their wedding reception, in the receiving line, Lyndon turned to Sheila and said with panic in his voice, "Oh, my God, what does it mean to be married?" Sheila was appalled and furious, but she smiled brightly and said, "I guess we're about to find out!"

Sheila and Lyndon separated one and one-half years later. Sheila felt that the marriage failed primarily because of Lyndon's fear of intimacy, which went much deeper than she had imagined, deeper than even he had realized. They were both quite certain that this would not have emerged if they had merely lived together; something about being married brought out his most intense fears. At the time of the separation, Lyndon also suggested that Sheila was greatly to blame, because of what he called her deep dependency needs. She did not really *feel* dependent, but two things conspired to convince her that he was right: the fact that "everyone knows" that females are dependent and her mislabeling as "dependency" her feeling of connectedness and her capacity for warmth and love.

Sheila and Lyndon have remained on cordial terms, seeing each other for dinner every few years when he comes to a conference in the city to which she has moved. Years after their divorce, Lyndon told Sheila that his psychoanalysis taught him, "There was no way you could have made that marriage work. I was too frightened of intimacy. You did all that anyone could have done."

During their marriage, Sheila had had another major, disappointing surprise: Lyndon was threatened by her intelligence. She had never been intellectually competitive, and she genuinely enjoyed other people's intelligence. For months she was unable to see how competitive Lyndon was with her, because she hated to believe that someone she loved could have such petty feelings. She also found it hard to understand how anyone could need to outdo someone he cared for instead of taking pride in what she accomplished; by contrast, she delighted in his accomplishments.

Furthermore, over the months, Sheila became aware of another side of Lyndon, through incidents such as the following: Sheila had worked hard all day and suggested to Lyndon that they go to a movie that night. He said he didn't feel like going, so she asked if he would mind if she went on her own. He said that was fine. She dressed, put on her coat, and as she started to leave, Lyndon looked up from the rocking chair in which he was curled and pleaded, like a small child, "Don't leave me here alone." Sheila had never suspected how much Lyndon feared being alone. In fact, it was Lyndon, not Sheila, who had strong dependency needs; so strong were they that he felt that if he gave them free rein Sheila would swallow him up.

Making a decision about whether or not to stay in a relationship is like weighing something on a balance scale. If the relationship is 90 percent good and 10 percent bad, you stay in it, of course, and the same goes for an 80–20 split. When it gets to 70 or 60 percent good, you stay or leave depending upon the particular nature of the bad part and whether or not the 70 or 60 percent is really terrific.

Sometimes what is good is in the relationship itself—he has a great sense of humor or capacity for tenderness, he's a great lover, or he's genuinely proud of the work you do. Sometimes what is good comes from somewhere else—staying in the relationship gives you economic security or helps you to keep a sense of your identity as his wife or his woman.

Women who question a man's behavior can lose their sense of being "appropriately" feminine, the social approval attendant on being a good wife and a feminine woman, love or attachment, and economic support from their husbands. This leaves most women virtually no real choice, and it exposes them to being mislabeled masochistic. In fact, if there were such a thing as a genuine masochist, she or he would choose pain if offered pleasure or self-esteem *without* pain. This choice, however, is not what is offered to women.

In 1941 Theodor Reik wrote that the so-called masochist enjoys not the pain but what is "bought" with the pain. Few have taken serious note of what Reik said.

In male-female relationships, at least six aims can be achieved through some suffering, and all of these are healthy, desirable goals in themselves. They cause trouble when the person who helps you to reach those goals is also the person who causes you substantial pain. Then, it's time to see if you can attain those goals on your own or with people who bring you less pain or none at all.

The first goal is attainment of *a sense of self-esteem or even a sense that one really exists*. Reik said that staying in an upsetting situation in order to enhance one's self-esteem is different only in degree from the behavior of saints and martyrs, who are willing to suffer in order to be a part of a higher good. For Sheila, putting up with some of Lyndon's hangups helped her to feel that she was a *real* woman, a woman who could be patient when someone she loved had his own troubles.

After she and Lyndon were divorced, Sheila became involved with Arthur, a man quite a bit older than she who had an international reputation for the excellent work he had done in his field, which was related to hers. She thought that at last she had found a man who was successful enough not to be threatened by her intelligence and achievements. Both she and Arthur believed that Arthur was a genius and that Sheila was only fairly bright, but bright enough to appreciate Arthur's genius. Sheila's self-esteem, then, was enhanced by Arthur's choice of her as a sounding board, as the woman most worthy of his regard. When he told her that her ideas were not very good, she accepted his criticism because she believed he was right; since he was so smart, he could judge whether or not she was any good.

Although she mislabels such women's behavior "masochism," Jessica Benjamin's comment in her 1983 paper, "Master and Slave: The Fantasy of Erotic Domination," is a stunningly accurate summary of such relationships: "Masochism is a search for recognition of the self by another who alone is powerful enough to bestow this recognition."

Sheila and Arthur's story may sound familiar to you because it is so typical. One of the most famous examples of this kind of relationship was that of Zelda and F. Scott Fitzgerald. According to Zelda's biographer, Nancy Milford, some of the material for Scott's novel *Tender Is the Night* was taken from Zelda's letters, and Scott drew on some of her writing for *This Side of Paradise*. Furthermore, according to Milford, although Zelda wrote most of a short story called "Our Own Movie Queen," it was published under Scott's name alone, and Zelda wrote articles that were attributed to them both.

One example of how Sheila and Arthur related to each other in this regard will suffice. When Sheila was a graduate student, she and Arthur attended a conference in a foreign country. The subject of the conference was one with which Sheila had only limited familiarity but about which Arthur was one of the world's authorities. The night before Arthur was to give a commentary on five papers that other people were to present ahead of him, Arthur said to Sheila, "I've read all these papers and I can't find any themes or ideas that would tie them all together. Would you look at them for me and see what you think?"

Sheila's heart pounded as she read, because she wanted to be of some use to Arthur but feared that she was way out of her depth. After spending several hours reading the papers, thinking about them, and making notes, she gave Arthur her opinion. He smiled and said, "Good! That's just what I had decided to say!" For the first time, Sheila found the strength to get angry at Arthur. "But you told me you couldn't think of anything to say! Why didn't you tell me what you thought and ask me to read the papers and see if I agreed?" "Oh," he replied patronizingly, "I didn't want you to be influenced by what I thought." Then she really got angry. "How dare you think that I have so little intellectual backbone that I would think something was brilliant just because you said it!" she cried.

Next morning, she heard Arthur suavely present her ideas, nearly word for word as she had spoken them. He added a few witty remarks, which greatly amused the audience. A week later, back at home, Sheila was typing up the text of Arthur's talk from the conference, since he had been asked to publish it in a prestigious journal. As she prepared the title page, having typed the manuscript, she asked him in a joking tone of voice, "How come my name isn't on this as a coauthor?" Sheila believes that if Arthur had responded calmly, she probably would have let the matter drop. However, he bristled—no doubt because he knew she was right—and tried to make excuses by saying, "I had the ideas first." She countered, "But I had the same ideas within hours of when you did, we discussed them together ahead of time, and you presented them in just the words I had used!" So her name went on the paper—as second author. She now realizes that Arthur had probably never read the papers and simply wanted to save himself the bother of slogging through them.

Had Arthur been a fellow graduate student, or had he not seemed so brilliant, Sheila would have gained less self-esteem by staying with him and helping him with his work. As it was, she put up with the frustration and the humiliation of his telling her that she was less smart than he, because he said she was so much smarter than *other* women. That is a familiar pattern in female-male relationships. A man will attempt to ensure a woman's loyalty by setting her up against other women, making her feel that she is better because this particular man has chosen her. Although the women's movement has raised women's awareness of this male tactic, the current experience of my patients, my students, members of my audiences when I lecture, my friends, and myself show that the problem persists. It appears to diminish in effectiveness in proportion to women's economic and emotional dependence on men.

A subcategory of women who endure some pain in order to gain self-esteem is women in relationships with married men. A journalist planning to write an article about this topic told me that she firmly believed that the women were masochistic. However, many women prefer to have a relationship that gives them some self-esteem—even if it means the man is often unavailable to them—than to have a constant relationship with a less attentive man or with no one at all. This latter possibility is very common, in view of the 123:100 ratio of single women to single men, especially when one considers that a large proportion of those 100 men are gay.

Sometimes it's not even self-esteem that is gained through endurance of pain or misery; it is something even more fundamental—the feeling that one exists. This can come from the recognition that "I suffer, therefore, I am." It can also come from someone else's recognition of your misery: If he sees how unhappy I am, at least he sees me, at least we both know I'm alive. Like the child who can get attention only by misbehaving, being punished may hurt, but it is better than getting no attention at all.

A second aim of women who remain in unhappy relationships with men is *to win or keep their love, or at least the hope of being loved.* If you love your partner because of his good qualities, even if he sometimes treats you badly you may hope that if you are patient with his bad behavior he will be grateful and will love you that much more. Many women who become involved with married men—in addition to seeking self-esteem, as mentioned earlier—also fit this category. Or you may simply put up with his behavior in the spirit of enduring the bad in order to keep his love. As a wise friend, who works as a registered massage therapist with people who suffer from chronic physical pain, said, "Feeling empty or lonely can be worse than feeling pain." He told me the story of a woman who had had intense pain in her neck and shoulder muscles for years. These were the muscles she tensed when she felt angry or frightened. On one occasion, she had a sudden memory of having tensed these muscles when her rather punitive parents were mocking her. The pain gave her an excuse to escape to her room, where she found a little peace and quiet, a refuge from her parents' rejection. The pain also gave her something to think about besides her hurt feelings. By thinking about her aching body, she could avoid the sense of loneliness and worthlessness that her parents made her feel. I would add that focusing on the pain can help you avoid facing the depressing fact that a person you love may not love you or may not be capable of showing love for you.

How many aches and pains are born of such feelings? Physical pain can result from the tensing of a whole host of muscles—in the back, the shoulders and neck, the jaw, the hands and arms, the stomach. Muscles that remain tense can lead to the misalignment of the spine and the pinching of nerves, all of which can be extremely painful. Rarely does anyone completely fake illness and pain, but in some relationships physical pain is the only way to get the other person to show that he cares. And depression and tension can lead to genuine physical changes that cause real physical suffering.

Another version of the suffering-in-order-to-be-loved theme involves the myth that women have enormous capacity for destructiveness. Images of Cleopatra, Circe, witches with supernatural powers to do evil, Lady Macbeth, and the housewife who drains her husband of all his energy and his seed come to mind.

Where does the "demanding woman" image come from? In part, it comes from the fact that, since women are supposed to *give* nurturance, not *ask* for it, any request they make of a man can be regarded as excessive. In addition, since women, not men, are considered the emotional sex, and "emotional" has been classified as opposed to "rational," women's needs are perceived to be under little or no rational control; they are thought to be boundless and unmeetable. Furthermore, recent work on the Victorian era has suggested that a major source of some men's visions of women as loose and lascivious has been their anxiety about their own sexual adequacy. This information helps us to understand current myths and fears about women's potentially overpowering needs, since contemporary men who fear that they are sexually inadequate often attempt to deal with that fear by casting women as impossibly demanding both sexually and emotionally—"It's not that *I* can't do enough; it's that *she* wants too much." In a society that has long taught women that men should be the center of their lives, it is as if some collective unconscious has taken note of the fact that one cannot make enormous demands and place severe restrictions on women without expecting that they will want considerable compensation in some form, whether in sexual activity, emotional tribute, or material goods.

In her work on masochism, Gertrud Lenzer pointed out that in the original "masochism" scenario by Count von Sacher-Masoch, it is the man who desires and the woman who is desired, and—as in the Marquis de Sade's earlier work—the man who asks to be whipped and beaten by the woman. These male writers apparently felt vulnerable to women's sexual charms and in their stories conveyed the belief that, given a bit of power over a man, a woman becomes remorselessly cruel. When I speak to women's groups of all kinds, I find that one of the women's greatest worries is their knowledge of how quick men are to believe that women are evil and powerful and of how vulnerable to women this makes them feel. The women do not feel powerful, but they know that men fear them. They try to allay men's fears by appearing less threatening, like animals that present their throats to their potential attackers as a sign that they are harmless. The "presentation of the throat" by women takes various forms, allowing themselves to be mistreated emotionally or physically or showing that they can be hurt by the man's behavior. The hope is that, "If I show him I am so harmless that *he* can hurt *me,* he won't be afraid of me, he won't feel—or make me feel—that I am some kind of witch—and he will love me." As Karen Horney wrote in 1939 in *New Ways of Psychoanalysis,* women's endurance of suffering is an attempt "to gain safety and satisfaction in life through inconspicuousness and dependency." And Theodor Reik has said that the "masochist" makes sure that his or her failings and sufferings are *seen* by the other person in the relationship, as a way of saying, "I'm not threatening—I'm not even much good, so you shouldn't be afraid of me." Indeed, much of the traditional feminine role has consisted of appearing dependent and becoming as inconspicuous as possible. In *Body Politics,* social scientist Nancy Henley documented the many ways in which females are taught to take up as little room as possible—crossing their legs, keeping their arms and legs close to their bodies at all times, wearing corsets and other restrictive clothing in days gone by.

A slightly different form of enduring pain in the hope of being loved is illustrated by Ingrid, a 60-year-old woman who wanted to go to Japan with her 65-year-old husband, Robert. Robert feared that leaving his business for the month-long trip would mean losing a great deal of money. Much of his self-esteem as a man comes from feeling that he is a "good provider," since he grew up in poverty. Ingrid, understanding his fear of having to struggle like his father, gave up her dream of the trip. Was she masochistic? No, but she knew that if she kept pushing for the trip, Robert would feel so threatened that he would become more distant from her and she would jeopardize their normally loving relationship. She may also have felt, in a related form of suffering-in-order-to-be-loved, that he would value her even more because of her willingness to endure disappointment for his sake.

Similarly, Sheila hoped that if she was patient and understanding about Lyndon's inadequacies, he would feel grateful toward her. She knew that to criticize him could only confirm his fear of her as a powerful, angry woman, because he frequently told her under those circumstances that she was too powerful and angry. She never understood how he could consider her both powerful and dependent at the same time, although she knew that he felt both ways about her.

It is maddening that these two views of women exist throughout society, but only rarely does anyone question the logic of their coexistence. In *The Mermaid and the Minotaur* Dorothy Dinnerstein suggests that the explanation lies in the fact that most males are raised primarily by mothers and, thus, learn to regard women as unduly powerful. At the same time, growing boys are taught that they are supposed to be independent, particularly of women's influence, and one way they deal with this is to regard males as independent and women as dependent, incapable of controlling them. Thus, men fear that women have a great deal of power over them, and believing that women are dependent helps to reverse the power balance that makes them so uncomfortable. Both myths—about women's power and about women's dependency—serve as strong controls over women's behavior. That, perhaps, is what enables them to coexist—that they serve to maintain the current balance of power.

A third reason why women endure pain in their relationships with men is *that they love the person who causes the pain* (though not *because* he causes them pain). Sheila certainly loved Lyndon for all of the reasons described earlier. Like most women, she had been taught that loving someone means being patient with him, overlooking his faults, and helping him to become a better person. This is considered a part of maturity, especially for women. To walk out on someone you love, just because he has caused you some unhappiness, is considered immature and unwomanly.

Similarly, Ingrid, whose husband was reluctant to take her to Japan, should not be called masochistic. We should instead acknowledge that because she loves him, she has some respect for, and patience with, his feelings and fears, and thus did not insist on taking the trip.

In describing how she became addicted to drugs, Barbara Gordon relates in *I'm Dancing as Fast as I Can* the history of her relationship with her lover Eric, who at first treated her well and later made her his prisoner, both physically and psychologically. Trying to understand how he gained so much control over her, Gordon writes:

> I went back to my room and lay on the cot, remembering Eric as I had loved him. How he smelled, how he smiled, how he made love. I turned over and buried my face in the pillow. Why did you do it, Eric? Why did you let me stay in the apartment? Why didn't you get me to a hospital? And then, from a very deep part of me, I asked myself another question. Why did you let him do it? Because I loved him. That was the only answer. I loved him.

This passage illustrates that often it is not that the woman desires the pain her lover causes her but rather that the good features of the relationship—either current or remembered—make the unhappiness worth enduring. We can understand this pattern more clearly if we think about this type of situation apart from the sex of the people involved. We may ask, "Is it reasonable to stay in a relationship that has brought you a great deal of happiness if the other person does some cruel things? Or should you leave immediately?" The reasonable answer would seem to be that your past experience suggests that your loved one has the capacity to care about you and to treat you well. It is only logical to regard the bad behavior as a temporary aberration, perhaps a result of some current stress, and to help him work it out *because you love him*. To consider immediate desertion seems inhumane and selfish. But at what point do you decide that the cruelty is excessive and permanent? That is an individual decision that has to include consideration of what other alternatives you have, how much your present situation hurts, his apparent motivation to change, and so on.

A fourth aim, as mentioned in Chapter 2, the *expiation of guilt,* is an aim of some women who stay in painful relationships. Guilt is no doubt one of the most excruciating of all feelings to endure, and most people will do almost anything to dispel it. Because women are encouraged more than men to worry about other people's feelings *and* to uphold moral standards, when they believe they have hurt someone's feelings or behaved immorally, they tend to feel guilty. The guilt that makes them willing to endure unhappiness may be of recent origin, or it may be the guilt they learned to feel as very young girls. We are somehow less surprised, less jarred, to see a little girl who frequently says, "I'm sorry" or "Would it be all right if I did X?" than by seeing such behavior in a little boy. Little girls learn, above all, not to allow their needs to get in the way of other people's needs. So if they feel they have slipped up, they feel intensely guilty. Thus, women in interpersonal relationships are far more likely than men to feel guilty and ashamed about asserting their right to have some of their own needs met.

In her book, *The Total Woman,* Marabel Morgan describes the end of the day syndrome in a "traditional" family, in which the husband comes home from work, tired and tense, wanting peace and quiet and comfort. The housewife, says Morgan, also feels like saying, "Me! Me! Meet my needs!" Morgan's "solution" for a happy marriage is for the woman to forget about her needs and to meet her husband's instead. (Morgan's promise is that this will make him so happy that when a wife "fill[s] his cup" she'll get the "overflow.") Morgan never discusses whether the wife might occasionally deserve to have *her* needs met first. Her book and its twin, Helen Andelin's *Fascinating Womanhood,* both made the bestseller list because there was a huge market for this kind of advice, which played into what many men wanted in their wives, as well as the beliefs of millions of women about the nature of morally upright feminine behavior. For many men, these books spoke to their longings to have their own needs met before having to give to anyone else (and who hasn't sometimes had such longings?), although this fantasy is only fleeting for people who want egalitarian, *mutually* caring relationships. What some women found appealing about Morgan's and Andelin's advice was that they suggested that enduring whatever suffering he dishes out helps you work off your guilt about your unfeminine wish to have some of your own needs met.

Some women in "traditional" family arrangements also feel guilty because their men go out into the world, where they develop high blood pressure and ulcers, in order to do their best for their wives and children. Although no one thinks the world of paid work is easy, what is too often overlooked by both partners in such families is how difficult it is to take the traditional woman's role, to shoulder virtually the entire burden of child rearing, and to keep the family running as smoothly and wholesomely as an idealized television sitcom. Women who fill the traditional wife and mother roles are made to feel that they are "getting away" with something because they don't have to face the big bad world out there. Never mind what it takes as a wife and mother to deal with the responsibility for the lives and happiness of a number of other people, the media image (and often their husbands' image) of such women is of self-indulgent narcissists who spend lots of time having their hair done and shopping for new clothes. Seen in that light, enduring mistreatment from the husband when he comes home from the rough outside world can seem little enough payment for one's "easy" ride as a housewife.

A housewife who also works outside the home is even more susceptible to guilt, because she is not home all day to prepare meals and remember to get out a candle for the meatloaf (to celebrate Johnny's home run!), as Marabel Morgan says a good woman should do.

Although she was far from a Total Woman, Sheila felt horribly guilty every time Lyndon seemed threatened by her achievements at work. She knew enough psychological theory to believe that her accomplishments made him feel "castrated," and most women will tell you there is no quicker way to feel ashamed and unwomanly than to be accused of psychologically castrating their men, robbing them of their masculine identity. So Sheila felt she owed it to Lyndon to put up with his insults and demeaning comments, to atone for her sin of achievement.

In this connection, in *Fascinating Womanhood,* Helen Andelin makes one of the most guilt-inducing statements ever written. By describing masculine pride as extremely sensitive and fragile, she declares that one of women's primary duties is at all costs to avoid damaging that pride. Such a warning causes women to worry that any time they have differed with their husbands, any time they have had a different idea or— heaven forbid—a better one, they have done their husbands a horrible wrong. Once again, women are made to choose between denying their own needs and feelings—for which they may be called masochists—and asserting themselves, knowing that they will have to pay for that behavior—for which they may also be called masochists.

The fifth aim, related to the expiation of guilt as a product of suffering, is the *allaying of anxiety.* For women whose husbands periodically humiliate or abuse them, emotionally or physically, the waiting period before the next assault can arouse intense anxiety. These women may find that the only way to stop the anxiety is to precipitate the assault as soon as possible, to get it over with for the time being. Some battered wives say that the only aspect of their lives over which they have any control is the *timing* of the beatings they receive. Theodor Reik called the precipitation of an upsetting incident for this purpose an attempt to "bind anxiety," to "master" the event; I would also call it a way to meet the basic, healthy human need of avoiding feeling (and being) completely helpless.

Particularly if your man feels guilty after abusing or insulting you, and if his guilt leads him to show you a little warmth and attention, you may bring on the painful situation in order to attain the positive things that follow it. Sheila knew that Arthur was likely to hear about it if a paper she presented at a conference was well received. She knew that he would tell other people that he was proud of her but would tell her only what he found in her ideas to criticize. So, like an animal presenting its throat, she sometimes told Arthur that her presentation had gone well but that she had had trouble answering a question from a member of the audience, and she would ask Arthur's advice for handling such a situation in the future.

The sixth aim that a woman can seek through suffering—especially a woman who has few economic or social resources and is involved with a man who mistreats her—can be a *chance to show her strength*. As Reik has written, by submitting to punishment one can sometimes show rebelliousness, an attitude that says, "In spite of this, I shall endure." Reik calls this an effort "to save [one's] internal independence when [one] has to give up the external one." Sheila certainly felt that she was being tempered through learning to endure Lyndon's coldness toward her and then Arthur's assaults on her self-esteem. After all, part of what it means to be a Good Woman—in addition to appearing weak and dependent so as to be unthreatening—is, almost paradoxically, to be strong enough to withstand whatever your man sends your way. In other words, women are to be alternately weak and strong, as it suits men.

In her pursuit of Total Womanhood, Marabel Morgan admiringly relates the following story of an exemplary wife. Morgan has just instructed the woman reader to make Plan A for each day but to be ready to switch to Plan B when something interferes, and to have Plans C and D ready for further emergencies. The purpose of having all these plans in readiness is to enable you to remain calm, so that when your husband comes home from work and it's "Me! Me!" time, you are tranquil enough to drop everything and meet his needs. Morgan writes:

> A neighbor trudged into my house the other day looking like a tired Phyllis Diller. She was laughing, not crying, when she said, 'Well, I'm down to Plan G now, but would you believe, I haven't lost my cool yet? It's amazing how differently I see problems now. It's almost a challenge to see if I can make Plan B work as well as my original plan. This ABC business is like a game I play with the fates of the day, and I'm winning!' Here was a happy and flexible Total Woman.

I think of the woman's "obligation" to protect her husband from stress, so that *he* won't have ulcers and heart attacks, and I wonder what will happen to a wife who has to remain calm and even find excitement and challenge in repeated upheavals in her daily life. In addition to causing physical disorders among women, there is no doubt that such behavior contributes to the high rates of depression and drug use among wives.

Sheila felt that her patience with both Lyndon's and Arthur's mistreatment of her—mistreatment that sprang from the men's own inadequacies and fears—was a sign of her strength. She would have preferred to live without that mistreatment, but since it was part of her marriages, she used it to enhance her self-image and her real capacity to be strong.

In the examples just given, the women came to feel stronger simply through enduring. Two variations on the theme of strength through suffering are worthy of note. The first is that one way to acquire power is through making the other person feel guilty, unappealing though that may be. So, when my friend Marianne quietly endures her husband's periodic coldness, he sometimes feels guilty, and this gives her a certain kind of control over him. No doubt, she would gladly give up her power in return for genuine warmth from him; but when one already feels rejected and shut out one doesn't also want to feel altogether powerless.

The other variation on this theme is that the victim of mistreatment can derive vicarious strength through her identification with the mistreater. When Arthur would criticize her work, for example, Sheila could think to herself, "He wouldn't even bother to criticize most people's work, but because he is such a brilliant man he is in a position to recognize good work, and he thinks mine is good enough to spend time critiquing."

In trying to understand why women stay in unhappy relationships with men it is helpful to consider a phenomenon that psychiatrists call *folie à deux,* which means an insanity shared by two. The term is applied to couples in which one of the members is psychotic and the other member—usually a woman who is dependent on the man—becomes thoroughly caught up in the psychotic's delusional system. They come to share the delusion, for example, that the man is the savior and that the world is persecuting him because no one knows his real identity. It occurred to me that this was a description, although in milder form, of a large proportion of marriages and female-male relationships. I believe that the term is relevant to many relationships in which women are dependent on their men and the couple creates and maintains the delusion—in the sense of an erroneous belief—that the husband is extremely special and must be protected and defended at all costs. In 1984, counselor Gretchen Grinnell observed in her presentation at the Women's Institute of the American Orthopsychiatric Association convention that the men in such relationships "indoctrinate the women into their belief systems and are very paranoid," two characteristics of the classic *folie à deux.*

Sheila's marriage to the brilliant Arthur was just such a relationship. The wives who stood by their lawbreaking husbands in the Watergate and other well-known white-collar crime scandals have often been admired for their loyalty. As philosopher Kathryn Morgan has observed, the traditional "woman in love" is supposed to yield her autonomy to the man: "Self-abnegating self-sacrifice [is supposed to be] morally fulfilling for a real woman."

In our society, the strict division of behavior into "masculine" and "feminine" and the threat of ostracism if your behavior is "wrong" for your sex constitute the most powerful force keeping women in *folie à deux* relationships with men. As in many societies, we have allowed the powers that be to divide the world into two groups of people. The members of Group A are taught to be concerned with and sensitive to relationships and feelings, to be skilled at interacting with others and at giving them emotional support and comfort. The members of Group B either are not taught much about relationships and emotions, or they may even be taught that to be concerned about such things is wrong or bad for them. Group A members are, of course, women, and Group B members are men. Then, we insist that one member of Group A pair up with one member of Group B and that they live happily ever after! When a woman asks her male partner to show her a little warmth and affection or to talk with her about a problem in their relationship, she feels that she is asking for very little, and he feels that she is being incredibly demanding. In a way, they are both right. She isn't really asking for much, no more than most women have learned to give with ease. But for one who has never learned to do these things, doesn't know whether he can do them, or even feels he should be ashamed to do them, she is asking for the moon. Philosopher Ronnie deSousa has described this situation by saying, "What every woman wants in a man is another woman," another person who *can* express feelings and talk about what needs to be discussed in relationships. The less expressive person in a relationship tends to have much of the power, since the other person often has to worry about how the less expressive one is feeling and to try, with little feedback, to win his approval. According to Gloria Steinem, that is one reason so many women love to watch soap operas on television: The

men on those shows spend a great deal of time talking about
feelings and relationships—far more than most real-life men.
They even seem to enjoy it, and by and large the other characters in the show do not put them down for doing so.

In Olive Schreiner's classic novel, *The Story of an African Farm,* Schreiner poignantly describes this division of
roles and the passive, helpless position in which it places
women. She shows how traditionally feminine behavior is the
way to be a successful woman, that is, to catch a husband.
As one of her female characters says:

> A little bitterness, a little longing when we are young, a
> little futile searching for work, a little passionate striving
> for room for the exercise of our powers—and then we
> go with the drove. A woman must march with her regi-
> ment. In the end she must be trodden down or go with
> it; and if she is wise she goes. . . . A little weeping, a
> little wheedling, a little self-degradation, a little careful
> use of our advantages, and then some man will say—
> "Come be my wife!". . . Men are like the earth and
> we are the moon; we turn always one side to them, and
> they think there is no other, because they don't see it—
> but there is.

The authors of *Total Woman* and *Fascinating Womanhood* urge us to consider this hiding of one side of ourselves
from men as our sacred duty, not as a tragic way to have to
behave and a way of depriving a love relationship of its potential. Morgan advises women who feel upset to "call a girl
friend as your sounding board. Release your steam on her instead of on your tired husband." We are not supposed to
wonder why it is the wife's sacred duty to be her husband's
sounding board at a moment's notice, no matter what has
happened during her day, or why it is all right to burden one's
woman friends, since they have to give a great deal of energy
to being *their* men's sounding boards. Morgan writes suc-

cinctly about husband and wife: "He doesn't need your advice or leadership in times of trouble. He needs your ear, not your mouth."

Women who behave passively and self-effacingly are promised their reward: a husband. Rosemary Daniell writes from her own experience: "According to the myth, there exists, like the diploma at the end of a course, a perfect, or perfectible, man for every woman who has learned her skills." If he is not perfect, the fault must surely lie in her; she has not learned to give or to suffer enough.

Because a woman's fundamental obligation is to help her husband, she must find out whatever he wants her to do and then set about doing it. Morgan was horrified that the night her husband proposed marriage, he prefaced his proposal by a long recitation, through which she drowsed, waking only as he proposed, realizing that the recitation had been his description of what he wanted in a wife! She writes: "I couldn't admit I had slept through it all. I should have been awake. I could have saved myself and Charlie years of misery." How sad that she was about to marry a man with whom she did not feel comfortable enough to ask him to repeat his recitation; how sad that she was about to marry him but had no idea what he wanted; and how sad that she would have *done* whatever he asked if she had only known what it was. (And what does it say about her feelings for her husband that she fell asleep during his proposal speech!)

Letting us know that this is the way marriage *should* be, Morgan advises us to make lists of things we have to do and says:

> When your husband asks you to do something, he expects it to be done without reminding you. The next time he delegates a job to you, write it down. Give it top priority on your list. Many a husband is so convinced that this plan works that now, instead of asking his wife to do anything for him, he just writes it down on her master sheet.

In such relationships, women's self-esteem comes to depend on behaving in accordance with the rules. No matter what her husband does to her, a wife is to give him "unqualified acceptance," say Morgan and Andelin, but *he* is not expected to meet *her* needs. Their books read like manuals for masochism: "It is only when a woman surrenders her life to her husband, reveres and worships him, and is willing to serve him, that she becomes really beautiful to him."

It is supposed to be an added bonus if your man is a little brutal, since part of the Good Woman's role—part of what makes her feel proud of herself—is to tame the man. Furthermore, not being allowed to wield real power themselves, women can feel powerful if they are married to men who *do* wield it, even if it is at their expense.

What is particularly poignant about these books is that nearly every example of a wife's benefiting from her patience and endurance is of her husband giving her some material goods or even money. Outstanding because of their rarity are instances of a husband telling his wife he loves her, and no example is given of a husband showing any interest in listening to his wife's feelings; the closest any husband in Morgan's book comes to that is telling his wife that she can go ahead and redecorate the family room as she has been dying to do.

In *The Hearts of Men: American Dreams and the Flight from Commitment,* Barbara Ehrenreich describes how, during the 1960s, the *Playboy* philosophy exacerbated the division between masculine and feminine and added to the macho image and the flight from a close, committed relationship with a woman. Before that time, a Real Man was supposed to provide financial support for his wife and children, go with them on family outings on weekends, and take a real role in the family. But Hugh Hefner and his cohorts made those attitudes seem unmasculine, letting oneself be trapped like a wimp under some woman's thumb. Men's love of home and hearth was redefined as something about which any Real Man should be ashamed; instead, a man should crave ever more elaborate stereo systems and automobiles and ever more beautiful women—simultaneously or successively—but with ever less commitment and feeling. Since a Real Woman is less womanly if she wants her man to be less of a Real Man, women have been forced to put up with diminishing allegiance and affection from their men. If a woman demands more, she is accused of being unfeminine and castrating, but if she puts up with her man's lack of affection and involvement, she is called masochistic.

As for the men, a society that gives them unlimited power over women produces not only power-hungry men but many sadistic and vicious men as well. Rosemary Daniell writes that ". . . my lover, I was beginning to learn, liked not only reluctance, but humiliation, even fear. I knew his passion for hunting deer in North Georgia with razor-tipped arrows; now I recalled how he had told me in his other, literary voice— that 'the deer loved to be hunted.' " Men can come to believe that the victim loves to be mistreated.

Since it is the rare man who feels he can express a range of feelings and still be a Real Man, many women seek out men who are intense and exciting. They do this because intensity sometimes goes with some expression of feeling, and even when that feeling is only sexual passion or jealousy, it can seem better than simple coldness and absence of emotion. Daniell writes: "There's no doubt about it, Southern men have, and freely express, 'feelin's.' Add to that their desire to excel as lovers, their vulnerability to, even expectation of, female moods, and one begins to understand their charm." Those qualities can make it worth putting up with the abusiveness or even violence that may go with them.

I was stunned when, at a recent feminist conference, a woman (I'll call her Janet) who is famous for her tireless work on behalf of victims of rape and wife battering, made the following statement to me after hearing that I had written an article called "The Myth of Women's Masochism": "You must send me a copy of your article, because *I* know these women don't enjoy their pain, but it's much better if I have the word of a professional to back up my assertions." She paused and then said quietly, "As for me, though, I always go for the men who treat me badly. I guess I really am a masochist." Like many women, she was quick to see pathology in her own behavior, even though she could see the health and strength in others. It took only a couple of minutes with her to discover what she really finds attractive in these men, since she does not need to suffer. She is an extremely bright, energetic woman who has a passion for life and throws herself wholeheartedly into whatever she takes on. The typical undemonstrative American male has no appeal for her. She responds with excitement to men who can show some intensity and some passion for *something,* whether it is their work, or cleaning up the environment, or political activity. Unfortunately, since men are so often taught to hide their feelings, they are likely to find it hard to regulate the expression of them, so that they show either nothing at all or unbridled feeling. The latter is great when the feeling is either love or intellectual excitement, but when the feeling is rage it can be horrible. Janet's choice, then, is between a man who is so controlled that he can never match her intensity, and a more emotional man, who may also give vent to strong negative feelings. It is not surprising, I think, that such a woman would choose the latter option, but it is certainly not masochistic. As one woman wrote, after she had extricated herself from a bad marriage, she found that she missed her husband but did not miss his hostility and mistrust.

A slightly different—but important—way of looking at Janet's situation was suggested to me by Ronnie deSousa, who said that because women are encouraged to be in touch with their feelings, they often experience life more fully, letting life *affect* them. Some misname this "masochism" when it entails fully experiencing upsetting feelings, but it is often more accurate to call it being fully alive and open to a wide range of experience. When a woman mourns the loss of a loved one, weeping more and longer than the men who loved the deceased, she is often said to "wallow" in her grief, as though she enjoyed it. Psychotherapists know that fully experiencing the sense of loss leads to a healthier recovery, but even they sometimes call such women masochists.

In creating the myth of the New Man, who does show his feelings, the media have vastly complicated women's attempts to extricate themselves from unsatisfactory relationships with men by clouding their vision of their male partners. The media have given women the impression that there are large numbers of New Men out there, waiting to enter into loving, sensitive, egalitarian relationships with women. It is potentially harmful to believe in this myth. Of course, there are more and more men who are sincerely trying to be sensitive to women's needs and concerns, but they are still a rare breed. There is nothing new about women wanting to find such men; women have always loved men who read them poetry, because that romantic act suggests that they have some emotional sensitivity and capacity for expressing feelings. But we face several serious dangers if we believe that New Men are everywhere.

In the first place, many men are "passing" as New Men by saying things like "I cry at movies" or "I believe in making my needs and feelings clear to you." Crying at movies that have nothing to do with your relationship with him is nicely unthreatening, but is he touched or upset when *you* are emotionally moved or anguished? Similarly, there is nothing new about men making their needs and feelings known to women. This is not to say that all men are good at this but simply that they have traditionally been better at making their own needs known than at responding to the needs of their women. A genuine New Man would be one who cares about the feelings and needs of his partner and makes that caring clear. The first danger, then, is that we will mistakenly identify as "new" the man who happens to be better than most at making *his own* needs or feelings clear but who is hopelessly bad at responding to ours. In her book, *The Cinderella Complex*, Colette Dowling argues that women are dependent and are raised to want someone else to take care of them. In fact, though, men are at least as dependent as women, but we rarely notice men's dependency needs because they are usually being met by women (their mothers, their wives, or both) and because men are taught to conceal their dependency. There is nothing new about a man who tries to get women to meet his dependency needs; what is rare is one who will *admit* that he has them.

Another reason the myth that New Men are numerous is dangerous to women is that it plays into the handicap under which women are already operating—their tendency to take blame upon themselves. Thus, when her husband says, "I'm terrific, because I make breakfast for the kids," a woman may think, "He's right. That does make him better than most husbands, so why do I still feel so angry at him and so ungrateful?" The answer is that making breakfast is about the *only* untraditional thing he does; yet he wants her and all their friends to believe that he is a New Man. As women, we are taught to be appreciative of what others do for us, and we are taught not to expect much—in the realms of sharing of housework and child care and sensitivity to our feelings—from men. So when we get a crumb of New Man-type behavior, we believe we should be thoroughly satisfied and feel greedy if we want more. These feelings are intensified by our knowledge that, even if he is only 5 percent a New Man, that does make him better than most of our male alternatives. So we try to suppress our resentment for his failure to take half of the burdens or to be sensitive to us a little more often, fearful that if we don't suppress those feelings we risk losing him and being left with no one or with someone even worse.

The bind is even more difficult for women who sincerely sympathize with the difficulty men have in becoming liberated. It is clear that massive social support for New Man behavior—especially from other men—is still sadly lacking. It takes real guts for men to change, because most of the behavior a New Man takes on is behavior that has been considered low status as a result of its association with women:

housework, child care, expression of feelings, and sensitivity to the feelings of others. Knowing what our men are up against in trying to change makes us even more susceptible to the temptation to settle for less than what we deserve.

It must be obvious from the foregoing what needs to change. The strict division of behavior into "masculine" and "feminine" must be abolished. Women must be encouraged to be more self-assertive so that they do not have to depend for self-expression on their men, and men must be encouraged to show more warm and tender feelings. Furthermore, the work currently associated primarily with women—housekeeping and child care—must be valued far more highly, to raise women's self-esteem and to free them from enduring embarrassment about their undervalued work in order to feel like Real Women.

Finally, women must learn to recognize when the other person in their relationship is at fault and not be controlled by the threat that the other person will think they are not feminine or patient enough if they refuse to shoulder all the blame.

At the lowest point in my own life a few years ago I was feeling extremely depressed and powerless. Two incidents had particularly intensified those feelings. One was a disagreement I had had with a coworker, who wanted me to handle in a certain way a matter related to some research we were doing. I felt strongly that it should be handled quite differently, and we had made our opinions clear to each other. The second incident involved the tail end of a relationship I had had with a man I'll call Bruno, who used to call me insulting names when he was angry at me. (That's the kind of treatment I'd never stand for now, but when one is younger and has less self-esteem one sometimes puts up with such things, hoping that being good will make them improve.) Bruno and I had had a disagreement and, as usual, he had told me that if I did not agree to do what he wanted, I was a "disgusting bitch." I spent two days feeling massively depressed, but finally had a flash of insight. I realized that in both situations I was being controlled by the threat that if I did not go along with the other person's wishes, they would dislike me. Once I was conscious of that dilemma, I had enough self-respect to feel that I could risk disapproval, since I believed that my viewpoint was really factually and morally correct in both cases.

The next time I spoke with my colleague, I was able to stand my ground. Whether or not my opinion prevailed mattered less than that I no longer felt that her disapproval would mean that I was a lousy person. Then I telephoned Bruno and told him calmly but decisively that I would not give way in my decision. Before he could speak, I said calmly, "And I want you to know that the reason I am doing this is that I am a disgusting bitch." He was speechless. Our interactions were never the same after that, because I had taken away the powerful weapon he had used against me for so long. No longer could I be controlled by his opinion of me. It had taken intensive work, through psychotherapy and the support of some dear friends and family, to reach that point, but it was the turning point of my emotional life. Never again have I felt so depressed. And when I have noticed any feelings of depression, I have stopped and asked myself, "Who is holding over me the threat that they will not think I am a good woman if I don't do what they want?" (Or about whom do I have that worry, whether or not they are threatening me?) Every time I have asked that question, I have found that some such fear has been lurking, and I have been able to deal with it, understanding what is happening rather than being unconsciously controlled by the automatic "feminine" tendency to try to do what other people want.

Often it is youth or inexperience that keeps women in relationships with men who treat them badly. There is a great deal to be said for experience, since it can bring insight. As a character in the film *The Natural* says, we have two parts to our lives—the part we learn from, and the part we live after that. This is especially true of women, much of whose upbringing could appropriately be called "blindness training" or "How to fail to see that your husband has faults and to blame yourself for what goes wrong." It is men who are supposed to be rational and see things clearly; women are supposed to have a sunny, trusting optimism and rose-colored glasses. Given some experience, a little social support, and the passage of enough time to realize that not *everything* could possibly be their fault, most women can learn to extricate themselves from bad relationships and gain strength and insight in the process. Ann Landers received the following letter from a woman who did just that:

I worked while my husband attended college. During those four years our two children were born. We lived on carrots, oatmeal and powdered milk. I bought no clothes for seven years.

Once he asked me what I wanted for my birthday, and I said, "I'd love to eat out and go to a movie." "It's too expensive." (It would have been around $10.) Instead, he gave me an iron skillet that cost $11.

During all those years, the children and I had no vacations, no meals away from home, and very little pleasure. We put up with daddy's temper tantrums, when he knocked holes in the wall with his fists and slapped us around.

After a while he was traveling for a government agency, going to such exotic places as Bermuda, Hawaii, and Japan. At the same time he refused to take his family to the ocean for a weekend.

Naturally, when he traveled, his pockets were full of government money and it was easy to pick up women wherever he went. He has a good deal of charm when he decides to use it. When I learned he had been traveling with a variety of female companions, we separated.

After the divorce his star began to rise. Today he has a much younger wife, a home on the water, and a salary approaching $70,000 per year. He also has two sons who despise him, and an ex-wife who hates his guts.

Many times I have asked myself why I stayed with him. I know now it was because I was a dependent person. I grew up at a time when your father took care of you until you married, then your husband took care of you for the rest of your life.

If I have anything to thank the louse for, it is that he pushed me into the "cold, cruel world," and when put to the test, I did very well for myself. Today I am an independent person with confidence and self-assurance. If I saw him on the street I would look the other way.

Women have much to tell us about their motivation if we would only listen to them. The Ann Landers story is not the tale of a woman who, given a choice, longs for a return of her suffering. It is instead the story of the end of a woman's suffering and the beginning of her growth.

CHAPTER 6

Women's Bodies

The widespread social view is that women can have it all [career and family] if they try hard but the same culture prescribes an increasingly rigid standard of feminine beauty. The bulimic women symbolize this impossible dream by trying to have their cake and eat it too—only to discover that it makes them sick. —PSYCHOLOGIST JUDITH LAZERSON

Society tells women to starve, paint, pinch, push, and otherwise distort our bodies in order to be thin, colorful, busty, hippy, and firm—but not too thin, colorful, busty, hippy, and firm. We are taught to do these things to appear attractive and we learn that being attractive—besides being nurturant and "nice"—is the route to Real Womanhood. We are also told that women are supposed to have babies, but soon after giving birth we are to return to our slender, youthful appearance, despite the major physical upheavals of pregnancy and delivery and despite the much-interrupted sleep that goes with having a newborn and exhausts most new mothers. We also learn early that old women are neither attractive nor dignified in the eyes of men, even old men.

The concern with our bodies begins very early. Little girls worry about whether they are too fat or too thin, too tall or too short, and pretty enough. The experience of many girls differs only in degree from that of the little girls that Carol Pogash calls "Real Live Dolls" in her *Redbook* article about beauty contests for little girls: "At the age of six Dawn entered her first beauty pageant. She was cute but lacked poise, and unlike the other little girls, she wore no makeup. She lost, and cried right on the stage. 'That was when I knew she had competitive blood in her,' says her mother."

Imagine caring whether your six-year-old is poised and whether she has the drive to compete on the basis of her looks! Dawn's story goes on: "To the Hinkes, winning is everything, and being naturally beautiful—with golden hazel eyes and an open face—clearly isn't enough. A month before each pageant, Dawn cuts down on cookies and cake, sometimes switching to Weight Watchers dinners." Training to become anorexic starts very early. Furthermore, for Dawn, "Roller skating and biking are forbidden, too, because she's got to keep her soon-to-be-judged face and body bruise-free."

> Today's contest is a streamlined affair. Girls are not asked to exhibit any talent or model bathing suits while wearing high heels. Still, dresses run as high as $100 and the competition is so stiff that Barbara Hinke won't reveal where she finds Dawn's pageant clothes. Families caught up in the pageant parade make it a way of life, taking vacations around their daughters' week-long national competitions and spending their restaurant and movie money on making a little winner.

Put yourself in Dawn's place. Her family never goes to a movie or out to dinner because every cent goes into an investment in her beauty. What an intolerable burden to place on a young child. If she wins, she feels more powerful than it is healthy for a child to feel; worse still, she feels that her success comes not from anything she *does* but simply from *how she looks* (over which she has little control) and what she *does not do,* like roller skating and other normal childhood activities. If she loses, then she has let her whole family down; all of her family's need to succeed has been invested in her and she has disappointed them. Altogether this is one very effective way to make a child feel that she has unreal power to hurt and destroy.

Pogash reports that new pageants appear almost weekly and take place throughout the United States, and that the "one thing all pageants do insist on is the old-fashioned pretty-girl dress and behavior."

Many books have been written about the impossible standards of beauty that are set for females and about the serious psychological and physical damage to which those standards have led. But even women who *are* beautiful do not have it made. It is common knowledge that most beautiful women do not *believe* that they are beautiful. In part, this is because when beauty is made such an important part of the definition of the female role, we can never be good enough. Furthermore, if a beautiful woman feels she should be even *more* beautiful, at least that gives her something to work for, rather than having to be content with simply existing, passively, waiting to be admired.

Ironically, however, when a beautiful woman grows older, it is no longer clear what she can be. When young, she is a potential sex object, a sought-after decoration for the arm of an important man at parties. If, as she ages, a woman loses her conventional beauty—and it is often believed that an older woman cannot be beautiful, *because* she is old—then she loses her value because she lacks both beauty and youth. Conversely, even a barely middle-aged woman who seeks a position of dignity and power cannot afford to be very attractive. If she is too beautiful either she is thought to lack intelligence (dumb but beautiful), or her beauty is somehow thought to interfere with her credibility. John F. Kennedy was regarded as both dashingly handsome and very dignified. By contrast, a beautiful, dignified woman in her late thirties or early forties who was recently mentioned as a possible candidate for an important public office in Toronto was advised by a knowledgeable colleague not to run, because she was not "frumpy" enough. Thus, women who are regarded as beautiful often suffer because of the assumption that they are stupid or simply decorative, and they live in fear of losing their beauty, which has been the only valued part of themselves. Women who are not regarded as attractive suffer because they lack a crucial ingredient of true femininity; and even beautiful women who have proved their intelligence and competence need to make sure they are not *too* beautiful if they want to acquire more dignity and power.

Weight is an important aspect of women's appearance, and in this connection there are many times in the course of a woman's life when she is given impossible choices because of the masochism myth. About women and weight problems I can speak from extensive personal experience. When I was a ballet dancer and a cheerleader in high school, my body was in good shape, and I was not overweight. I thought I was too heavy, though, for two reasons. One was that the fashionable ideal was a thin, straight-up-and-down body, and mine had too many curves to fit that image, and the other was that, because I exercised so much, I had developed what are now regarded as "shapely calves" but what were then called by some of my male classmates "football players' calves," making me self-conscious and embarrassed.

Females are expected to be thin, and that thinness is made so important to their "femininity" that many growing girls and women feel that they are never thin enough. If they are overweight or consider themselves to be overweight they suffer, feeling ugly and unfeminine. But if they constantly diet, they suffer from not only the physical deprivation but also the emotional drain of having to be constantly vigilant about their meals and bodies. Either way, one suffers and is in danger of being called masochistic: "You must really get something out of being laughed at and rejected, since you let yourself get so fat!" or "You must really enjoy suffering. Look at the way you starve yourself!'' In its extreme—and increasingly common—form, the obsession with thinness leads to a pair of clinical syndromes called "bulimia" and "anorexia," both of which are far more commonly seen in women than in men. The former involves compulsive or binge eating, followed by induced vomiting or purging through massive doses of laxatives; the latter involves starving oneself. Both result from a pathological need to be thin.

In a review of the research and clinical literature on the subject, as well as some careful research of her own, psychologist Judith Lazerson found that these women have what is called a high "external locus of control," that they regard themselves as having little control over their lives and are very dependent on other people. They try desperately to meet an exaggerated ideal of femininity as it is traditionally defined in North America. Many of these women become seriously underweight, and some, like singer Karen Carpenter, eventually die from the disorder. Becoming extremely thin is a way not only to be traditionally feminine but also, paradoxically, to avoid the challenge of becoming womanly by acquiring a body like that of a preadolescent male and, in some cases, causing delay or cessation of menstruation. It is not yet fully understood *why*, in individual cases, eating-disordered females have such anxiety about feminine standards, but psychologist David Garner, a specialist in these disorders, believes that one major factor is the media image of an unattainable feminine physical ideal. Furthermore, in view of the myriad of difficulties inherent in the traditional feminine role, as discussed in the preceding chapters, one can well understand why some growing girls feel frightened at the prospect of assuming the highly demanding role of mature, autonomous women in our society. Feminist author Susie Orbach has suggested that women who only binge-eat are in revolt against existing standards of feminine beauty. The lives of these women, too, are controlled by an obsession with these standards, and they suffer both from being overweight and from the effort to become thin.

These girls and women are caught in the masochism trap. Having developed a terror of being fat (and, therefore, unfeminine), many of these women become excessively thin. So indoctrinated have they been with traditional ideas about feminine beauty, however, that if they did *not* diet or purge compulsively, they would also be miserable, for these very thin women sincerely believe themselves to be overweight and have grossly distorted ideas of their body size. Thus, they apparently diet and purge to *avoid* the rejection or misery that they believe will come with being overweight or physically womanly, but—as I have witnessed—their doctors and their families often call them masochists.

In her own research, Lazerson relates how bulimics stick to rigid diets while becoming obsessed with trying to get around them. She reports that the women she studied tended to come from unhappy families in which the fathers were often alcoholic and had physically or verbally abused their wives. The wives had reacted passively and tried to pacify the angry husbands, while the daughters tried to intercede to protect their mothers. The bulimic women, then, had not had models during childhood of women who could be strong or whose identity was any different from the traditionally passive one. Similar histories are often found for anorexics. To "take control" of one's life by binge-eating, vomiting, or self-starvation seems to be the only way these women feel that they can have some control over their lives while remaining "feminine." This requires that they smother their anger and assertiveness and put all their energy into preoccupations with food and their bodies. One of the women studied by Lazerson wrote about her "constant fear of losing control, and if I give in I will be at the mercy of a repulsive gorger." Of course, some therapists believe that the symptoms of these patients are in part indirect ways of expressing some of the anger and self-assertion that they dare not show more directly; by causing intense worry to people who care about them, they punish those who helped to feed their fears of obesity and womanliness.

As have most women, bulimics and anorexics have internalized the belief that they can never be good enough; consequently, their self-esteem is abysmally low. Lazerson writes: "It is as if fixing or rearranging the usually quite normal, and often attractive body, will correct the interpersonal and deep dissatisfaction with the self." Lazerson says that her patients believed they could only win approval and affection by being thin.

For such reasons, many of the people now working with women who have eating disorders believe that their treatment must involve an emphasis on self-acceptance. Self-acceptance is a rare commodity in women, since our upbringing has so often emphasized a constant striving for perfection. Being a woman means always having to say you're sorry, feeling you can never relax. Women who attempt to enhance their self-esteem by becoming thinner, leading to eating disorders, do not feel better once they become thin. They report feeling depressed, disgusted with themselves, and frustrated no matter what they do. Preventive measures are essential. They must take the form of relieving the pressure on women, both to fit a particular (impossible!) physical type and to be as self-denying as necessary to meet prescriptions for feminine behavior.

Women who are overweight face both unnecessary humiliation and unnecessary frustration. The humiliation comes from the classification of the overweight woman as unfeminine and unable to control her presumably gargantuan appetite, and the unnecessary frustration comes from the unavailability to women of a wealth of reliable, useful information on weight gain in women. The former is a result of rigid stereotypes about physical appearance, but the reasons for the latter are more complex. First, the relevant information has largely been in the possession of people who, compared to physicians, have relatively low status—nutritionists, most of whom are women. Do most of us go to nutritionists for advice about our bodies? No, we go to medical doctors, because we believe that they have the answers, although we are learning that in medical school students are taught very little about nutrition. It is sad that M.D.s who are often willing to refer patients to other kinds of *medical* specialists—urologists, oncologists, and so on—rarely make referrals outside of the medical profession. After a nutritionist helped me to lose weight, my physician expressed amazement at the amount of weight I had lost and the way the entire shape of my body had changed. I gave him the nutritionist's name and address, but in the eighteen months since then he has yet to refer anyone to her.

The other reason for the unavailability of helpful information for overweight women is that, like the people who have the information to offer, those who stand to benefit the most from such help are relatively low-status people: women. More women than men have weight problems because of physical factors: the extra layer of fat in women's bodies and the physical changes related to menstruation, childbearing, and menopause, including the effects of female hormones on water retention and weight gain.

If women were given this kind of information early in their lives, it seems likely that many of our physical problems could be prevented or minimized. Our society's priorities become clear when we compare this lack of emphasis on prevention of women's health problems with the research and large sums of money that have been spent to inform the public about more male-oriented problems, like coronary disorders. When nutritionists and dietitians tried to spread the word to women, they were often mocked and dismissed by physicians, so that patients who wanted to stay in their physicians' good graces either had to steer clear of other kinds of professionals or conceal their sources of help from their doctors. Society has neglected its ability to help overweight women but has continued to accuse them of doing something damaging to themselves.

My own experience with weight gain illustrates the shame, sense of helplessness, and poor health that result from the relative unavailability of the proper information. Keep in mind as you read my story that through it all, well-meaning friends, relatives, and physicians kept asking me, "Why do you do this to yourself?"

In graduate school I started to gain weight, and at the end of graduate school, when I was 25 and had my first baby, I had gained 35 pounds. Two years later, I gained 50 pounds during my second pregnancy. Why I gained so much weight was a mystery to me. I did eat more when I was pregnant than when I was not, but so did most women I knew, and they didn't gain nearly that much. When I asked my doctor for an explanation, all he could say was that I must be eating a lot more than I would "admit to." I felt ashamed and believed that the weight gain was really my fault, that there was something that I was doing wrong. When my second child was born, I lost only the number of pounds that she weighed at birth, and even when I stopped nursing, I was still more than 40 pounds over my prepregnancy weight.

Each time I saw my family doctor he handed me diet plans. I told him, "If I ate everything on this diet plan, I would *gain* weight." He replied, "If you eat less than this, and you're still so fat, you must be eating all the wrong things." I told him that I mostly ate meats, cheeses, fruits, and vegetables. He said, "Well, you must be eating peanut butter in bed." Every time I left his office, I was in tears.

Finally, in desperation, I put myself on a 150-calorie a day diet. I would eat nothing except a cup of mushrooms with lemon juice and garlic powder or a cup of strawberries or green beans, and over a period of weeks, I lost 20 pounds. However, I was depressed, tired, and irritable. When I went off the diet and began to eat the kinds of small, healthy meals that people of normal weight eat, my weight quickly shot back up to its previous level.

I went to an endocrinologist, who told me, "In medical school they taught us that women who weigh as much as you and say they eat as little as you do are lying about what they eat. But I want you to know that I believe you." I burst into tears, because someone finally believed me! The endocrinologist ran a lot of tests, but when the laboratory reports came back, she told me, "Something is wrong with your body, but we don't quite know what it is. I'm just as sorry as I can be. Call me once a year, and I'll let you know if any discoveries have been made that might help you."

I was miserable. I felt that just seeing me could ruin the day for passersby on the street and was sure that no one could talk to me without thinking constantly, "She is disgustingly fat." In no other area of my life had such strenuous efforts produced such minimal results.

Women's failure to lose weight and keep it off reinforces the belief that women have vast needs and appetites that they cannot control. I found that if you tell people that something is wrong with your body, that if you eat the same amount they do, you will gain three times as much weight as they do, and that if you diet you will lose one-third as much as they do, they think you are making excuses.

One day a friend told me about a woman named Carola Barczak, who runs a weight-loss salon in Toronto. I told him that I had tried everything and wasn't about to throw away good money on a slick weight-loss place, but reluctantly I went to see Carola. She quietly explained her methods to me and said they could "change the whole shape of your body."

After briefly examining me and asking me a long list of questions, Carola told me that I was malnourished. "I know that sounds strange to you," she said, "because you are overweight. But I think you have an enzyme deficiency, so that your body isn't able to break food down into forms that it can use to run your various organs and bodily processes. So your body doesn't work properly, and much of the food you take in is stored as fat." That sounded logical, but I didn't dare to believe it, because I didn't want to get my hopes up. I had spent too many years feeling that my weight was beyond my control. Furthermore, if she was right, I would feel very angry at not having known about this problem for all those miserable years.

On a Monday night I began taking enzymes with my meals, as well as other vitamin and mineral supplements that

Carola recommended. On Tuesday I ate an enormous lunch at 12:30 and was starved by 2:30, when I ate two large pieces of chicken. By 4:30 I was famished again. I had never felt so hungry in my life! I called Carola and told her what was happening. She said, "Don't panic. You are coming out of a malnourished state. Eat when you are hungry, but don't eat junk." I told her that I was not panicking, that indeed my hunger suggested to me that her diagnosis had been right, that the enzymes were allowing me to *use* my food in a way I had not been able to do before.

For two weeks I ate like a pig but did not gain an ounce. Previously, if I had eaten like that I would have gained 15 pounds in as many days. My friends started telling me that I looked as though I had *lost* 10 pounds, even though my weight had not changed at all. Carola told me that I was losing fat but gaining muscle, which kept my weight stable but made me look trimmer.

On the Wednesday after I started taking the supplements, I called Carola again. It was July 1983, the hottest summer in Toronto in years. For many years I had felt like the princess and the pea when it came to heat. One bit of heat, and I rushed to the nearest air conditioner. I am not claustrophobic, but I thought I knew how claustrophobics must feel—when I got at all warm, I felt as though my skin were going to split. I was ashamed and thought my sensitivity to heat was a sign of moral weakness. Another symptom I had had for years, but did not connect with this heat sensitivity, was that I did not sweat. I could sit in a sauna, and as the people around me dripped with sweat, I would barely begin to "glow." This was terribly feminine and ladylike, of course, but when I mentioned it to my doctor, he said, "Gee, that's not normal. We should check that out." It turned out, however, that he didn't know what the cause was, and he never mentioned it again. On the Wednesday in question I had left my air-conditioned office and emerged into 95-degree heat, expecting to panic. Instead, I began to sweat and did *not* feel uncomfortable. When I called Carola to tell her, I said, "You didn't even ask me about sweating, but I haven't sweated in years, so this must be related to the supplements I've started taking.'' She responded that sweating is one way that the body gets rid of waste materials. Sweating is a sign that your body is working properly, which explained the panic I had felt when I couldn't sweat. When something toxic is in your body, and you can't get rid of it in the normal ways, something unhealthy is happening to you.

After a few months of feeling symptom after symptom disappear—problems I had attributed to the aging process; ''I guess once you're over 18, things start to fall apart''—I decided to try some of Carola's other recommendations.

Within three months I was 32 pounds lighter and had lost a total of 50 inches in 14 places. Furthermore, my layers of cellulite were gone. As Carola explains in one of her tapes about nutrition and physiology, North American doctors say that cellulite is just a fancy name for fat and that if you just diet and exercise the cellulite will go away. European doctors, says Carola, know that that is not true, that you can be skinny and still have cellulite, because cellulite is so hard that diet and exercise do not budge it. Furthermore, she says that cellulite is a real health problem. Once formed, the chunks of fat impede circulation, leading to a wide variety of problems in women's legs; then, because circulation is poor, still more cellulite forms. Ever since graduate school I had noticed that if I bumped my thigh on the side of a chair, I felt as though knives were going through my flesh. I had never understood why. Carola explained that was because when cellulite forms it can pinch the nerves and make them more sensitive to pain.

Through such information, Carola has given me a great gift—not just the weight loss but also real control over my body and, for the first time, a great deal of knowledge about how my body works and how to tell when something is wrong.

Perhaps the best news is that the beneficial effects last. I spent more than two weeks in South America last summer. I had been told not to drink tap water or to eat fresh fruits and vegetables to avoid getting gastrointestinal infections from unfamiliar bacteria. I did as I was told, but that meant I ate more fattening and salty foods than usual. I was sure that I would gain 10 pounds, since my body used to work that way. In fact, I did not gain an ounce.

Needless to say, not every woman is overweight because of an enzyme deficiency, but there are a variety of deficiencies and imbalances that some nutritionists are able to identify and remedy fairly easily. Carola told another client I referred to her that her colon seemed to have become coated with old fecal matter. When that happens, the body does not cleanse itself or eliminate waste material efficiently or completely. All Carola did was to instruct my friend to swallow a special cleansing powder, and without changing the way that she was eating, without exercising, my friend lost 30 pounds in three months. Her cheeks became pinker and her eyes clearer, too, as mine had done when I began using my food and getting rid of toxic material properly.

I know from personal experience that many overweight women do not bring their trouble on themselves; it is simply that no one has made the relevant information available to them. Of course, many of the people who accuse them of "doing this to themselves" also lack the information to draw a different conclusion.

The area of weight is a no-win situation for women. We are regarded as unattractive and unfeminine because of our extra weight. But if we do manage to lose some weight and feel good about having done so, people roll their eyes and say, "Vanity, thy name is woman!" Either way, we feel uncomfortable about our appearance. Fat is not feminine in North America, and vanity is not compatible with the self-sacrificing, selfless aspect of feminine identity.

Even some feminists can put overweight women in a position where they have two unpleasant choices by saying that women should not try to lose weight, since what we need is to be liberated from excessive worry about our appearance. Is it politically correct for a fat feminist to want to lose weight? The first thing to realize in considering this is that men are not placed in a similar position. Can you imagine asking if it is all right for a *man* to want to lose weight? Of course not. He will be admired for wanting to feel and be healthier, more attractive, and fit. Beyond those reasons, however, as for a man, changing a woman's weight can be important for her— feminist or not—for three additional reasons:

(1) Excess weight is often a sign that the body is not working well, that one is not healthy.
(2) Our bodies are very important to us, and it is crucial to understand how they work, to be able to read their signals when things go wrong, and to have some real control over them.
(3) It is not vain to want to create something that is more, rather than less, esthetically pleasing. We can do this with our own bodies *without* accepting the old belief that being pretty matters desperately, defines our entire identity, and is more important than anything else about us. We can develop our bodies as we wish without becoming obsessed by appearance and without supporting the attitude that physical attractiveness is the hallmark of womanhood.

Feminists have not criticized women for body building, which also is healthy and improves one's appearance. Can it be that this activity has escaped criticism because it is associated with males? It would be ironic for us to believe that we *should not* lose excess weight, just because men think we *should,* but to think we *can* develop our muscles, because men have always done so. It is not in women's interests either to adopt a standard because it has been applied to men or to reject one because men promote it. Either way, we are allowing ourselves to be controlled by men's standards, on the one hand striving to reach them and on the other hand reacting against them. We must be free to decide what is good for us *apart from* what men traditionally believe.

Weight loss is only one area related to women's bodies

in which physicians have misinformed, or inadequately informed, women. Another major source of trouble, about which much has been written, is the poor application, or misapplication, of medical research and knowledge to a wide range of women's problems. I shall discuss only a few in detail here but refer the reader to relevant articles that frequently appear in magazines like *Ms. Magazine* and the Toronto-based *Healthsharing,* and physician Robert Mendelsohn's excellent book, *Malepractice.* The principal difficulty is that most doctors are men, most of the researchers with access to research funds are men, and most of the people who decide which research projects should receive funding are men. One well-known fact that illustrates the consequences of this male orientation is that the focus of birth control research has been on finding pills for women to take (before their ultimate effects were fully known) and developing equipment to be placed in women's bodies before its effectiveness or its side effects had been adequately explored. Men have not been subjected to equally untested, risky, or ineffective methods of birth control. Many of the problems with the birth control pill, diaphragms, and intrauterine devices are now well known, but some lesser known facts about birth control illustrate the point effectively.

I had an IUD inserted before I later gave birth to my children. I told the doctor as he inserted it that I was due to leave town the following week and asked what to do if the initial pain he told me to expect should continue. "Oh, just grab the string, and yank it out," he said. When I was a thousand miles away from home the following week, the pain became excruciating, so I tried what he had recommended and almost tore my cervix. When I returned home, I learned that the IUD had been improperly inserted. And, of course, the instruction to yank it out verged on the unethical.

In their 1984 book, *The Doctors' Anti-Breast-Cancer Diet,* Dr. Sherwood Gorbach, David Zimmerman, and Margo Woods explain that antibiotics can decrease the birth control pill's effectiveness. This is documented medical information, but it has *not* been widely disseminated. And it is primarily women who are left to raise the children who are conceived while they are on the Pill, and it is women—far more than men—who are viciously attacked if they choose not to carry to term pregnancies that result from their physicians' failure to inform them about factors that reduce the Pill's effectiveness.

Another bit of important birth control information that has not been made available to women involves the use of spermicidal foam. An article appeared in a medical journal a few years ago about the increased incidence of birth defects in children who were conceived when their parents were using foam. There is no warning on the packages of this over the counter method of birth control, and rare is the physician who mentions this report to a patient. But who is likely to shoulder the burden of raising a child with a birth defect? Its mother. Suffering has often been thus carelessly imposed on women by physicians, medical researchers, and drug-approval boards. Then the women who are left to deal with the unhappy consequences are branded as desirous of suffering.

Feminist and antiracist activist Flo Kennedy has repeatedly made the point that the men who condemn women for having abortions are never the men who stay up with the unaborted children when they have fevers or who seek in desperation and often in vain for a job that will get them off welfare to support those children adequately. And in a recent symposium on "Fetal Rights," Janet Gallagher quoted Dr. Margery Shaw, a physician and lawyer, as suggesting that any woman who knows the fetus she is carrying is defective and chooses *not* to abort should be held legally liable to that child when it is born. In the same symposium, Barbara Katz-Rothman pointed out that our culture has a horror of infanticide but forces women into it (through abortion) by failing to provide an economic, social, and emotional environment that is supportive to people who are raising defective babies. Whether they have abortions or not, women are the ones who suffer and thereby provide further "evidence" of female "masochism."

Older women in our society are victims of the conjunction of male-dominated medical and mental health professions and the stereotype of the aging woman as lacking both physical beauty and dignity. As if feeling unattractive and undignified were not enough, women growing older have had too little access to medical information that might ease the physical pains and discomforts of menopause and other physiological changes and have been led by social prescriptions into the likely depression of the empty nest syndrome.

In regard to the problems related to menopause, many of these have often been attributed to woman's hysterical nature, to her inability to cope psychologically with aging. Although it should not surprise us to find women having such difficulty in a society that offers older women few supports or rewards and a great deal of unhappiness, it is *not* the primary reason for menopausal hot flashes, insomnia, and increasing vaginal dryness. These are hormonally based symptoms. In the area of medical assistance for menopause, as in the area of birth control for women, drug treatments have been implemented before their side effects were adequately explored. Here, too, nutritionists have helpful information to offer, but it has not been widely publicized for the same reasons that nutritionists' information about women and weight loss has not been broadly disseminated. There are, for example, natural remedies familiar to nutritionists and naturopaths (who, like physicians, vary in their dependability and helpfulness) that can reduce the side effects of menopause by making the process happen gradually, so that the body is not subjected to sudden, major hormonal swings. According to Carola Barczak, at least three types of treatment have been found helpful for easing menopausal symptoms: herbs such as cohosh and wild yams that contain mild forms of natural estrogen, supplements called protomorphogens, and vitamins and minerals such as B6 and zinc, which can moderate hot flashes.

With regard to other physical changes that aging women experience, we have all heard about older women who become bedridden because of a broken hip. Like many others, I had the impression that older women were prone to broken hips and that their bones, once broken, were slow to mend. That impression was correct, but only in recent years has the term "osteoporosis" become familiar to the general public, and only lately has it been identified as a disorder more commonly found in aging women than in aging men. Most important, it is a disorder that one can do a great deal to prevent or diminish. Osteoporosis is the name for increasing brittleness of bones, and it is caused by the loss of calcium and other nutrients from the bones that comes with aging. Women after menopause lose at least five times as much bone calcium per year as men of the same age, and women's greater longevity makes osteoporosis even more of a "woman's problem." As women were informed in *Ms. Magazine*'s special 1984 issue on "Our Bodies," all women over 30 years of age should take calcium supplements for this reason. What was not mentioned there, however, and what many people do not know, according to Carola Barczak, is that if magnesium is not taken with the calcium, magnesium is taken from elsewhere in our bodies in order to work with the calcium tablets, leaving us magnesium-deficient (which can lead, among other things, to muscle twitches and prematurely gray hair). According to Carola and to naturopath Daria Love, other synergistic nutrients such as Vitamin C are often required as well to effect bone restoration. What also impedes osteoporosis is exercise. Of course, only within the last decade have women been encouraged to exercise, and even today the sight of older women on bicycles or on jogging tracks frequently occasions mirth.

Women often have not been informed by their physicians that they should take calcium-magnesium supplements and exercise as they get older, and this has led to a frequency of osteoporosis in older women that is needlessly and tragically high.

Inadequate information and restrictive social stereotypes and employment policies have led to avoidable mental health problems in aging women. The inability of a woman who has been out of the paid work force for years to find a job has been a major cause of depression in middle-aged women, a depression that often begins or intensifies when her children leave home. This has been called the empty nest syndrome. For decades, mental health professionals have nodded knowingly and talked about this syndrome without objecting to the aspects of socialization that make it almost inevitable. If we encourage women to feel that they should stay home and raise their children, is it any wonder that they become depressed when their work seems to be done? It is a telling point that this pattern in women has acquired the empty nest label but that the analogous problem—depression in men who retire from a job—has no special title. As psychologist Phyllis Chesler demonstrated in *Women and Madness,* understandable emotional responses in women are often labeled as pathological, but understandable emotional responses in men are not classified as signs of disturbance. Her children have left home and she's depressed—it's the empty nest syndrome. He's retired from his job and depressed because he's so bored—no wonder, after all those years of doing important work! Since the social arrangements that lead to depression have not been the focus of most psychotherapy, women who are assigned this label have been treated as though the mental illness comes from within them, as though they had set themselves up to suffer this depression. Sure, they should have known that when the children left home they would feel depressed; but in a society that restricted women's options, how much could they do—take up a hobby?

Furthermore, as feminist social worker Rachel Josefowitz Siegel relates in her 1983 article on "Change and Creativity in Midlife," if a woman goes to a therapist for help with this kind of depression, she may well find her sexuality becoming the main topic of the therapy work, and this will get her nowhere.

Women's interpretations of their responses to physical problems often have been distorted by the masochism myth.

One therapist told me that a woman patient came to see her, claiming to be a masochist. The patient—an overworked single parent—explained that she felt she was a masochist because when she caught mononucleosis and had to stay in bed for two weeks she enjoyed it. The therapist suggested that the enjoyment had not been of the discomfort from her illness but rather of the time to rest, but the patient had been so indoctrinated with the myth that she kept searching for further "proof" of her masochism.

It is clear that, because of social prescriptions and myths about women's appearance, physical condition, and the meaning of aging, many aspects of women's bodies have become sources of discomfort, pain, and sorrow to them. Once again, however, the women themselves often have been blamed for bringing that suffering on themselves through their vanity, their lack of preparedness, and their presumed lack of intelligence and resourcefulness. It is of fundamental importance that useful information be made available to women about their bodies, that the exclusive and often misused power of physicians be controlled, and that we keep clearly in view the importance of trying to alter the social arrangements that frequently lead women to be valued largely for their appearance and youth. The excitement now being generated about the enduring strength and attractiveness of such mature women as Gloria Steinem, Lena Horne, Geraldine Ferraro, and Ruth Gordon shows that change is possible, even though a great deal remains to be done.

CHAPTER 7

Women as Victims
of Violence

*Any self-respecting John Wayne fan will tell you that all women
really want to be slapped around occasionally.*

—ANDREA BLANCH

Feminist Gloria Steinem and pornographic movie star Linda
Lovelace would seem an unlikely pair of allies. But in an article in *Ms. Magazine* in 1980, "The Real Linda Lovelace,"
Steinem showed how the myth that Lovelace loved to be sexually used and humiliated was created by her husband, Chuck
Traynor, who kept her his prisoner and knew how to "work
the media." According to Steinem, Traynor boasted, "When
I first dated [Linda] she was so shy, it shocked her to be seen
nude by a man. . . . *I created Linda Lovelace*." He "created" her, says Lovelace, by putting a gun to her head, forcing her into prostitution, while having her watched through a
peephole to prevent her escape, having water forced up her
rectum with a garden hose if she refused to expose herself in

restaurants, and training her to relax her throat muscles so that she could perform fellatio on the full length of a penis without choking.

At a party where Lovelace was forced to do her fellatio act for a line-up of men, Gerry Damian became "creatively inspired" to do the film *Deep Throat,* about a woman whose clitoris was in her throat, making her constantly eager for fellatio. In the movie Linda Lovelace was shown smiling throughout her ordeal, to make the moviegoer think that she was having a good time.

According to Steinem's article, however, the truth is that Lovelace spent years as a sexual prisoner, cut off from all normal human contact, being beaten, tortured, and raped by her husband so severely that she suffered permanent rectal damage and permanent injury to the blood vessels in her legs. She tried three times to escape before she was successful, and her escape was engineered at great risk, because she had reason to believe that Traynor kept grenades and a machine gun in a van outside his house. Lovelace had spent months working to appear trustworthy to him so that he would lower his guard, and she allied herself with his secretary and arranged to obtain disguises. She also worked hard on herself to turn her terror into nagging fear, writes Steinem, so that she would have the nerve to go through with the escape plans. She had appealed to the police for help, but they had told her they could do nothing "until the man with the gun is in the room with you," and reporters had refused to believe her story. After all, once a porn star always an object of contempt.

Steinem says that Lovelace's autobiography, *Ordeal,* "attacks the myth of female masochism that insists women enjoy sexual domination and even pain, but prostitution and pornography are big businesses built on that myth." Pornography is different from erotica, of course, since the latter gives the same importance to the woman's pleasure as to the man's and dignity to both sexes.

Why did Lovelace become involved with Traynor? He was nice and gentlemanly to her at first and had no sexual relationship with her at all. He offered her an apartment as a refuge from her strict, authoritarian parents. And then, she says, he did a 180-degree turn and she became a prisoner.

People ask her, though, what *attracted* her to this man and this life, as though what had drawn her to him was his cruelty. Steinem writes, "If you accept the truth of Linda's story, the questions are enraging, like saying, 'What in your background led you to a concentration camp?' No one asks how we can stop raising men who fit Linda's terrified description of Chuck Traynor." Until we can stop raising such men, says Steinem, the solution is for women to bond together to rescue each other, particularly in supportive shelters for battered women. Such suggestions have been put into action vigorously only within the past decade, and this change came about because a small but growing number of people began to reject the myth that women victims of violence were masochists who were happy to stay where they were.

Violence against women continues, however. Existing shelters and services for the victims are far too few to meet the need, and conservative governments tend to be quick to cut back on these services. Sadly, too, there is still no shortage of men whose desire for power over women and whose ruthlessness toward them make them victimizers. When Steinem wrote her article in 1980, Traynor was married to his next porn star, Marilyn Chambers, and Steinem wrote at that time:

> As for Chuck Traynor himself, he is still the husband and manager of Marilyn Chambers.
>
> Larry Fields, a columnist for the Philadelphia *Daily News,* remembers interviewing them both for his column a few years ago when Marilyn was performing a song-and-dance act in a local nightclub. . . .
>
> While Traynor was answering questions on Marilyn's behalf, she asked him for permission to go to the bathroom. Permission was refused. "Not right now," Fields remembers him saying to her. And when she ob-

jected that she was about to appear onstage: "Just sit there and shut up."

When Fields objected, Traynor was adamant. "I don't tell you how to write your column," he said angrily. "Don't tell me how to treat my broads."

Some people would argue that Lovelace was a masochist, but in truth she escaped because she did not want to suffer. Although she escaped, Traynor's sadism continues unchecked.

Pornography reinforces the view that women like to suffer sexually and that suffering can be equated with female sexuality in general. I am not just talking about the porn rags that show pictures of women grinning and cutting their labia or the photo layout of hanging women that caused a recent issue of *Penthouse* magazine to be banned in Canada. I am talking about the glorification of the abuse of women that pervades our society. Within the past two months I saw the following within four blocks of my house:

◇ In a clothing shop window, a male mannequin was suspended in a threatening, violent, and sexual pose over a female mannequin, which lay limply on the floor.

◇ In a jewelry store window, diamonds and other jewels were displayed on the ears of a row of models of women's heads—but in every case one half of the head looked as though it had been violently blown away.

These scenes parallel the current wave of violence against women in movies. Pornography teaches men that they have, and deserve to have, sexual power over women and that it is masculine and glamorous to exercise and abuse that power. A police sergeant working with a police pornography squad reported, "I couldn't believe the stuff I was seeing when I first joined the squad, and now it's even worse . . . desecration of corpses, you name it. . . . the clear message is that

women love rape, they love sex with pain." Sally Roesch
Wagner writes in *Against Sadomasochism* that she even regards the "cult of romance" and the plethora of romance
novels as reinforcing this view: "Through romance we learn
to be passive, to wait and to submit to the pain and humiliation of loving someone who has power over us." The message of the cult of romance is that women need to be overpowered and the message of hard-core porn is that, because
women are passive, they need to be raped. Wagner points out
that as porn grows more sadistic, romance novels grow more
masochistic. In pornography, women are often described as
being bound and loving it. Wagner believes that as women
assume more real power in society, some men feel increasingly threatened and need more urgently to believe that women
really want to be overpowered and made to suffer. Researchers like psychologist James V. P. Check and his colleagues
have found that simple exposure to hard-core pornography increases both women's and men's inclinations to believe that
women like to be hurt, and people with traditional sex-role
orientations are more likely than others to believe that a woman
assault victim is to blame for the assault.

Women in pornography are the subjects of both physical
and emotional violence and are made to appear less human,
less worthy of respect than other people. They are even reduced to the inhuman, as objects or tools for men's use.

Feminist journalist Susan Cole has written:

Once out of the ivory tower and into the real world, we
discover the *actual* harm pornography causes. It is easy
to get the evidence. Talk to women. Surveying some of
the victims of battery, I have encountered women who
openly confess that their sex lives changed considerably
once their husbands got into pornography. The pornography, often from magazines, gave their spouses all kinds
of ideas about what was sexy, and made their spouses
wonder why their wives were not being sexy in the way

the pornographic models were sexy. Many of these women report being forced to replicate sexual acts in the pornography.

A woman who discovers that her man buys pornographic materials is in a difficult position. If she objects, she is likely to be accused of being sexually stodgy, having no sense of humor, as though porn were funny! But if she remains silent she will suffer from the knowledge that he responds to porn, and she will always wonder what he thinks of her as they "make love." Is he imagining her gagged and chained? Would he find her more stimulating if she were? Writer Anne Cameron described this dilemma in an open letter to a woman who had written to a newspaper about her experience:

> . . . you found violent hard porn in an intimate friend's bedroom cupboard, and now nothing is making much sense. You probably feel used. You probably wonder how many times you thought your friend and companion, a renowned professional who has often been asked to act in an official capacity for women's groups, turned to you after being turned on by porn. . . .
> You're not going to change his mind. You aren't going to be able to sit down and rationally discuss this. There isn't going to be the tender scene from a daytime soap where he looks at you with tear-dewed eyes and says, "I didn't realize what it was really all about. Please, help me get over this terrible addiction. You're right, and I've been insensitive." And if he *does* say it, he isn't going to mean it. . . . This man, you thought, was . . . your proof that not "all" men were pains in the face, and you have probably defended your relationship with him. And now there you are, and there he is, and there is that collection of hate stuff, and where does that leave you?
> . . . I have seen feminists look pained but not protest when their gentle sensitive men made remarks that

were downright stupid. We still accept "boys will be boys." Only when we are up against suitcases full of misogyny do we react. And then we are told we have "overreacted," and our anger is discounted and denied, and if we express it loudly we are told we are not "real women" because "real women do not get that angry."

And what can you *do*. Well, you could invest a few dollars in some printed stickers and attach them to his office door, his office window, the side of the office building, maybe his car, his friends' doors, and let as many people as possible know "Mr. Perfect Collects Dirty Pictures.". . .

You have to realize he will not like you any more. He will not smile and say, one of the things I admire about you is your mind. He will not say, possibly the most exciting thing about you is your precise logic. . . .

A surprising number of people still believe that a woman victim of violence must have brought it on herself. Even at a convention of feminist academics and clinicians last summer, I was stunned at the expression of such attitudes by a large number of women, some of whom work directly with victims of battering and rape. Although some people have begun to acknowledge that rapists often approach women from behind, before a rapist has a chance to see whether the woman has "asked for it," and although some will acknowledge that abused wives often stay with their abusers for very good, nonmasochistic reasons, such lip service to an enlightened viewpoint often simply covers up a more deep-seated, long-standing belief that female victims of violence ask for it and even enjoy it.

In the late 1960s, Americans learned that it was no longer acceptable to say that they hated blacks, even if they felt that way. Their hatred and fear did not magically disappear; they just learned not to talk about them. Similarly, as a result of feminists' efforts to stop victim-blaming, many people who continue to regard women as bringing violence upon themselves no longer acknowledge their belief so openly. As long as people assume that women are masochistic, they will tend to seek the "little thing" the victim must have done to bring the violence on herself. By contrast, this is *not* how the motives of male victims of violence are usually interpreted. For most audiences, the rape of a man by another man in the movie *Deliverance* was simply horrifying and undeserved; no one said the guy loved it or really wanted it. Similar rape scenes with woman victims do not always elicit such responses.

Although pornographic materials are rife with examples of supposedly sexually masochistic women, as Theodor Reik wrote in *Masochism in Modern Man,* "masochism as a perversion is rare among women." And after a recent review of the research and clinical literature on the subject, Andreas Spengler concluded in 1983 in *S and M: Studies in Sadomasochism* that "the number of women prepared to enter sadomasochistic relationships . . . appears to be extremely small."

For the most part, however, even mental health workers have commonly assumed that women who have been beaten by their husbands or their boyfriends have brought the beatings on themselves or even enjoyed them and needed to be beaten. In one example of this practice, three authors wrote in the journal *Archives of General Psychiatry* about violence "fulfilling masochistic needs of the wife" and being "necessary for the wife's . . . equilibrium." Irene Gilman wrote in the journal *Psychiatry* about Sigmund Freud's view that masochism is the woman's way of avoiding Oedipal feelings, because she fears losing her mother's love. So, goes the argument, she provokes the male's (father-figure's) aggression to punish herself for desiring her father and to show her mother that she has given up that desire. And in the journal *Social Casework* in 1976 Beverly B. Nichols described how, because of the Freudian view that the woman provokes the abuse, social workers ask the batterers what the women did to provoke them and often accept the batterers' explanations. Elaine Hilberman makes the same point, saying that the woman who complains of having been abused "is suspected of fabrication, provocation, or seduction. . . ."

Such attitudes have a history of respectability. Nicole Walton-Allen's 1984 psychology master's thesis includes this useful summary:

> It could almost be said that from the beginning . . . wifebeating has been a part of human existence. Although the transition from group marriages and extended relationships to monogamous pairings provided women with protection from an "open season on rape," it also induced the complete subjugation of women to the authority of men (Brownmiller, 1975). With the advent of pairing marriage, the man assumed control of the household and came to regard his wife as his property. Her status was reduced to satisfying his lust, bearing his children and tending to the home (Martin, 1976). The church also sanctioned the subjection of women to their husbands, utilizing the twisted rationalization that Eve's behavior in the Garden of Eden signified the inherent evil of women (Davidson, 1977). Constantine, the first Christian emperor, was most remembered for his torturing and eventual murder of his wife (Davidson, 1977). Even the Apostles perpetuated this misogynistic view, with Paul emphasizing the "man is not of the woman, but the woman of the man. Neither was the man created for the woman but the woman for the man" (I Corinthians 11: 8,9) and "Wives, submit yourselves unto your own husbands, as unto the Lord, for the husband is the head of the wife" (Ephesians 5).
>
> During the Enlightenment in Europe in the 1700s, such inspired writers as Rousseau continued to preach the shackling of women to the whim of men. Quoted by a pioneer of women's rights, Mary Wollstonecraft (1792, p. 180), Rousseau was noted to espouse the belief that ". . . formed to obey a being so imperfect as man, often

full of vices, and always full of faults, she ought to learn betimes to suffer injustices and to bear the insults of a husband without complaint; it is not for his sake, but for her own, that she should be of mild disposition. The pervasiveness and ill-nature of women only serve to aggravate their own misfortunes and the misconduct of their husbands." . . . . In the U.S. prior to 1871, a husband was allowed to beat his wife with a stick no bigger than his thumb [hence the term "rule of thumb," for which I now substitute "guideline"], pull her hair, choke her, spit in her face and kick her about the floor (Davidson, 1977). Furthermore, while the court of law acknowledged the husband's right of "chastisement," the battered wife was not allowed to "vex, discredit or shame" the family by seeking any legal protection (Martin, 1978).

Is it true that battered women need the violence? Do they try to provoke it? Psychologist Don Dutton, a researcher who has worked extensively with batterers in Vancouver, Canada, was asked those questions by a psychiatrist at a recent professional meeting. Dutton replied that, before he began to work with these men he had asked himself the same questions. In group meetings with batterers, however, he said that when he asked the men themselves to describe what led to the battering incidents, they not infrequently said something like: "It was Friday, and I'd gotten my paycheck, so I went out and cashed it and got roaring drunk. Then I came home late, and my wife was asleep, so I woke her up and beat her." Clearly, the sleeping wife had not provoked the abuse. According to another battered wife her husband would "knock me in the head," saying, "Here's for what you did today. If you didn't do it today you'll do it tomorrow."

According to the traditional argument, even if women don't provoke the abuse, they must enjoy it, because why else would they stay? Dr. Dutton and his colleague, psychologist and family violence expert Dr. Susan Lee Painter, have proposed a compelling, coherent explanation *other than masoch-*

ism for why women stay with their batterers. They call it the theory of "traumatic bonding." They point out that physical abuse leaves women victims exhausted, emotionally and physically hurt and drained, and thus in desperate need of some human warmth and comfort. When the women are in this particularly needy state, the men who have abused them are often still at home and sometimes even feeling guilty; thus, whatever warmth or affection these men offer tends to be accepted by the women, because they are in such need. It is not the abusive side of their abusers to which these women bond but the warmer, affectionate side that meets their healthy need to be loved and cared for.

But even if they do not actually *enjoy* the beatings, do the women somehow elicit them? Hilberman believes that abusers are men who, for whatever reason, do not control their aggression and regard women and girls as "legitimate targets" for their hostility. She says: "The basic fact of the victim's femaleness is used by the offender to justify the assault. . . ." In this connection, I recall my own amazement at the reaction of one of my close male friends when he came on the scene just after a belligerent automobile repair man had gotten angry at my claim that my car was under warranty and had shoved me. Because of that, and because of my sheer frustration about the generally unpleasant scene, I had burst into tears. As my friend entered the garage, I told him what had happened, but he did and said nothing. Later, he confessed that he assumed I had been lying about the man having pushed me, because "when women get upset and cry, they lie." Using this kind of "logic," men can regard women as deserving of whatever they get, simply because they are women. In fact, it is well recognized that many abusers are alcoholics, psychotics, deeply immature men, or "bullies," as analyst Natalie Shainess calls them. What abusive men describe as "triggers" in their wives' behavior that set off their abuse include breaking an egg yolk or wearing their hair in a pony tail. In 1979 psychiatrist Alexandra Symonds related in a *Journal of American Psychotherapy* article a case in which the husband beat his wife with a broomstick because their baby vomited in the highchair during dinner, and family therapist Michele Bograd notes that "Family therapists sometimes appear unwilling to acknowledge that some battered women *are* innocent victims whose sole 'collaboration' was standing within arm's reach of their husbands." Shainess points out that " 'to trigger' does not mean 'to be responsible for.' " By contrast, we would not say that a child elicited a beating by accidentally spilling a glass of milk and thereby hold the child responsible for its parent's loss of control. We might say that at the end of a hard day we can imagine losing control over spilled milk, but we would probably not use that kind of argument to *justify* the beating of a child in the way that women's behavior is said to "trigger" their husbands' abuse of them. What accounts for this difference? In part it is our tendency to believe that children should be protected by their parents rather than hurt by them. In part it is the pair of myths about women that were mentioned earlier—women as either smothering, emotionally draining and demanding or cold and rejecting—for if we classify women's behavior as fitting into one of these two types, then it is easy to believe that either type can drive men to lose control and thus make women responsible for their own beatings.

There is one more myth that feeds this belief, and that is the myth that male humans have stronger aggressive drives than female humans. Therefore, we cannot expect the poor dears to control their aggression any more than we learned (from boys) in high school that we could expect them to control their sexual feelings once *girls* had aroused them. From my own research and inspection of the enormous body of research done by others on sex differences in aggression, if I were to state my conclusion in a headline, it would be: "Little girls are as aggressive as little boys if they think no one is looking." If children believe that someone is watching them, the sex difference increases, with boys becoming more aggressive than girls. Males learn early that it is all right, even "all boy," to give vent to their aggression, and females learn early that it is unfeminine to do so. The evidence does not suggest that males are somehow innately incapable of controlling their aggression. Furthermore, as suggested in the work of psychologists Cannie Stark-Adamec and Robert Adamec, it seems grossly unfair not to hold males responsible for their aggression but to hold females responsible for all of the "evil" things that they are alleged to do (as embodied in the myths about women). It has long been assumed that hormonal factors lead males to be more aggressive than females, in particular that the males' testosterone is what gives rise to aggression. Some recent research has shown, however, that the cause-effect relationship also works in the reverse direction: dominant, aggressive behavior can lead to an increase in testosterone. Thus, if we train males to behave aggressively, we raise their testosterone level, and understanding this makes it clear that the issue is far more complex than the widely believed assumption that males are inevitably aggressive because of their hormones.

In our society too few people are shocked if a man says he slapped his wife around in order to "teach her" not to nag him about his drinking. In *Psychology Today* in 1970, R. Stark and J. McEvoy reported their research showing that one in four Americans explicitly takes the view that there is a good reason for a husband to hit his wife and vice versa. Of course, the "vice versa" is a far less frequent occurrence.

If it were true that women look for abuse, we should be able to discover whether they knew before marriage that their husbands would beat them. According to Eva Vincze, who runs a shelter for battered wives in Virginia, many of the women were beaten by the men before they were married, but the reasons for the beatings seemed to the wives to be attributable to the men's jealousy. The women tended to feel that marriage would solve the problem: "I thought once he owned me, he would stop the battering" or, "I thought that he was afraid I would leave him at the altar and run off with some other guy. All the time we were engaged, the only reason he hit me was when he imagined I had been stepping out on him. I believed that once we were married he would feel sure of me, and his jealous rages would stop.''

By contrast, there is Linda Lovelace's description of the reversal of Chuck Traynor's behavior once he married her, when he changed from an apparently considerate, kind person to a torturer. What Lovelace had in common with the women who hoped that marriage would stop the abuse was their traditional feminine faith in the fundamental goodness of their men.

Once the women see that the beatings continue, why do they stay? Many of the reasons are now familiar to you: for economic reasons, because they have no way to support themselves or their children; they fear harming their children by depriving them of their father or precipitating a divorce; they have few sources of love and support, so they are very dependent on these men. Barbara Star reported in the mental health journal *Victimology* in 1978 that she had found in her research that battered wives are not submissive people but do tend to repress anger and to have few coping abilities. She concluded that ''these factors point to passivity, rather than the need for maltreatment, as the more appropriate rationale underlying the endurance of physical abuse.'' She wrote further that the women perceived themselves as unable to bring about changes in their environment and ''believe that any action will only make a bad situation worse.'' Passivity and a sense of powerlessness over one's environment are, as we have seen, elements basic to the feminine image.

Many women, sensing that something is seriously wrong with their husbands, believe that they would be bad women to ''hit them while they are down'' by leaving them. Not realizing that it is not within their power to help these men very much, they stay through a misguided attempt to help someone whom they may love and who has probably shown them some love and kindness in the past. As one therapy patient said, ''Yes, my husband used to beat me, but eight-month periods would go by when he wouldn't. And the Christian ethic is that you stay married forever.''

California wife abuse archivist and social activist Laura X reports that "battered women often tell me their husbands can't get an erection unless they beat the woman first," and for a dependent woman with poor self-esteem to risk feeling she has "unmanned" her already troubled husband by refusing to allow him the one way he can become sexually aroused is too big a risk for her to take. She would surely believe she had failed to be a supportive, sympathetic wife.

Alexandra Symonds explains that many battered women are isolated, and this makes them more dependent than most women on their husbands. Among the battered women whom I have seen, their isolation comes sometimes from their naturally reserved natures but more often from the fact that their husbands are immature, dependent, and very possessive. These men want total loyalty and obedience, and they fear that any friendships their wives have could undermine their wives' loyalty to them. Thus, these women feel that they are unworthy wives if they venture to tell a woman friend about their fears of, and frustration with, their husbands. This keeps them more isolated, so that even if they want to leave their husbands, they have nowhere to go. Kathy Kaplan, now in her late twenties and serving a 30-years-to-life sentence for finally killing the husband who violently abused her for years, said, according to a newspaper article, that when her husband got into financial trouble

> . . . he would take her to a motel room and tell her that some men would be visiting, adding: "It's your turn to earn your keep."
>
> "He was on amphetamines," Kaplan says, "and one night when he got drunk he said he'd fix me so no other man would ever want me."
>
> Kaplan lost consciousness when her husband raped her with a knife.
>
> "He took me to a doctor who never looked at my face, stitched me up and didn't even ask how I came to have such injuries," she recalls.

"I thought I was the only one in the world going through this kind of experience. . . . I didn't know there were people who could help."

Symonds has also said that the woman victims are often frozen with fear of these men, and—like good, traditional women—they believe that they can stave off the violence if only *they* try hard enough to be "good" by becoming as obedient and cooperative as possible. Most women have serious defects in their self-esteem, and so it is easy to convince them that virtually anything that goes wrong in a relationship is their fault. The corollary of this is that if they try hard to avoid doing anything that might upset their abuser, the abuse might stop. The poor self-esteem of these women can lead them to think that if the one who loves you treats you like garbage, what might the rest of the world do to you? as an abused wife asked family violence specialist Richard Gelles. How, indeed, could these women take the risk of leaving? Their self-esteem stands to be undermined even further if, by walking out, they destroy the image other people may have of them as partners in a happy, stable marriage. They fear feeling, and being seen to be, failures at marriage, inadequate wives who couldn't make a go of their relationships.

An often overlooked point is that, as researcher Diana Russell has written, "It is often assumed that if an abused wife will only decide to leave her marriage, abuse will end," but the cases she studied show this is not true. In many abusive situations, she reports, wives stay because their husbands simply will not let them go. She gives examples of one woman whose husband repeatedly kidnapped her after they were separated, and the police said they could not protect her; another woman whose husband tried several times to murder her; and yet another whose husband's threat to kill her was so serious that she had to leave the state.

· This is similar to the position of prostitutes who have brutal pimps. According to a recent investigation, prostitutes who try to break away from their pimps are usually beaten or subjected to death threats.

There is one further, important psychological factor that sometimes leads abused women actually to elicit abuse, and that is the fundamental human need to feel that they have some control over their lives. It is unbearable to wait helplessly for a beating that a woman knows will come; she needs to believe that she can avoid the beating by behaving in certain ways and not behaving in others. For some women, as discussed earlier, the belief that they have some control is all they have left. Laura X, who has had extensive contact over many years with battered wives, says that some women have told her that things got so bad that when they knew the abuse was coming, they *would* elicit it, just to get it over with and to give themselves the feeling that if they could not avoid the beating, at least they could control *when* it would happen.

In trying to gain some sense of control through understanding and through making an effort to be good women—by not believing that their men are irrational, self-centered, and unable to control their impulses—most abused wives hold four beliefs, according to psychiatrist Elaine Hilberman:

(1) Violence is "normal," that it happens to most wives;
(2) Their man's violence is rational, that he abused them because he is physically or mentally sick, alcoholic, unemployed, or under other stress;
(3) Violence is justified, that they deserve it because they have been bad, provocative, or challenging; and
(4) Violence is controllable if the women can only be good, quiet, and compliant enough.

It is particularly poignant that women try to believe that their men's violence is due to illness or stress, even though few would justify their own harsh behavior on such grounds. The tragedy of the fourth belief is that behaving in a totally compliant way further undermines the woman's self-esteem, making her an even more likely victim of abuse. As Hilberman summarizes the situation, a woman stays in such relationships to "protect her husband and her marriage, at the expense of her self-esteem and autonomy and, possibly, her life."

Nicole Walton-Allen has listed some of the psychological factors that make it difficult for an abused woman to leave her man:

◇ *shock* that the person who says he loves her can treat her so terribly (to leave would be to acknowledge the awful reality of the situation);

◇ *guilt* that she feels she has contributed to her own beatings or has fueled her abuser's anger;

◇ *depression* that she is locked in a relationship that seems hopeless and joyless (depression makes it even harder to help oneself);

◇ *shame* that anyone would consider her so detestable as to beat her (and leaving is to admit to the world that this has been the case);

◇ *humiliation* that she has allowed anyone to take advantage of her to such a degree; and

◇ *low self-esteem,* which contributes to her physical and psychological immobilization, keeping her locked in her situation and clouding her ability to take stock of her life and come to rational conclusions.

There is one more myth related to battered women that needs to be put to rest and that is the myth that battered women come from homes where they, as children, saw their mothers being battered. There is no evidence to support this simplistic theory. It is true that among battered wives a large number saw their fathers beat their mothers, but the same is true for wives who are *not* beaten. We live in a society that condones violence, particularly male violence, that believes violence is "natural," particularly for men and that, therefore, we cannot control it very much, especially if women continue to "elicit" it. We do not use the same logic and say that people should feel free to urinate and defecate whenever and wherever they feel like it, on the grounds that these, too, are "natural" impulses. But because women are considered legitimate objects of aggression, wife abuse has been tacitly condoned. Throughout our society there is ample opportunity for men to learn that women deserve abuse, and there is ample opportunity for women to develop such poor self-esteem and such a sense that women ought to depend totally on their husbands that they become too isolated and depressed to leave abusive relationships. Many people today, because of the women's movement, believe that men no longer consider women to be legitimate targets of aggression. It is a tempting belief; most of us would prefer to think that the world is getting better. However, there is no evidence that the incidence of wife abuse and rape is declining.

Since not all women are in a position to wait for men to bring their contempt and aggression toward women under control, how can and do women extricate themselves from violent relationships? In their work as counselors of battered women, Eva Vincze found in Virginia, as did Erica Rothman and Kit Munson in North Carolina, that the most important factors are to help women improve their self-esteem, to provide sources of warmth and support other than from their abusers, and to help them feel more powerful and take more control over their lives. Obviously, it is crucial, too, to help them examine their assumptions about what it means to be a "good woman" or a "good wife," and to enable them to see that those terms should not involve putting up with whatever a man dishes out. A number of counselors have found that it is extremely helpful to have the court remove the man from the home, giving both him and the woman the clear message that society will no longer condone physical violence as a way for men to express their frustration. Vincze stresses the importance of "empowering the woman to see she doesn't *deserve* to be battered *and* that she needn't be totally dependent on the man."

The general public is often distressingly oblivious of battered wives' real reasons for staying with their abusers. When Nicole Walton-Allen and I surveyed lay people about spouse abuse, we found that although many said a battered wife would stay with her husband because she is a masochist, no one gave that interpretation of the behavior of a battered husband who stayed with his wife.

"Conventional wisdom" has long held that not only battered wives but also women who get raped somehow asked for it. Only recently have most women realized how shocking and unfair it has been for the courts to allow rapists to go free because their victims had had previous, voluntary sexual contact with the rapist (as with a man who comes back to rape his former girlfriend or his ex-wife) or even because they had had previous sexual experience at all. Judges' decisions have been filled with observations about the victims walking alone at night or wearing "seductive" clothes when they were raped, implying that the women brought the rape on themselves. Such comments are not typically made about men who are murdered or robbed—or raped—while walking alone at night, and previous sexual experience is not usually an issue when men are raped. Feminist author Susan Griffin has pointed out, according to the Federal Commission on Crimes of Violence, "Though provocation . . . may consist only of 'a gesture'. . . only 4 percent of reported rapes involved any precipitative behavior by the woman." Even men who say that they have never committed rape become aroused when they watch depictions of rape in which the victim is portrayed as sexually stimulated by the assault, and Griffin notes that, in order to prove we don't want to be raped and in order to avoid being raped, we often lead very restricted lives. "The fear of rape keeps women off the streets at night. Keeps women at home. Keeps women passive and modest for fear that they be thought provocative.''

Not only have women been accused of behaving ''seductively'' toward rapists (as, for example, by wearing a short skirt), but rapists have often been excused for the crime because they are unemployed or because they have been the victim of some social mistreatment such as racism or poverty. A widely known psychological phenomenon is people's distaste for victims; this seems to be related to the wish to avoid being associated with victims or being thought to be one. But the double standard has been applied consistently in the area of rape: *male* rape victims have usually been regarded sympathetically, *female* rape victims as having asked for it, and male perpetrators with female victims as having raped for ''understandable'' reasons.

It is supposedly ''common knowledge'' that many women have fantasies of being raped. Maria Marcus suggested in *A Taste for Pain: On Masochism and Female Sexuality* that of all women who report having sexual fantasies, 25 percent have fantasies that they call ''rape fantasies.'' If that were true, surely that might prove that women are masochists. But did you ever talk to someone who actually had been raped who continued to have anything that could be called ''rape fantasies?'' In a *Village Voice* article titled ''The Rape Fantasies of Women: Up From Disrepute,'' Signe Hammer tells the story of a friend who used to have what she described as ''rape fantasies''—until she was raped. Hammer found that women who were molested as children, not surprisingly, did not later have erotic rape fantasies. Hammer says about herself that ''while I may have my rape fantasies, I have an intense dislike of the sort of man who really needs to overpower women.'' It should be noted that Hammer's misuse of the term ''rape fantasies'' here adds to the confusion, although her statement illustrates the important point that what are called ''rape fantasies'' have little or nothing to do with any real wish to be overpowered and raped.

In a similar vein, Molly Haskell wrote in a 1976 *Ms. Magazine* article called "Rape Fantasy: The 2,000-Year-Old Misunderstanding," that the term is a serious misnomer:

> For a woman to fantasize rape in the correct sense of the term would be to fantasize not love or lust but mutilation, and no sane women—and very few insane ones—express such a desire, even unconsciously. . . . "A rape fantasy," says Lois Gould, "has nothing to do with the *Daily News* rape, with the physical pain of ripping your vagina open. The fantasy takes you up to the point of physical interaction." . . . "A rape fantasy," said another friend, "has nothing to do with having a couple of teeth knocked out. It's when Robert Redford won't take no for an answer."

Haskell goes on to explain that the prevailing male version of what is called a woman's rape fantasy—what is generally accepted in popular culture, psychiatric literature, and courts of law—"is based on the assumption that women are masochistic and want to be taken by force." She points out that Helene Deutsch gave the term "rape fantasy"

> a pivotal place in the female psyche, while allowing it to stand indiscriminately for daydreams and night dreams; wish fulfillments and fears; adolescent and adult fantasies; the fantasies of a borderline psychotic and those of a relatively normal, functioning woman. . . . Helene Deutsch thus paved the way for the diverse associations of a term that was problematic enough to begin with to become politicized as a general sexual rule for women. No one assumed that because men had castration anxieties—*i.e.*, fantasies—they wanted to be castrated.

Haskell also quotes psychiatrist Robert Seidenberg as saying that "rape fantasy" has been completely misinterpreted by his colleagues as a masochistic desire rather than as the woman's way of expressing what has been going on all of her life.

What are called rape fantasies usually consist primarily of one of three elements, or of some combination of the three:

(1) The wish that some man will find you so devastatingly desirable that he cannot control his aroused sexuality;
(2) The wish to be able to trust someone so completely that you could feel that you could put yourself completely in his hands, sexually; and
(3) The wish to have the man make all the sexual advances, so that you would not have to risk appearing "too" sexual and, therefore, "unfeminine" in the traditional sense.

None of these is masochistic. The first is about being desired; as Haskell notes, "the emphasis is on the prelude, and an aura of sensuality, a sort of generalized voluptuousness in which the woman's needs and desirability are the controlling motifs. . . . the all-important element is that the men 'go mad with desire.' " The second element in "rape fantasies" is about being able to focus completely on one's own sexual enjoyment. The third leads to a phenomenon that Dr. Carol Cassell, in her book *Swept Away: Why Women Fear Their Own Sexuality,* calls women's need to be sexually "swept away." She demonstrates how, even today, many women feel reluctant to express their sexual feelings and have to "justify" such feelings by convincing themselves that they are "in love" or that the control of sexuality has been taken out of their hands.

Haskell observes that occasionally a rape fantasy does involve violence, but then "it is of a very special kind—an expression of fear rather than desire . . . or the reworking of sexual traumas."

Women have long been taught that females are supposed to be sexually passive. As Linda Phelps says in her 1979 paper on "Female Sexual Alienation":

If we come to view male-dominated heterosexuality as the only healthy form of sex, it is because we are bombarded with that model for our sexual fantasies long before we experience sex itself. Sexual images of conquest and submission pervade our imagination from an early age and determine how we will later look upon and experience sex.

Since "normal" female sexuality and rape both imply passivity, many women have slipped easily into misusing the term "rape fantasies" when pairing images of their own passive sexuality with those of men desperately desiring them.

This image of the sexually passive, defenseless woman persists in part because, as Haskell observes, we never hear about the thousands of times a man makes advances to a woman and she says "no" and walks away: ". . . the account that appears in public print is a very one-sided one, and very conducive to the stereotypes of masochistic women and masterful men."

Even "pseudo-rape" fantasies change as women change and become stronger, according to Ti-Grace Atkinson, another feminist theorist. She says that as women assert themselves more, their sexual fantasies lose their "masochistic" character, so that in their fantasies they become sexually more active, less the passive recipient or victim of the man's sex drive.

A significant kind of rape that has only been legally recognized and publicly acknowledged much in the last decade is marital rape. Fourteen percent of the women surveyed by Diana Russell in her book, *Rape in Marriage,* reported that they had been raped by their husbands, but according to Russell many more women who had had similar experiences didn't call them "rape." They called it "doing their duty."

A couple who had moved to North America about ten years ago came to see me because they had been having problems with their young son. The wife was very angry at her husband, and the couple quarreled continually. As we talked, it emerged that the husband had raped his wife, and that was why she was so angry. When she reported this to me, I turned to him and asked him to comment, expecting him to make some attempt to deny it. But he grinned broadly and said, "You must understand that in my culture this is the way a man shows that he loves a woman." His wife's understandably furious reaction had been turned into impotent rage by the male portion of his culture's support of his action. But it is not so different in traditional North American culture. A male respondent in *The Hite Report* reported that a psychiatrist had told him that he should have raped his wife, since she had refused to sleep with him.

Although feminists have been working to see that laws are passed against marital rape, the law changes slowly, and not all judges are in sympathy with the new attitudes and statutes. Until recently, according to laws throughout the continent, a husband had a right to have intercourse with his wife regardless of her wishes and regardless of whether he physically or emotionally coerced her. Indeed, there was no such thing as rape in marriage; it was called exercising one's "conjugal rights," and a woman who refused her husband's sexual advances was the one who was breaking the marriage contract. Thus, both legal and cultural factors made it nearly impossible for a raped wife to seek moral or legal redress. The rationale exonerating married rapists often was that women's sex drive is weaker than men's and, therefore, the husband needed to force his wife to have sex.

Forty-two percent of the raped wives studied by Russell left their marriages, and in another 17 percent of cases the marriage ended although it was unclear what role the woman played in ending it. Only one-fifth of the raped wives were still married to their rapists at the time of the study. The fact that so many women walked out reveals how determined they were to avoid pain, particularly in view of the courage it took to leave. For example, one woman reported that her rapist/husband had fractured their child's skull for making a noise, so she was convinced that he would try to kill her if she left him. Furthermore, raped wives often have a hard time finding friends and relatives who will support their leaving. Another woman in Russell's study described how her husband's daughter, the manager of their apartment building, and a bartender all helped her husband try to get her back, even though her health and life were in danger.

According to Russell, raped wives rarely blame themselves for the rape, but among those women who do stay in their marriages, the biggest reason for doing so is self-blame. However, the wives who stay are also more likely than those who leave to be Third World women, to have traditional expectations, and to believe there is a high likelihood of being raped outside of marriage. Thus, the women who stay appear to do so because of a variety of social-cultural pressures, not because of their masochism. Other information suggests that raped wives are quite right not to blame themselves, because except for the fact that wife rape usually begins when the wife is young, many kinds of women are raped by their husbands. There does not seem to be one particular type that "asks for it." What *is* determined by the wife's characteristics is how she handles the experience. Perhaps Russell's most important finding is that there is no evidence that women enjoy being raped by their husbands. Only two of the 87 victims had been raped by two separate husbands; ". . . it is very rare for victims of this form of abuse to repeat 'their mistake,' " says Russell. Even a woman whose father had beaten her mother regarded her husband's violence against her as intolerable, and another woman said, "I would never put myself at the mercy of a man again."

What about the claim that some women are sexual masochists, aroused not necessarily by rape but by being tied up in chains, gagged, and pinched with nipple clamps, burned with dripping hot wax, defiled, and humiliated in grotesque ways? Charles Brenner, a psychoanalyst, has defined sexual masochism as "the seeking of unpleasure, by which is meant physical or mental pain, discomfort, or wretchedness, for the sake of sexual pleasure. . . ." As noted earlier, reports of such behavior among women are extremely rare. Psychologist Julia Sherman has pointed out that although Kinsey's famous statistics show that far more men than women are "sexual masochists," the term is more often applied to women. In the 1983 book *S and M: Studies in Sadomasochism* Thomas S. Weinberg, having examined the research literature about sadomasochistic relationships from sociological perspectives, concluded, "It does not seem to be the case that 'submissive' women seek out dominant men." He had found no evidence to support this widely held belief. Furthermore, in the same book, Paul Gebhard specified that even the people called "sexual masochists" do not find pain attractive per se but only "pain" that is inflicted on them as part of a prearranged situation. "Accidental pain is not perceived as pleasurable or sexual." A woman who might participate in a sadomasochism scene that she helps to plan is *not* aroused if she twists her ankle during her preparations.

Theodor Reik wrote in *Masochism in Modern Man* as long ago as 1941 that "the suffering of pain, being beaten or tied up, disgrace and humiliations, do not belong to the sexual aims of the normal woman." More recently, psychiatrist Robert Robertiello wrote in 1970 that there is an important distinction between masochistic submission, which involves making oneself *less than* another person, and surrender, which involves "the letting go and giving one's self to the activity one is involved in." The latter was described by Robertiello as "very desirable and not at all masochistic behavior." Few people, however, have listened to Reik and Robertiello; most have continued to believe that women are sexually masochistic, in part because they confuse surrender with submission.

In view of the rarity of true female sexual masochism, why has it become a widely accepted belief that women are sexual masochists? Some men wish to believe that women like to suffer, since it makes them feel powerful to know they can make other people feel this way. The famous sexual guru Havelock Ellis wrote in *Love and Pain* that "Among mammals the male wins the female very largely by the display of

force. The infliction of pain must inevitably be a frequent indirect result of the exertion of power.'' It's the animal argument again—if we interpret animals' behavior in certain ways,
then we can use (or misuse) it to justify human males' mistreatment of human females. Ellis went on to write: ''Within
the limits consistent with normal and healthy life, what men
are impelled to give women love to receive. So that we need
not unduly deprecate the 'cruelty' of men within these limits,
nor unduly commiserate the women who are subjected to it.''
Sigmund Freud believed that as soon as woman is degraded,
man's sexuality and pleasure can be developed fully—men's
need to feel powerful and potent feeds on the subjection of
women. One might expect that such a statement would be made
in a tone of some moral outrage, but Freud makes it as though
it were simply descriptive, with no exploration of how this
came to be and with no sign of dismay or protest.

Modern developments in birth control are used to justify
the view of women as fair game for all men unless a woman
has one man (usually a husband) to protect her, according to
Sally Roesch Wagner in *Against Sadomasochism*. According
to this kind of thinking, the Pill presumably removed the
woman's vulnerability by eliminating the risk of pregnancy,
so women now risk no more than men in sexual encounters
and, therefore, no longer merit men's protection.

Most feminists have been uncomfortable with the view
of women as sexual masochists, but recently a group of lesbians in a book called *Coming to Power* wrote that lesbian
sadomasochism exists, is worthy of respect, and is far more
interesting and sexually arousing than what they call ''vanilla
sex.'' They do not appear to represent the majority of lesbians or of feminist lesbians, but their claims must be evalu-
ated, particularly since, as they point out, most manifestations of women's sexuality have been unthinkingly condemned
or misinterpreted at some time or another. First of all, most
of the book's contributors are not describing enjoyment of
suffering but rather intensification or prolonging of sexual
sensation.

A writer who calls herself Juicy Lucy writes: "[My whip is of] very soft leather, 8 thongs about 18" long with a wood & leather handle, & at the beginning of sex I only like it lightly. As things progress, lightly isn't enough. Be very clear about this—this is not a beating I'm talking about. This is an intensification of sensation, a heightened stimulation of certain areas & it *feels* good to me." Other writers in the book describe the use of techniques designed to prolong sexual arousal or to experience their lovers' strength. For most people, prolongation of sexual arousal is not painful but is intensely pleasurable, and the experiencing of one's partner as strong can certainly be arousing and pleasurable without involving any suffering. As Pat Califia wrote in 1983 in *Sapphistry: The Book of Lesbian Sexuality*:

> Discomfort, stress or actual pain can contribute to some women's sexual pleasure. First of all, these sensations increase tension, speed up breathing, and reproduce or intensify many of the physiological changes associated with arousal. This is also a way to express trust or devotion to a lover. . . . Breaking through mental and physical barriers creates a feeling of elation.

Still other writers in *Coming to Power* describe techniques for exploring the limits of their sexual and sensual feelings, again not activities that are by definition painful. In this regard Califia notes, "The lesbian who self-identifies as a sadomasochist uses roles, power exchanges, and intense sensations for sexual gratification." The authors of other chapters describe the feeling of trusting their partners so totally that they can give up all control over the progress of the sexual encounter to them. This surely is not masochism either.

In a chapter called "If I Ask You to Tie Me Up, Will You Still Want to Love Me?" Juicy Lucy says: "By saying 'sadist' & 'masochist' I do not mean that I or any of those other dykes consciously decided to cause pain. Pain is simply the inevitable result of unacknowledged power roles. I have never known lesbians to say to each other something like, 'Let's start a relationship & hurt each other a lot, OK?'' Thus, although she is using the term "masochist," she does not mean it to signify the enjoyment or seeking of pain.

Now, so far none of the experiences described constitutes actual enjoyment of pain. Indeed, an entire chapter in *Coming to Power* is devoted to the care that must be taken to protect the passive partner from real pain and to make sure that the encounter will not involve real danger. A woman who describes herself as a lesbian sadomasochist told me that the one time she really hurt someone—accidentally causing her to bite her lip—she felt terribly sorry. She also said that if she and a lover were having an argument, they would not have an S and M encounter, because there would be a danger of hurting each other physically and because anger mars the complete trust that is necessary for such sexual scenes. The only genuine pain any of the authors of chapters in *Coming to Power* describes is used to expiate the guilt that they have been taught to feel about being sexually aroused. There, too, the ultimate aim is pleasure—to get beyond the guilt so that unhampered sexual enjoyment can be felt. In calling "masochistic" such practices as the prolonging of sexual excitement, the authors follow in the misguided footsteps of Theodor Reik, who in 1940 had mislabeled as "masochistic" the willingness to endure pain in order to achieve some ultimate relief or pleasure.

One other feature of lesbian sadomasochism was described by a practitioner in this way: Physical pain and pleasure both involve a high level of arousal, and it is worth risking pain in order to create a level of physical arousal that can bring intense pleasure.

Califia's definition of lesbian sadomasochism provides a concise summary that shows that, although submission may play a role, pain and humiliation per se are not the aims: "Sadomasochism is defined here as an erotic ritual that involves acting out fantasies in which one partner is sexually dominant and the other partner is sexually submissive."

I have a close friend who is a feminist and who, when she heard that I was writing this chapter, confessed that she feels aroused when reading descriptions of some sexual masochists' fantasies. She figured that must mean she is masochistic. "Nonsense," I told her, "I'll bet that what you find arousing is not the idea of pain but rather the idea of prolonging arousal or being made to feel intense stimulation, which these writers have called masochism but which is not that at all." That suggestion rang true, she said. When we find certain images or fantasies arousing, we do not have to accept other people's labels or interpretations of our feelings.

Another group of women, many but not all of them lesbian feminists, wrote a book called *Against Sadomasochism: A Radical Feminist Analysis,* in which they made many of the points I have just made and went even further. One woman who had formerly been involved in sexual masochism said that when she suffered actual physical pain it was in an attempt to "release a great deal of emotional pain," not to suffer for the sake of suffering. And in the same book, feminist Robin Morgan writes quite accurately that even most women who become aroused by fantasies of sexual masochism are immediately turned *off* by real masochism. I think Reik came close when he described something that he had mislabeled "masochism"—the prolonging of sexual arousal—as being like "the joyful anticipation of children at Christmas who are waiting with fevered excitement for Santa Claus."

One other important point about prolonging excitement needs to be made. Many women do not feel comfortable about asking their sexual partners to do what feels good to them. For such women, so-called masochistic fantasies or actual "masochistic" deferring of orgasm might be the only way they can prolong their arousal if they are in bed with a man (or a woman) who cares only about rushing ahead to his or her own orgasm.

One woman in *Against Sadomasochism* wrote about a friend of hers who had become involved with a woman lover who really hurt her physically. The friend then tried suicide "to end the pain." No masochist she. Another former sexual masochist managed to quit that kind of life but needed constant reassurance that she was not inherently masochistic. She and her abusive partner had shared the belief in the victim's need to suffer. Because the victim was emotionally dependent on her partner, it took a great deal of emotional support from friends for her to learn to identify the many healthy motives and strengths she had. Only in this way could she revise her accustomed view of herself as inescapably a victim.

One more form of violence against women that warrants examination is father-daughter incest. The traditional clinical interpretation involved blaming both of the females involved: the mother and the daughter. It was said that the mother did not like sex and therefore palmed her daughter off on her husband as a sexual object, to get some relief for herself. The daughter was regarded as seductive and highly sexual, seducing her helpless father into an incestuous relationship. The father's normal masculine lack of control over his sexuality was used as his excuse.

Recent theories, thanks to front-line workers like Norma Totah and Dr. Suzanne Sgroi, who were brave enough to take a new look at father-daughter incest, have shown that this is not so. What *is* typical is that both parents are highly insecure, dependent people, who desperately need to maintain their marriage. The husband attempts to do this in the stereotypically male way, by making demands on the members of his family, in Archie Bunker style, issuing orders and insisting that his needs be met immediately. The wife attempts to keep the marriage together by responding to his requests, à la Edith Bunker, not feeling free to question the legitimacy of those demands. Indeed, as a "good wife" who wants to keep the family together, if any feeling that her husband might be wrong comes near her consciousness, she suppresses it. It is easy to understand that for such a couple sex is often problematic. The husband is easily threatened by anything that may "go wrong" in bed and he perceives any assertiveness on his wife's part as "castrating." He often finds his daughter less threatening and turns to her. The daughter—raised in the midst of this insecure, interdependent famiy—senses that refusing her father's sexual demands would destroy him. She cannot tell her mother, because to bring this out in the open would destroy the family, the prospect of which is the source of the family's most profound terror.

It has not been unusual to hear clinicians claim that the daughters who are victims of incest with their fathers, in addition to being "seductive," were also masochistic and thereby precipitated the incest. Understanding how these families really operate, however, makes it clear that for many of these girls, putting up with the pain and shame of their fathers' sexual assaults on them is less fearful than taking the risk of destroying their families altogether.

A number of years ago Florence Rush tried to call the public's attention to the fact that the pleas of these girls for help had too often gone unheeded. They would finally get up the courage to tell someone and their stories would be nervously ignored or cast aside as fabrications, products of the girls' overactive, oversexed adolescent imaginations. This reaction is far less common today, but it still is common. Rush poignantly described the effect that this societal avoidance had on the girls, making them feel both crazy and evil. She also explained how Sigmund Freud, on hearing many of his women patients describe scenes of childhood sexual assaults by their fathers or other male relatives, at first believed that their stories were true. When his own father died, however, he felt guilty about what he believed was his mistreatment of his father and needed to believe that fathers in general were good people. In part to support this need, he reclassified the women's reports as fantasies or wish fulfillment. When Rush wrote about this in 1980 in her excellent book, *The Best Kept Secret: Sexual Abuse of Children,* it made hardly a ripple in the mental health professions or among the general public, although it warranted a tidal wave. But a few years later a male psychoanalyst, Jeffrey Masson, wrote something similar, after having carefully inspected materials in the Freud Archives, and was attacked in a deeply personal way, called hysterical, manipulative, and deceitful. These attacks deflected attention from the facts he presented by focusing on his personal sexual life and his "betrayal" of the guardians of the Freud Archives. When Rush, a female social worker, told the story of Freud and the incest cover-up, the male psychoanalysts did not think it even worth bothering to criticize, but when one of their own told the same story it was necessary to punish him. From the work of Rush and Masson it is clear that when female victims of suffering inflicted by men have tried to tell their stories, they have often been disbelieved and even humiliated for coming forward. If you keep quiet, you suffer in silence and wonder whether this makes you masochistic; if you tell, you are punished and mocked for telling and thereby made to suffer anyway, so the telling can be seen as a sign of your masochism.

Particularly in relation to women as victims of violence, it is important to understand the danger of the continuing belief in women's masochism. Freud believed that men's sadism and women's masochism were instinctual, rooted in the unconscious. As Kathleen Barry points out in *Female Sexual Slavery*, Freud thereby moved the responsibility for men's cruelty to women from the individual man to the abstract realm of instinct and the unconscious; the implication is that men cannot prevent their sadism any more than women can prevent their masochism. And the more we believe that women are innately, inevitably sexually masochistic, the less will we believe that women can take control of their sexuality and become free simply to enjoy it.

What can we do to combat such views of women? First, we can refuse to believe that women are masochists. This refusal is of profound importance for several reasons. As Hilde Hein wrote in her paper, "Sadomasochism and the Liberal Tradition," to allow the degradation of women is to make us all less human: "To degrade someone, even with that person's expressed consent, is to *endorse* the degradation of persons. It is to affirm that the abuse of persons is *acceptable*.

For if some people may be humiliated and despised, all may be.'' Second, we can disavow the mistaken belief that women are willing victims. Erich Fromm is reported to have said, ''The fact that millions of people take part in a delusion doesn't make it sane.'' And finally, we can recognize that the fight to vanquish that belief is in an important sense a fight for our freedom. Adrienne Rich calls ''the worst thing of all . . . the failure to want our freedom passionately enough.''

Gloria Steinem in her article about Linda Lovelace describes how a society set to believe that women are sexual masochists responds when a woman tells the truth:

> Once [Linda] started giving her own answers to questions and trying to explain her years of coercion, she discovered that reporters were reluctant to rush into print. Her story was depressing, not glamorous or titillating at all. Because she had been passed around like a sexual trading coin, sometimes to men who were famous, there was also fear of lawsuits.

And, finally, Steinem asks the ''most popular'' question about Linda Lovelace:

> *If she really wanted to, couldn't she have escaped sooner?*
> Linda explains as best she can. As I watch her, I come to believe the question should be different: *Where did she find the courage to escape at all?*
> Inside the patience with which she answers these questions—the result of childhood training to be a ''good girl'' that may make victims of us all—there is some core of strength and stubbornness that is itself the answer. She *will* make people understand. She will *not* give up.
> In the microcosm of this one woman, there is a familiar miracle: the way in which women survive—and fight back.
> And a fight there must be.

CHAPTER 8

Women at Work

For women as a group, the future holds terrifying insecurity: We are increasingly dependent on our own resources, but in a society and an economy that never intended to admit us as independent persons. . . . —BARBARA EHRENREICH

In the work place, as at home, women are often forced to choose the lesser of two (or more) evils and then are blamed for bringing their unhappiness on themselves. Women have always been underpaid and underpromoted and, what's more, have learned to swallow the "justification" for this. It has not been unusual to hear women say, "I don't mind being paid about half as much as a man who does my kind of work, because after all he has to support his family," or, "He would feel threatened if I got paid as much as he does." According to Jan Mears, a Toronto consultant on the quality of working life, the "head of household" argument has recently been vigorously revived by management and by working men and women, especially in response to economically stringent times.

There are substantial barriers that women encounter in business even at the point of trying to enter the work force, fed by what Anthony Astrachan called in a 1984 *Ms. Magazine* article men's conscious and unconscious anger and fear that women at work will deprive men of power. Sometimes the most stark manifestations of sexism at work are kept among "the boys." One incident of this type was told to me by a man called Malcolm and also illustrates how racism frequently goes hand in hand with sexism. Abner, a business executive, asked Malcolm to interview a prospective employee who was East Indian. Malcolm found her to be extremely intelligent and hardworking and to have an excellent employment history. After the interview, before hearing Malcolm's opinion of the applicant, Abner told him, "You know, I haven't interviewed her myself, but since she's Indian, she's got two strikes against her." "Why two?" asked Malcolm. "She's also a woman," was the reply. Malcolm was expected to laugh and agree. If he had not, he would have been accused of "siding with women"—a low-status thing to do, a betrayal of the old boys who run the company (not one of the executives in their company is female).

Another method for discouraging women from obtaining job or career training and for silencing us about unfair treatment at work has been to make us feel lucky even to be considered for a particular kind of work. I once was told that I might well be discriminated against because of my sex, and at the time I felt that this was perfectly reasonable. When I applied to graduate school in 1969, the man who chaired the department where I eventually got my Ph.D. informed me in a preadmission interview: "Your grades and your graduate record examination scores are good, and so are your letters of recommendation. We may well accept you into our program. We always do end up taking a couple of women [that turned out to be exactly what they did take—two women and six men]. *But* we are reluctant to do so, because no matter what they say at the beginning, at some point in their training or in their career, women drop out to have children—and they *should*—but it means a loss to the profession. We spend time training women to be psychologists, and then they take time out to have and raise children.''

I remember feeling ashamed of women for being so unfair to the profession of psychology. I felt inclined to swear to him that either I would never have children (but he had just told me that I *should* have them) or that if I had children I'd stay up all night and work weekends, so as not to let the profession down. This kind of encounter is less likely to happen today, because the women's movement has stressed the principle that child rearing is an essential part of society's work and that the people who do this work deserve to be supported rather than being made to feel they've let their profession down. Furthermore, one can now point to large bodies of research data that show women actually miss fewer work days than men, even though it is usually the mother who takes time off from work when the children are sick *and* even though only women have morning sickness, swollen ankles, and sometimes severe exhaustion as a result of pregnancy; sleep deprivation because of nursing newborns in the middle of the night; and menstrual and menopausal difficulties. I won't speculate on why men manage to miss more work than women; the fact is that, as most women have long suspected, women as a group are remarkably conscientious about holding up their side (whether it's at home or at work), even when they are doing two jobs at once. The major loss to the professions and to other work places comes not from women's days of missed work but rather from the reluctance of employers, professional training schools, and factories to give women the training and the chance to prove what they can do.

The stereotype of femininity that society teaches us also stands in the way of girls and women receiving adequate education and training for work. In relation to this, I decided to examine why it should be that the school records of male and female students who are underachieving—that is, receiving lower grades than they are capable of earning—show that by the end of high school, the male underachievers have usually been underachieving from the time they entered school. The underachieving girls, however, are usually normal achievers, or even superachievers, until the end of grade school or the beginning of junior high school. Now, some people have said that this is easy to explain, that the increase in female hormones at puberty suddenly makes the girls less intelligent. However, psychology master's student Laurie Case and I set out to test our theory about this pattern. We suspected that underachieving girls would have narrower ideas about what constitutes acceptable "feminine" behavior than would the girls whose achievement remained high. In other words, if you think that girls have to be cute and not noticeably intelligent, then you had better make sure—as puberty arrives and you become interested in boys—that you don't show your intelligence.

I had a very bright friend a few years ahead of me in high school who wanted desperately to be elected homecoming queen. When she entered high school, she made sure to score poorly on several tests each grading period, because the names of honor roll students were posted every six weeks; she feared that if her name went up on that list she would be considered unfeminine and would never be elected queen. She succeeded. She was elected homecoming queen and graduated with a much lower grade average than she might have had.

Laurie and I thought that girls whose achievement stayed high would have not only a broader sense of what is "feminine" but also a broader basis for their identity in general. That is, in answer to the question, "Who are you?" the achievers would be more likely to say, for instance, "I am a girl, and I am sixteen years old, and I am a Methodist, and I am intelligent, and I am a soccer player, and I knit, and I have good friends, and I am a daughter, and I am a big sister," whereas the underachievers would be more likely to say, for example, "I am a girl, and I like boys, and I like clothes, and I don't do too well in school." In other words, the underachievers' sense of *who they are* would simply depend on

fewer and more traditional things. It would be more important for them to let their grades slide in order to remain
"feminine" and thereby maintain their sense of their identity. Lengthy interviews and questionnaires showed that our
suspicions were correct.

When girls begin to let their achievement slip as early as
grade school and junior high school, it does not seem to be
because of their "need to fail." Instead, it seems largely attributable to the socially imposed stereotypes about what is
acceptable for females and to socially imposed punishments
("You're not a real woman," "You're not feminine," "No
man will ever want you") for women who succeed too well.

Judith, for example, began to underachieve after she
learned from her best friend, Melissa, that the reason Tom
had never asked her out on a date during the two years that
she had had a crush on him was that she always scored higher
than he did on their math tests. The "feminine" stereotype
has presented many girls with an impossible choice: Either
they can minimize their intellectual abilities and their competence, in order to have the potentially happy and socially
acceptable experience of "getting a man," or they can develop their abilities but risk ostracism because men will be
afraid of them. In either case, an important part of themselves may have to be suppressed.

Traditionally, women at work have learned that they can
be regarded as competent *or* as nurturant and supportive, but
not both. Women can be seen as unthreatening and supportive, in which case, as we have noted in several contexts, they
are in danger of being regarded as *overly* emotional and,
therefore, incompetent. Or they can be seen as capable workers, in which case they are in danger of threatening their male
coworkers' and bosses' need for achievement and, therefore,
as "castrating." The former type of woman will not be given
raises or promotions, because she is not considered the kind
of worker who will advance and help the company grow; her
value lies in keeping up the other workers' morale, going for
coffee, and helping to defuse interpersonal problems among

workers. The latter type of woman may be denied raises and promotions because she is too threatening.

Traditionally, women have been guided toward the "nurturant" alternative of the "competent or nurturant" choice and have taken the responsibility for the "mood" and "spirit" of the workers in their offices or factories; but these concerns can lead them to neglect their own needs on the job. For example, women have been trained not to appear so bright and creative that the men at work feel they have been surpassed. They have been taught to behave this way for the men's sakes—so they won't feel threatened and inadequate—and for their own sakes, because the men, who usually have the power, will not help them to advance on the job if they are perceived as threatening. As a result, many women have concealed some of their intelligence, creativity, and ability and have focused instead on being nurturant and supportive to their (especially male) coworkers and bosses.

It is hard for a woman to be regarded as "one of the guys" or a "team player" in many work places, because the men still hold most of the power. If a woman tries to be one of the guys, she is in danger of being regarded as "seductive" (as, for example, if she goes out for a beer with them after work, when many of the real business deals are made) or as trying to be "too masculine" or sticking her nose where it doesn't belong. But if she does *not* try to be one of the boys, she will be perceived as "one of the girls," with all the low-status associations that has in the majority of work places (partly because women usually have lower-status jobs than men), or she will be considered aloof.

To advance in the work world, which is largely controlled by men, a woman usually has to win the approval of the men who are in power. To do this, she often risks alienating herself from the other women at work, who are not advancing as fast as she is and who will understandably regard her as having gone over to the "other side." Ellen, a secretary in an insurance office, was studying to become an insurance salesperson. Since most of the salespeople who could give her valuable advice were male, she had lunch with them increasingly often, which meant that she had lunch less frequently with her female coworkers. She thereby distanced herself from her women friends, which she regretted. But if she had not allied herself with the men, she would have had far less chance of making any career advancement.

Even when women have overcome all of these barriers and have obtained the same jobs as men, it is usually assumed that they had different reasons from masculine ones for going into that kind of work. For example, in my own profession, although many people assume (often incorrectly) that male psychologists are gentler and less macho than most males, the typical attitude is that male psychologists know a lot about human behavior, whereas female psychologists want to help people. Indeed, this is true of what many people assume about men compared with women in any of the "helping" professions.

As a result of the women's movement, it has become less acceptable to try to justify underpaying and underpromoting women on the grounds that that's the way things should be. Ironically, however, the conservative forces in society have grasped eagerly at a concept that psychologist Matina Horner originally put forth in an effort to *help* women—the concept she called "motive to avoid success," which has become popularly known as "women's fear of success." Every time I lecture on women and masochism, someone tells me a story about a promotion she has not received at work and claims that she is living proof of women's need to fail and fear of success. For example, one woman told me that she had worked longer hours and sold more real estate than the men in her office, but when one of them received a promotion for which she had hoped, she began ruminating about the details of her behavior at work, searching for what *she* had done that had kept her from being promoted. Months later, she learned that the company president had told a colleague that nothing could persuade him to put a woman in a supervisory position. When women describe such experiences, a moment's inquiry usually reveals clear evidence of misogyny at the woman's work place and a strong tradition of promoting even mediocre men over competent, hardworking women. Such women have learned to deflect blame onto a "fear of success," a thinly disguised synonym for "need to suffer." As usual, our self-blame leads us to suppress or even deny our anger at the people who control our fate—in this case, the bosses.

It is important to know what Horner actually wrote, so that we can think about this fear in a way that is helpful, not harmful, to women. For her doctoral dissertation, Horner—now president of Radcliffe College—explored her suspicion that some women's failure to achieve great things at work might involve motives other than their "achievement motivation." She wondered whether some women might be plagued by a "motive to avoid success." To test her hypothesis, she asked young adults to complete stories that began, for example, with the statement that a woman had just done very well in medical school. Horner looked at the story completions and found that many of the young adults associated the woman's success with unhappiness; either she had lost all her friends and lovers on the way to this academic success, or some disaster befell her after the success came.

Horner's results have been largely misinterpreted. They have often been taken to mean that women have an innate, self-defeating fear of success. So, when women failed, something within them was blamed. But what Horner's results really show is that traditionally women have been punished for succeeding—for instance, by losing boyfriends who wanted their women to be dumber or less successful than they—and often *learn* that they ought to avoid success. This is very different from believing that they have an innate drive to avoid success or need to fail. Once again, it's a question of where the trouble comes from—from within the woman or from without. If men had been taught that their success in school or in careers would lead women to lose interest in them, they, too, would probably have developed mixed or negative feelings about success.

For such reasons, as well as because of poor self-esteem, women have often learned that it is feminine to be silent and keep their opinions to themselves. I had not been taught that lesson, and when I was interested in a subject, I eagerly participated in class discussions. When I started teaching graduate school and had two very pretty women students who never said a word, I assumed that they were either not very smart or not very interested in the material I was teaching. Three weeks into the course I gave the students an essay exam and decided, on a whim, to read the students' answers without knowing who had written which test. Two of the exams showed far more perceptiveness and intelligence than the others, and when I checked to see who had written them, I found to my amazement that these dazzingly intelligent answers had been produced by the two silent women. Subsequently, I got to know them both and learned that they were extremely shy about speaking up in class, because they were sure that they were the least intelligent students there. Since that time, I have had a far greater appreciation for the way in which even very bright women are often made to feel deeply insecure about their intellectual abilities.

Both of these women wrote superb master's theses, which I suggested they present at a professional meeting. The quality of their theses surpassed much of what full-fledged psychologists often present at such conferences. When the day of the meeting arrived, they felt a kind of terror I have never before witnessed in such a situation. One of them said that when she is nervous her voice squeaks, and then as she hears herself squeak she feels more insecure, and the fear becomes worse and worse. The students and I discussed their concerns at some length and I tried to allay their anxiety. At the conference, they both made excellent presentations, looking far less nervous than they felt.

Were they masochistic to put themselves through that ordeal? Or would it have been more masochistic for them to remain paralyzed by their fears, avoiding new challenges and experiences, never testing the possibility that they might turn out to be better than they thought they would be?

According to psychiatrist Jean Baker Miller, a woman

who finds that she is working well and suddenly has fears or blocks is often feeling that to use "self-determined power for herself [in her work] is equivalent to *selfishness,* for she is not enhancing the power of others." Furthermore, writes Miller, if such a woman is self-sufficient and self-directed at work, "Her sense of identity . . . [may be] so bound up with being a person who *needs* that the prospect of *not needing*" may feel like "a loss of the known and familiar self."

Regardless of how assertive a woman may be, she is likely to be subjected to manifestations of misogyny in her work place. According to Anthony Astrachan, "Hostility toward women is most overt—and most sexual—in the blue-collar workplace, where centerfold pictures and harder-core porn photos are often displayed on the job." Indeed, writes Astrachan, many men find it difficult to think of any one working woman as both sexual and competent, and they attempt to deal with this by thinking of only one of her aspects:

> If we, in our minds, can transform a woman peer or power wielder into a wife or mother, whore or nun, we do two things: we deny that she is simultaneously competent and sexual; and even though we have not barred her from the workplace, we keep her out of the main arena of action, where we find her difficult to handle.

Although many women have been silenced, poor women have been the most silent, the most invisible women. Added in recent decades to the chronically poor have been the growing millions of women who have become impoverished through divorce. Low or unpaid alimony and child support have put hordes of women on the welfare rolls. To be on welfare is humiliating and makes one feel impotent, but the stories of mothers' frustrated attempts to get off welfare are tragic. Many welfare mothers have no job training and little education, some because they come from families who have been on welfare for generations, others because they have been housewives for most of their adult lives. In order to get a job, they need to find adequate day care for their children. If they can't find day care and miss work because their children are sick, they are in danger of being fired, for usually they can obtain only unskilled jobs in which they are easily replaced by men or by women without children. If they attempt to avoid this problem by acquiring training for higher-level jobs, these women must still pay for day care while they attend classes. While they are being trained, then, there is even less money than usual for feeding, housing, and clothing the children. And if because of their children's needs the women miss too many training classes, they will not be able to complete the course and get a job. Even for those who finish training courses, jobs are by no means guaranteed. Women on welfare can choose the misery of remaining on welfare or of fighting the tough battle to achieve something better. Either way, they suffer.

One obstacle that has been no respecter of income has been sexual harassment in the work place, a problem that, until recently, had no name. It was simply considered part of the job to put up with sexist jokes, comments about one's body and one's real or imagined sex life, and even sexual propositions. Such treatment implied directly or indirectly that if a woman did not at least tolerate such overtures she might lose her job. Although sexual harassment has been outlawed in many places, some people regard the laws as unfair restrictions on fellows who are just out to make a joke or have a good time. Women who bring charges of sexual harassment against their employers are often regarded as bitches who are out to cramp men's style or "break their balls." A woman who puts up with sexual harassment is made miserable. A woman who protests often (though, thankfully, less and less these days) becomes the target of rude, threatening, or ostracizing behavior, especially if she files a formal complaint. If she has to choose between two types of unhappiness and chooses silence, is that a sign of her inherent masochism? And the reality for countless women is that they have no choice: As sole support or a major support of a family, they need that job and have to shut up and tolerate the harassment.

In my own job before the start of a meeting of my colleagues, nearly all of whom were male, a man once asked me jovially what novel I was reading. "It's not a novel," I replied. "It's my appointment book." I was dating no one at the time, had not dated for a long time, and my book was filled with notes like "Meet students from testing course at 10 a.m.," "Get frozen green beans," and "Take kids to Hebrew School." Another male colleague grinned lasciviously and said to all present, "Wow, you can just imagine what kinds of things she's got in that book!" Because I was an unmarried female, he assumed that I had a wild sex life and he felt free to comment on it at a business meeting. In this situation, to disabuse him of his misguided notion would have meant telling him about the realities of my private life, and I simply did not want him to know anything about that; I already felt invaded. But to allow his fantasies to persist also made me feel invaded. And anything other than "going along" with him would have made me seem like a humorless bad sport.

Overt sexual harassment by now has received considerable negative publicity. One unfortunate consequence of this new public awareness of the problem, however, has been that much antiwoman feeling has not disappeared but only gone underground and become more subtle. It has taken the form of what I called "sex-based manipulation," by which I mean a range of unpleasant treatment to which women are subjected because they are female and most of their bosses are male. Such treatment has always gone on, but it has been intensified by all the attention that has been paid to overt sexual harassment. The history of the civil rights and women's movements has shown that when attention is called to a group's oppression, the biased attitudes do not vanish overnight; rather, when external restrictions are imposed (such as laws against sexual harassment), other, less overt forms of expression take their place.

Claire was an assembly-line worker in a food packaging factory. Every three months, the workers on the line that packaged the most food received a small bonus. Claire's working speed was sometimes slower than the speed of her coworkers because she took pride in her work and believed it was important to take a little extra time and care, since properly wrapped food lasts longer. When her line failed to win the bonus, her male foreman and her male coworkers accused her of "fretting" about her work. Men are rarely said to "fret," and this is only one of many sex-biased words that are used pejoratively against women; some others include "fussy," "needy," "dependent," "overemotional," and "oversensitive." Rather than being praised for her high standards and conscientiousness, Claire was criticized in a way that was partly determined by her sex. This vulnerability is increased by the fact that, as women, we tend to blame whatever happens on ourselves and to look to ourselves to improve the situation. Thus, instead of reacting to the criticism with justified anger, instead of feeling proud of her standards and concern for others, Claire joined with her critics in considering herself too fussy.

A few years ago I realized that I often felt inadequate and unhappy in my work, although in many ways I found work very gratifying. As I thought about the sources of my unhappiness, I began to realize how much was the result of what I call sex-based manipulation. It was a long time, though, before I dared to talk to my colleagues about it, because I suspected that what was really wrong was that I was incompetent. Finally, I got up the nerve to present my ideas to a group of women psychologists at a professional meeting, shaking with fear that instead of identifying a universal problem I was only exposing my own inadequacies. But as I spoke, smiles of recognition appeared on my listeners' faces, and they began to heave sighs of relief as they heard someone else talk about what she had been through and what they, in their own isolation, had feared was evidence of *their* incompetence.

One story I told them was about a woman patient of mine whom I shall call Ms. Berryman, a dignified welfare mother. Her six-year-old son had been taken into the care of the Children's Aid Society when Ms. Berryman left him with her aunt for a week so that she could try to find an apartment free of cockroaches. This was especially important because the child was blind and spent a great deal of time playing on the floor. During the time her son was at her aunt's house, her aunt and uncle quarreled, the aunt ran out of the house, and the angry uncle, left alone with the blind child, called the Children's Aid Society. The mother had cared for the child entirely on her own for six years and had rarely left him. Every few months, she would take him to a close relative's home and go away for two days, often on a drinking binge. But she never drank or was drunk in her son's presence, and she was an excellent mother who never abused or neglected him. In court, the Children's Aid workers said she was a bad mother because she had left her son with her aunt and because of her drinking. As a result of issues of court procedure and evidence, the case was adjourned several times before a decision was made and Ms. Berryman interpreted each adjournment as another attack on her mothering ability. Her poor self-esteem hit rock bottom and, with each adjournment, she began to wonder aloud whether she was such a bad mother that her son might not be better off with someone else.

A male psychiatrist whom I shall call Dr. Strong was my team leader. He instructed me that the focus of my work with Ms. Berryman should be on getting her to express "the negative side of her obvious ambivalence about her handicapped, burdensome child." I suggested that it was at least as important to help her rebuild her self-confidence, but Dr. Strong criticized this approach and said I was allowing my motherly feelings to get in the way of seeing what this patient really needed. Not only pejorative words like "fussy" but even potentially complimentary ones like "motherly" can become evidence of women's alleged incompetence.

My opinion about the appropriate therapy for this woman was thus devalued by being classified as an outgrowth of my supposedly stereotypically feminine motherliness. My belief in the importance of working on the patient's strengths was mistranslated as a wish to take care of my patient. This signified my *overinvolvement* and thus my "unprofessional" attitude toward her, requiring me to choose between, on the one hand, feeling unprofessional but encouraging Ms. Berryman's strengths and, on the other hand, treating my patient poorly in order to protect my self-esteem.

I also faced the dilemma of what to do with Dr. Strong's advice. I could follow it, thereby going against my clinical judgment and reinforcing both his view and mine of myself as fitting into the unappealing submissive-compliant female stereotype. Deciding that maintaining a pleasant relationship with my supervisor was more important than acting in the patient's best interests would have resulted in my feeling divided against myself. It would also have undermined my confidence in my clinical judgment—and rightly so, since I would not have been doing what was best for my patient. Dr. Strong and I would have believed—or acted as though we believed—that it was lucky for the patient that *he* was supervising me. My alternative—to stick to my plan for therapy—*might* have allowed me to believe that I was acting in my patient's interests. But this would have been a hard belief to sustain, since most women have learned that if we must choose between asserting ourselves and "admitting" that we are wrong, we should do the latter, especially since if we do not, we confirm the view that we are bitchy and castrating and often stand to be punished by the rejection of the men with whom we disagree. In the end, I chose to do what *I* thought was right, although it meant incurring my supervisor's wrath.

Equally insidious treatment of women at work occurs in all vocational fields. At a party recently, a bright, charming woman named Adele told me what happened to Judy, one of her coworkers at a clothing manufacturing house, a fine old company that had been run for decades by an all-male hierarchy. In the last few years they have hired a few capable women, who worked diligently and well. Judy was one of these women, and after a while she applied for a position as one of the company's five marketing directors. To her amazement, she got the promotion. Then, after several months in that job, she was fired. When such things happen, some kind of rumor usually circulates about the reason for the firing, but in Judy's case not a word was said. It remains a complete mystery. Naturally, the other women are reluctant to request promotions, because they strongly suspect that Judy was fired because of her sex, that these powerful, wealthy men were uncomfortable having a women in on their top-level meetings. Certainly, none of the other women has been encouraged to apply for promotions; indeed Judy's request for her promotion was entirely her own idea. The women at this company have no powerful male mentors, a serious problem since having upper-level mentors is one of the most important ways that employees learn the ropes at their work place and acquire the self-confidence they need for advancement.

As the women's movement and its aims increasingly have permeated society, women who are known to be supporters of the movement have sometimes come under suspicion at work. As if it isn't bad enough to have to work with women, some men find it intolerable to have to work with feminists. One consequence is that such men watch, hawkeyed, for signs that these women are participating in "inappropriate" activities. In one mental health clinic, a notice about a march in support of welfare mothers went up on the bulletin board in the staff lunchroom. A senior administrator called the notice "political" and said that it should be removed, because the board was not the proper place for political items. Among those notices that he considered appropriate were an announcement of a symposium on methods of administering psychotropic drugs, registration forms for a government-sponsored conference on the pros and cons of institutionalizing delinquent youths, and several newspaper cartoons that mocked feminism. Since those three items embodied far more traditional, conservative values than the notice about the welfare march, they were considered nonpolitical. The administrator claimed that the drug symposium and institutionalization conference were of clinical relevance and that the cartoons were just jokes.

The welfare mothers' march was, in fact, *directly* relevant to the mental health of both the mothers and their children. However, the differences seemed to be that the march was focused on women who had not come under therapists' power by being classified as patients and who, by virtue of organizing politically, were potentially powerful themselves.

Sometimes the sex-based manipulation is not so subtle. Consider this example, from my own experience, of the male's need to exercise power in a traditional way over females, even on matters that do not fall within his jurisdiction. A few years ago, I wrote a letter to the editor of a city newspaper, objecting to comments quoted in an article and attributed to another professional who worked in an institution related to my own. In the letter I totally omitted reference to my place of employment. I mailed the letter, and as I was telling a woman colleague what I had done, my male supervisor overheard and loudly commanded, "Don't send that letter!" A few days later, the letter was published. My supervisor came looking for me. Seething, he complained that, even though what I had written was correct, what I had said would make it hard for everyone in my agency to work with the other institution. As he grew more and more enraged, and his accusations about the enormity of what I had done came to be less and less related to what I had really written, I felt both puzzled and afraid. At last he exploded, and the reason for his rage burst from his lips: "You disobeyed me!" he bellowed, sounding for all the world like a furious father of a young teenager. I was 32 years old at the time.

Issues ranging from underpayment of women to sexual harassment and sex-based manipulation present women with impossible choices. With regard to each issue, society has placed barriers in women's paths, so that we often have to choose between improving our work situation but losing friends or self-respect and achieving no career advancement but living out the traditional female role, which may be problematic but at least brings the reward of being regarded as feminine and unthreatening. The causes of women's problems in the work place are multiple, but innate masochism is not one of them.

Sometimes, though far less often than for women, a man is called "masochistic." A man I know named Thomas left his native country for the first time at the age of 30, traveled halfway around the globe, and took a job in a subspecialty of his general field. He was paid through a research grant over which his supervisor had control. Thomas worked day and night for months, trying to learn the highly technical material he needed to understand the new research in which he was engaged. He never went to a movie, had meals out only because he could get back to work more quickly than if he went home for dinner, and made no friends. He lost sleep, night after night, because he was either working or worrying that he wasn't learning things fast enough. His boss gave him no encouragement, setting one superhuman deadline after another for him and chiding him when he failed to meet them. Because of the nature of the job—he was a kind of apprentice—Thomas was totally dependent on his supervisor, who was a cold, unkind man. Thomas spent more and more time working, thereby becoming increasingly isolated and depressed.

One day his supervisor told him that because he was so stupid, he was being fired. He humiliated Thomas, who at first reacted by agreeing that he must indeed be very stupid. However, he finally ventured to talk to another of the supervisor's employees and discovered that the supervisor had made equally vicious and unfair remarks to other employees as well. It was easier for Thomas to see that the other employees did not deserve the attacks than that he himself did not. He began to get angry, first in reaction to injustice against the other employees and then on his own behalf. Getting angry was the first step, because it meant realizing that the problem was not within himself. He recognized his shortcomings, such as his failure to confront his boss earlier with the fact that he was giving him impossible tasks. But he did realize that he was not as completely stupid as he had been told. Second, he developed other options, checking around quickly to see about other job possibilities, so that he was no longer at the mercy of this one man. As he did those things, his self-esteem began to improve for the first time all year, and his depression began to lift. At last, he went to the supervisor and in a balanced way acknowledged his own shortcomings but also told the supervisor in what ways he believed he had been unfairly treated. Feeling less impotent and better able to stand up for his rights improved his self-esteem still more and made him feel less trapped.

Hardly anyone would have interpreted Thomas's early behavior as masochistic. Since he is a man, his behavior was likely to have been interpreted as an intense need to achieve, consistent with the masculine role, not "sick" but only perhaps a little extreme. A woman who behaved in the same way would have been regarded as unfeminine and would have left herself open to the charge that she was a masochist. Nevertheless, the solutions for women in such situations are the same as for men: first, to look realistically at the source of the trouble, to see it as external to oneself when it *is* truly external to oneself; second, to find other job possibilities, where that is feasible, and to find friends and colleagues both at work and elsewhere, thereby preventing any one person from having too much control or importance in one's life; and, third, to improve one's self-esteem however one can.

For women there are other important steps to take. We have to familiarize ourselves with the realities of the work world for women. We have to stay aware of the extent to which women are underpaid and underpromoted and how women are subjected to sex-based manipulation. In this way we can distinguish between how much of our unhappiness is of our own making and how much comes from "out there." We have to keep talking to other women both at our own work place and at very different ones, women in jobs like ours, and women in jobs with more and less status and with higher and lower incomes than ours. We have to keep clearly in view the commonalities in our experiences that result from our being women and, therefore, being treated in similar ways. These insights can provide invaluable support and inspiration in the struggle to make the work place a better environment and a happier place for women.

CHAPTER 9

Women in Therapy

[After my suicide attempt] I started seeing Dr. L., a white man, who I also liked a lot. He's really helped me. But you know, no matter what I say, he brings it back to me. If I got bubonic plague it would still be my fault.

—FORMER MENTAL PATIENT

Every year millions of women who want to be free of the unnecessary psychic pain in their lives seek the help of psychologists, psychiatrists, and social workers. But since it is some mental health professionals who have been responsible for developing and perpetuating the belief in the myth of women's masochism, women as consumers of therapy services need to be aware that they may well have a therapist who believes in the myth. Some therapists do not hold that belief, but those who do are not likely to volunteer the information to prospective patients. A woman seeking psychotherapy may, without even stopping to investigate the possibility, become deeply involved with a therapist who accepts the myth and may thus be subjected to interpretations of her motives that will convince her that she needs to suffer. In this way, her "therapy" will leave her feeling even worse about herself than before and even less hopeful about the possibilities for change.

In my own clinical practice, I have heard women patients say things that many therapists would be quick to interpret as evidence of their masochism. One of my most intelligent patients told me one such story, and had I not asked her a crucial question, I would have had to consider seriously revising my theory.

After suppressing her anger for all 26 years of her life, terrified that it had the power to destroy people, Nancy had become good and angry at her boyfriend and had let him know it in no uncertain terms. Pleased to hear that she had finally shown some justifiable anger, I asked her what had happened next. "Oh," she said, "he was wonderful. He sat quietly at first, and then he said that I was right and he had been inconsiderate. Then he apologized. He even said he was glad I had told him how angry I was."

"What happened then?" I asked, suspecting I would hear that she had realized that her anger was not really dangerous and horrible.

"Then, I felt terrified!" she replied. "I began to shake with fear, and I wanted desperately to dig my fingernails into my skin and rip it from my body until I bled."

The thought occurred to me that here, surely, was a genuinely masochistic wish. But wanting to understand more about how she was feeling and what that image signified to her, I asked, "What did that mean?"

She said, "I felt overwhelmingly grateful that Joe had been so understanding and very guilty for having subjected him to my anger. It hadn't destroyed him this time, but it probably would the next time, and even if it didn't destroy him, my anger is so vicious that it isn't fair to take it out on such a wonderful man. The flesh I wanted to rip off was an embodiment of my anger, and if I could have torn it away from me, I would never again have had to worry about taking the major risk—to me and to others—of showing some rage."

No doubt some traditional therapists would have interpreted Nancy's image as a sign of her masochism, but I think that what she said should be taken at face value. What had seemed at first to be a perfectly masochistic image—a desire to tear at oneself and bleed after having been treated *well*—was in fact a manifestation of her lifelong belief that her anger could destroy others. Her impulse was the expression of her wish not to hurt others and not to risk losing the man she loved. Her apparently masochistic impulse actually represented her wish not to suffer and not to make others suffer.

It is important to find a therapist who wants to learn what a patient's words mean to the patient herself. Psychoanalyst Jeffrey Masson has described how rare it is for his colleagues to do this rather than imposing their own preconceptions on their patients. When I was a graduate student and did my first interview with a patient, I asked a black woman how she felt about beginning an academic program at Duke University in North Carolina. "It feels strange," she said. I assumed that I knew what she meant, since being one of a handful of black women in an advanced program at an almost entirely white university in the Deep South in 1969 had to be scary. But I asked her to explain the ways in which it seemed strange to her. She began to describe her sense of freedom at finally being away from her large, extended, loving family. She had lived with them until then, and although she was very close to them, she had longed to spend some time on her own, to become more independent. At that time in her life, what it meant to be one of a few black women in a Southern university was far less salient to her than what it meant to be away from her family for the first time. I realized then how dangerous it is simply to assume that we know what someone means, even when it seems obvious to us.

The women's movement has not modified the attitudes that most therapists have about women and masochism, and these therapists pass on their attitudes to their trainees. A graduate student named Janice came to see me last year, after she had read my paper on women's masochism, which had just been published. She was upset and told me the following story. She had been doing an internship at a local hospital, seeing patients for psychotherapy. One of her patients was Sylvia, a woman whose first husband, after they married, had refused to have any sexual relationship with her at all and had also begun to beat her. They were soon divorced and, some time later, Sylvia married another man. While married to her second husband, she became bulimic, going on massive eating binges and then forcing herself to vomit until her throat began to bleed. Janice's supervisor for this case was a psychiatrist, Dr. R. In their supervision sessions, Dr. R explained to Janice that Sylvia was a masochist. "You see how beautifully her masochism works," he said. "When her first husband isn't there any more to beat her, she *becomes* her first husband and forces herself to vomit until she bleeds. He's not there to hurt her, so she hurts herself."

Janice asked Dr. R to read my article, because after spending long sessions with Sylvia, she really did not believe that she enjoyed her suffering. Dr. R told Janice that I was missing the point. Sylvia, he said, like so many women, was displaying her unconscious need to suffer. It seemed to me that there was another explanation that made at least as much sense as his. The terrible experience of having a new husband refuse to sleep with his wife, and the effect it would have of making the wife feel unappealing, must surely have played a part in the development of Sylvia's disorder. According to Janice, Sylvia had left the marriage because her husband's rejection of her and the beatings were too terrible to bear. One can well imagine how scared a woman in her position would be when marrying for a second time. What would happen if her second husband did the same things to her? When people are frightened or anxious and their emotions are intensified, they often deal with those feelings by overeating. It may be the only way they can arrange to have some experiences that are pleasurable and over which they feel they have some control. It also can be a way to try to drown their sorrows. But one of the risks of overeating for a woman in this society is of becoming so overweight that a man will refuse to sleep with her. To avoid gaining weight, a woman who overate but wanted to remain attractive to men would have to force herself to vomit. I suggested this interpretation to Janice, who sighed with relief and said that it fitted what she knew about Sylvia and what Sylvia had told her.

I said that I thought the crucial question to ask in trying to understand apparently masochistic behavior is whether, if one could magically take away the pain, the patient would be pleased or would want it back. "I have a feeling," I said, "that if you could stop that woman's throat from bleeding she would be pleased."

As psychologist Phyllis Chesler showed in *Women and Madness*, therapists are quicker to label a woman emotionally disturbed than they are a man. One reason for this is the existence of the two types of myths about women. One is of woman as witch/castrator, woman as temptress, destroyer, imposer of impossible standards and demands—Eve and Pandora, among other mythological figures. The other is of woman as Earth Mother, the smothering or "eternal-feminine," pretty/passive/helpless type. Women and their therapists find it easy to regard women's behavior as falling into one of the handy myth categories, and both types of myths have their counterparts in the jargon of emotional disturbance. The witch type is called the "castrating woman" or the woman who has not been able to accept the feminine role and must try to outdo every man—instead of being appreciated as a person who has a healthy dose of self-esteem and achievement motivation. The Earth Mother type is often described as a woman who deals with her penis envy by having numerous children and over-investing herself in their achievements rather than as a woman who loves caring for children and simply is a good mother. The "smothering" mother is called just that or, perhaps, a "hysterical personality." Some women, like some men, do have emotional problems, but Chesler has shown that both healthy and disturbed women are far more likely to be considered disturbed than are both healthy and disturbed men.

Severely emotionally disturbed women are not the subject of this book, but many emotionally healthy women have needed some therapy, mislabeled themselves as disturbed, and looked in desperation to psychotherapists for help in becoming "healthier." Too often, such women have found therapists ready and willing to collude with them in looking at their own behavior as disturbed. A truly helpful therapist will point out that a woman patient has labeled her own behavior as "sick" and then will help her to understand how devaluing one's behavior is a classic part of the learned feminine role.

In this regard, as discussed in Chapter 4, because Erik Erikson is such a highly respected psychoanalyst, his claim that an emotionally healthy female does not have a sense of who she is until she knows "who will fill her inner space" has widely influenced other analysts in their clinical treatment of women. So, women who have not been satisfied to have men determine the meaning of their lives have often been categorized as disturbed, because they were "dissatisfied with the female role." If they accepted the female role, they were considered masochistic.

The assumption that a self-denying woman is a masochist is sometimes accompanied by the belief that being masochistic is normal for a woman or by the belief that being masochistic is sick, even for a woman, and sometimes—incredibly—by both beliefs. Finding unhappy women in their consulting rooms, traditional psychotherapists have frequently ignored those of women's problems that are socially imposed, such as how frightening it can be to have the sole responsibility for your child's happiness, or how depressing it can be for your boss to ignore your ideas because you are a woman. Traditional personality theorists have frequently ignored women's socially imposed problems and attributed them instead to women's "selfishness" or "unmeetable needs." When a therapist makes that kind of interpretation, women patients often try to show that they are good people by working to become "less selfish" and by suppressing some of their enormous "unmeetable" needs. Such behavior is then called masochistic.

Assumptions about what is normal behavior for a woman spread from therapists' offices and theorists' articles into the popular culture, complete with technical jargon (often misused). In a recent *Newsweek* article about Kathleen Sullivan's quick rise to the coanchor position on ABC's "World News This Morning," authors Harry F. Waters and Lucy Howard wrote:

> Colleagues find her easy to work with but, occasionally, an ego surfaces: she once dispatched an angry letter after a page in ABC's press department took a call from a reporter and didn't know who Kathleen Sullivan was. None of that diminishes her bosses' regard.

Although some people might say that Sullivan overreacted, if a man had written such a letter, it would hardly have been called a sign of "ego," and there is no way it would have been deemed necessary to explain that *his* bosses' regard was in no way diminished by an act which was in fact a perfectly reasonable, healthy response.

The problem of mislabeling women as masochists takes different forms in different schools of therapy. Some therapists of the "do your own thing and act on the basis of your feelings" type, such as some Gestalt or primal therapists, have encouraged women to think more about their own needs and feelings, thus helping them to avoid behavior that might be interpreted as masochistic. However, such therapists have often been stymied by the training their women patients have received over a lifetime to feel *guilty* about focusing on their own feelings when it means neglecting those of someone else. It's all very well for some therapists to say, "Figure out what you feel, and then act on it," but such advice is not enough to overcome years of guilt-inducing training for doing so. Nor can such exhortations overcome women's sense of panic as they wonder, "Who am I, then, if I am not a *real* woman, not a woman who puts other people's needs first?" Women should beware of therapists who take away their well-integrated identity without helping them to develop a new one that is equally rewarding. Women, after all, derive genuine *pleasure* and a sense of competence from being able to make people they love happy. So simply advising them to forget other people's feelings for once and think of themselves first can be a denial or suppression of a potentially, or actually, healthy and valuable part of a woman's life.

What has made it particularly hard for therapists to be helpful to women has been that no one knows what words to use. No terms have been available to help in labeling and thinking about much of women's behavior *except* terms of mental illness or deviation. Social psychologist Jeri Wine has done some important work in this connection by conducting a massive review of the research on sex differences in behavior. She found that when males have been shown to exhibit a particular kind of behavior more frequently than females, that behavior has usually been given a complimentary name, such as "assertiveness." This has happened even when the name has been a misnomer. Wine discovered that in many of the studies purporting to show that males were the more "assertive" sex what in fact was found was that males interrupted more than females. Wine also discovered that when females have been shown to display more of a particular kind of behavior than males, that behavior has generally been given a neutral or demeaning term. A prime example of this is "dependency" behavior. For a long time, women have been regarded as far more dependent than men, and the attribute does not have particularly admirable connotations. Trudi Yeger, a doctoral student in psychology at my institute, has pointed out that much of what has been called "dependent" behavior in schoolgirls has in fact been simply a show of interest in interpersonal relationships.

An extremely important shift from the patterns that Jeri

Wine identified has been accomplished by the group of clinical theorists working at the Stone Center at Wellesley College. They have taken a crucial step in expanding the possibilities for women in thinking about our mental health. They have created a new, accurate label for much of women's healthy, admirable behavior, calling it "relational ability" rather than "dependency" or "overwhelming need for affection" or "hysterical involvement in feelings and relationships."

Jean Baker Miller has observed that women are trained to focus, above all, on establishing and maintaining relationships. She has written:

> The sense of pleasing herself has been a very rare experience for most women. When they attain it, it is a newfound joy. Women often go on to find new and enhancing relationships, but if their goal is to secure the relationship first, they usually cannot find the beginning of the path. This, I believe, is because male-female relationships have been so effectively structured to deflect women away from their own reactions and fulfillment. In the past, this deflection had set in almost automatically, even before a liaison had been formed.

Thus, as a relationship begins, a woman is likely to try first to establish and maintain the relationship, looking to her own needs and wishes only later, whereas a man is less likely to focus on the establishment and maintenance of the relationship itself.

In addition, since women are said to be "naturally good" at forming relationships, when a couple has difficulties, both parties often believe that the woman primarily has (or should want to have) the skills to resolve the difficulties. This makes it hard for women to avoid taking most of the responsibility for the state of a relationship.

Women who do take on this responsibility usually become intensely angry after a time; they feel—realistically—

that their own needs are being overlooked. When they finally protest, their bottled-up anger is often expressed as rage, which seems out of proportion to the immediate precipitating incident. This makes it easy for the women (and their partners) to believe that their anger should be ignored because it is "hysterical" and "irrational." Or, although their anger is understandable, they may believe that it is unfeminine, and so instead of expressing their anger openly they turn it into more "feminine" wheedling and manipulation.

Therapist Michele Bograd has pointed out that, in her field of family therapy, therapists have traditionally focused on preserving the nuclear family, ignoring the harmful effects that traditional cultural practices can have on the family members. Thus, for such therapists family troubles are thought to arise because the individuals in the family are not carrying out the roles that are considered appropriate to the "typical" mother-father-children household. In countless case conferences I have heard my colleagues claim that a family's problems were the result of the father being too passive and the mother too assertive, but never have I heard the opposite said. Many family therapists sincerely believe that a woman who has an equal share of power in the family is the cause of a troubled family's "dysfunction," because her power makes the family nontraditional, and automatically flawed. This is yet another form of the "whatever is, is right" argument, and it has meant that many women in family therapy have been made to feel ashamed for standing up for their beliefs and rights. Sometimes, the wife-mother in family therapy feels depressed, because she has only been able to find a low-paying job or has been sexually harrassed at work. Rather than receiving support from the family therapist, she may well be told to keep her troubles to herself, since her major roles are mother and wife and she should not burden her family with her outside problems. Thus, the problems she has are cast as "her" concerns, too unimportant to be brought to the family therapy hour. I am even aware of cases in which the woman's desire to work at a paying job is blamed for the family's troubles—she is accused of investing too much energy in her work and not enough in her family—although that is rarely said about the husband. And Bograd gives the following illustration of a family therapist's work with an abusive husband and his wife:

> . . . a wife reminds her husband to fix a broken window; he feels infantilized and withdraws; she impatiently reminds him; he feels inadequate; she demands that he do as he promised; he angrily lashes out and slaps her. In this "neutral" description, the woman is described as demanding and aggressive, which are conventionally undesirable female qualities. . . . The husband's . . . violence is almost normalized as an understandable attempt to regain his "rightful" place in the marriage. . . .
> In the popular formulation of the overadequate battered woman/underadequate abusive man, the label "overadequate" has negative connotations—even though it refers to a battered woman's skills, resourcefulness, and survival abilities.

Bograd notes that some family therapists have recently begun advising such couples to separate for a while, so that the battered woman can acquire a different perspective on her situation or develop "the skills leading to her economic and psychological self-sufficiency." But that is not what the traditional family therapist does for a troubled family. Usually, the "treatment" is to try to make less assertive males more assertive and more assertive females less so, in order that they can conform to the traditional roles. It is assumed that the nuclear family is the best possible living unit and that it functions best when the roles are the sex-stereotypic ones. Bograd writes:

> When the battered woman is viewed as exerting control over her husband's violent actions, clinical interventions in conjoint therapy are sometimes aimed at helping her

develop traditional female characteristics. . . . The implication is that the women would not be battered if only they would become better wives or perfect the socially defined female role. To this end, battered women are sometimes taught to modify their demands, to temper their anger, and to become even more sensitive to their husbands' moods and wishes. Unfortunately, such behavior often corresponds to the behavior the husband expects from his wife—and uses physical force to obtain. . . .

Since the female stereotype includes powerlessness, and as Bograd says, "the powerless are regarded as bringing it on themselves," wives and mothers are kept in roles where they appear to be masochists.

Something similar happens in traditional marital therapy. Consider the following typical story.

Marilyn and Arnold were having frequent arguments about each other, about their children, about their house, about nothing at all, and they sought marital counseling. The psychiatrist was a kind, intelligent man who genuinely wanted to help them. However, all three of them—the couple and the therapist—became prisoners of sex-role stereotypes. Since Marilyn had been raised, like most women, to be aware of a range of feelings and to be generally willing to discuss them with the people to whom she felt close, she continued this practice in the therapy sessions. Indeed, because she wanted to make the marriage work, she made a firm commitment to do so, even though this often meant that she felt extremely vulnerable, describing how she felt and repeating the same stories, explanations, and feelings that she had gone over so many times with Arnold and getting little or no positive response from him. Arnold, having been raised as a traditional male—of British background—was reluctant to show any feelings at all or to talk to Marilyn or the therapist about his past. The three of them had agreed at the outset that honesty would be extremely important in their work together. Therefore, Marilyn was aghast when Arnold lied to the therapist about a former girlfriend. Arnold explained privately to Marilyn that the girlfriend was someone he had met when she was a patient at a hospital where he was a medical intern, and so he couldn't tell their therapist that, since the therapist would disapprove of him. For Arnold, saving face was far more important than working out his relationship with his wife.

A therapist can only work with what the couple presents to him or her as material. Each week, Marilyn opened up, trying to be as honest and undefensive as possible, and Arnold behaved sympathetically and supportively. Arnold never revealed anything about his behavior or his feelings that might put him in a bad light or that would provide material for discussion in therapy. He appeared to the therapist to be a sympathetic husband who had an extremely emotional wife. The therapist could not have known that Arnold responded very coldly when Marilyn tried to talk with him about these things at home. In no time, the focus of the therapy became Marilyn's feelings and fears. She became the patient. Her blood ran cold when, week after week, as they left the therapist's office, Arnold put his arm around her still shaking shoulders and said sweetly, "Why, darling, I didn't know you felt that way." This continued for months, and Marilyn put up with it because she had poor self-esteem and minimal social support, and Arnold's brief shows of compassion for her were just enough to make her feel ashamed of her resentment of him.

In this kind of couple therapy, because women are more likely to be open about their feelings than men, the problem quickly becomes perceived as the woman's, and this reinforces her tendency to feel that she must be bringing her problems on herself, seeking her suffering. After all, she sits there each week with a calm, rational, supportive therapist and husband, and it seems obvious to them all that the trouble comes from her.

In the former example, the therapist was merely limited. Some therapists are far worse. A journalist who was preparing to write an article about an aspect of contemporary child rearing called a noted therapist to ask him for his opinion on the matter. He said that he had a tape of a lecture that he had given on that subject and he would have it delivered to her office. When the journalist started to play the tape, she realized that the therapist had sent her the wrong one. It was a recording of a session that he had had with a wife and husband who had come to him for help with their marital problems. "I know I shouldn't have listened, but I was fascinated," she told me. What she heard was the wife reciting a litany of ways in which her husband had hurt her feelings deeply. The woman did not seem whiny or picky to the journalist, nor did the husband deny or disagree with any of what she said. After listening to the woman for a while, the therapist said that he wanted to speak to each member of the couple alone. When the therapist was alone with the wife, he told her that she was far too critical of her husband. When he was alone with the husband, he simply chuckled and recommended, "You should just go fuck someone else." Probably most therapists would not do such things. But it is important for women to know that some do and that such behavior is often only an exaggerated form of the general tendency to take the blame off husbands and place it on wives, encouraging men to take pleasure where they may and offering women little support in bringing more happiness to their lives.

Not all therapists make grave errors, of course. However, enough therapists of various kinds have done so that professional associations have found it necessary to establish firm guidelines about therapy and counseling with women to ensure that some of the more horrifying of these practices do not occur. In North America, many national and state-wide or (in Canada) province-wide psychological associations have developed, or are developing, ethical standards for therapy and counseling with women. The basis for establishing a standard is usually numerous carefully documented instances of the standard being ignored. It is distressing to consider the incidents that led to the adoption of standards such as, "The therapist/counselor recognizes physical violence and sexual abuse as crimes, and does not encourage the woman client to submit to them, to accept their legitimacy, or to feel guilty about being a victim'' and, ''The therapist/counselor avoids the use of language implying sexist bias, especially sexist jokes and the use of labels derogatory or demeaning to women.'' It takes no imagination to understand how such practices would enhance a woman patient's tendencies to blame herself for her problems and to feel that she brought them on herself. The myth of women's masochism tempts the clinician and the patient into victim-blaming. Instead of wondering what thoroughly human, understandable fears prevent a battered wife from leaving her husband, such a clinician, and the patient herself, often fall into the trap of attributing her decision to stay to her wish to suffer.

Some therapists—from many different schools of therapy—go even further to harm their patients. In her 1974 doctoral dissertation in psychology, Betsy Jean Belote reported her study of 25 women who had had sexual relations with their male psychotherapists. These were not women who set out to make sexual conquests of therapists in relationships in which the power balance was equal. Belote said that most of the women were in awe of their therapists, felt helpless, and were emotionally dependent on them. Naturally, they had gone to them for help because they were feeling in great distress, primarily in the form of depression. Most of the women were unmarried or separated, were living alone, and preferred male to female friendships. The women were an average of 16½ years younger than their therapists. Because they undervalued friendships with other women, and because they felt depressed, lived alone, and were so much younger than their therapists, these patients were particularly vulnerable to their therapists' sexual advances. Indeed, the women said that they felt that having sex with their therapists meant they were special, and this validated their self-worth. In this kind of situation, women with scant interpersonal resources in dependent positions go to therapists for help, and their therapists then use them for their own sexual ends. Incredibly, I have heard such women called masochistic, as though they had gone to the therapists in order to be sexually used.

I once counseled a 14-year-old girl who was shattered because her father's best friend, a 45-year-old man, had sexually assaulted her. Sobbing pitifully, she told me that she felt guilty, because she had always thought this man was handsome, so she was probably to blame. I told her, "I don't care if you thought he was the handsomest man in the world. I don't even care if you had fantasies about him or actually flirted with him. The point is that he is a grown man and you are very young and you did *not* ask for or deserve a sexual assault." The same goes for women therapy patients whose therapists have sex with them. It is not masochistic to go to a professional for help in an attempt to feel better. It *is* self-centered and unfeeling for a therapist to take advantage of a woman's low self-esteem and depression.

A friend once called to ask me for advice for her friend Audrey, an attractive, 25-year-old married to Sam, an up and coming young lawyer. When Audrey was pregnant with their first child, Sam began flagrantly having affairs with other women, making no effort to hide the fact from Audrey or from anyone else. Audrey was devastated, feeling unloved, unattractive, and lonely, as the birth of her baby approached. When she burst into tears several times each day and told Sam why she was upset, he sent her to a psychologist, telling her that she should seek help for her neurotic depression. Dr. K. was a large, slovenly man in his fifties. At first, he listened to Audrey in a supportive, fatherly way. She felt enormously grateful that someone was finally listening to her problems. Then he told her that she was obviously feeling unloved and unlovable. What she needed, said this married father of three children, was to feel what *real* love was like, and he volunteered to show her. He told her to lie down on his couch and take off her clothes, and he proceeded to have intercourse with her. He told her not to tell her husband or anyone else, since the

content of therapy hours is supposed to be totally confidential. It is not true, of course, that the patient has obligations
to the therapist with respect to confidentiality. As experienced psychoanalyst Graham Berman tells his patients, "What
you say here is confidential, not what *I* say here." In other
words, it is the professional's obligation to maintain confidentiality, but the patient can tell anyone what happens in her
sessions if she chooses. The point is for the patient to know
that what she says will be treated in confidence. The therapist
is obliged not to do anything that couldn't be talked about
publicly.

After several months, Audrey noticed that more and more
of the time during her twice-weekly sessions with Dr. K. was
being spent in sexual activities. She was feeling no less depressed and was starting to feel uncomfortable about her
"therapy," partly because her husband was paying for her
sexual encounters with the therapist. She told Dr. K. how she
felt, and he replied: "You are very special to me. You don't
need to feel funny about Sam paying for our time together,
because I am putting that money away in a special account
for us, and one day you and I will take a trip together. But I
can't stop sending bills to Sam, because then he would become suspicious."

Audrey's friend asked me what I thought Audrey should
do. I said that she should get herself another therapist, fast.
It took her months to do so. Why? Was she masochistic? Did
she like being sexually used? Of course not. But she was
pregnant at that time and later a new mother, so she felt very
much alone and in need of male approval and warmth. She
could not relinquish the only source of the few positive aspects of her life.

Audrey at last did find the strength to leave Dr. K. and
went to an excellent woman therapist. For a time she avoided
telling her new therapist about what had happened with Dr.
K. When she finally did, though, it turned out that she was
the third woman patient from whom the therapist had heard
similar stories about Dr. K. Fortunately, this woman was on

her area's professional ethics committee and Dr. K.'s conduct was brought to their notice. When the institution that employed him was made aware of what he had done, they moved him to another state and placed him in a well-paying administrative position. Only through years of work with her new therapist did Audrey begin to overcome the feeling that she had betrayed Dr. K. Still worse, when her husband found out about what had happened between Dr. K. and Audrey, he accused Audrey of seducing Dr. K. because she knew he was a married man and she could never have him. That "setup," he claimed, fed her masochism. Audrey stayed with her husband, because all her life she had been steeped in the Southern ideal of womanhood that includes the rule that a good wife is always patient and understanding with her husband.

Therapists who mistakenly construe the behavior of their women patients as masochistic do so not only in the consulting room but also in more public settings, such as professional meetings and conferences and in the media. A psychoanalyst I know does superb work with a variety of patients and in his practice takes great care to support women's strengths and to help them stop attributing "sick" motives such as masochism to themselves. I have never hesitated to refer patients to him. Imagine my surprise when I heard him speak at a convention of mental health professionals, where he presented the case history of a former patient in a way that seemed to place the blame for a sexual harassment incident on her, although he had given no information that would lead the audience to believe that she had behaved seductively or provocatively.

This young woman had gone to a professor for help in a course in which she was having trouble and the professor propositioned her. Frightened and perplexed, she fled. After giving the matter some thought, realizing that she still needed help to pass the course and hoping that she could ignore his proposition, she again went to him for help and he propositioned her again. The analyst reported that she had then gone to see her new therapist, who focused on helping her figure out why sex was such a loaded issue for her and exploring how her parents had dealt with sexuality. Not a word was said about the fact that the woman's fear, anger, and efforts to try again in the hope of a better outcome were normal, healthy responses to sexual harassment.

I knew that in his own consulting room this analyst would have taken care to support the woman in her healthy responses and to make sure that she realized that she had behaved appropriately. So during the question period I asked him to explain what he would have done if that patient had come to him. He was unable to say what he would have done and just kept repeating that the woman's family had always had trouble dealing with sexuality. It seemed that in front of his professional colleagues it was impossible for this intelligent, otherwise caring man to deviate from the traditional practice of blaming the woman for her misery. That is one reason why change in the mental health professions comes slowly. Therapists cannot know whether their colleagues are ready to hear statements in support of women's health and strength. They risk being regarded as incompetent and as having deserted the professional ranks if they say that a woman did not cause her own problems.

Indeed, therapists who take nontraditional views are often subjected to their colleagues' accusations that they are humorless and hysterical, or somehow weak because they have been fooled by women into "taking their side." Such accusations are often hurled by clinicians who behave as though calling assertive women "castrating" (instead of just "assertive," as would happen with men) is an act of rational judgment born of an inquiring mind and benevolent good humor. Such people often blame women's and men's refusal to accept rigid sex-based restrictions for a host of social evils, including delinquency, children's psychopathology, economic troubles, male sexual impotence, the breakdown of the nuclear family, and even the rape of women and girls. Women and therapists who do not accept the status quo of sex-role stereotyping actually are in danger of being blamed for contributing to some or all of these ills.

Psychiatrist Alexandra Symonds has described how mental

health professionals long believed that abused wives "needed" the pain and how strong was the pressure on the professionals to act on this view. She writes that they

> were all convinced that the solution to this violence was in helping the wife not provoke her husband, or in helping her to leave. Only on rare occasions were any of these hundreds of [case] conferences directed to recognizing or trying to deal with the disturbance in the husband. . . . we were responding in a stereotypic way to victims of crime. . . . It is now known that we all have an unconscious need to reject the victim.

Dr. Symonds suggests that one reason her colleagues had such trouble thinking about the women's point of view was that in the face of other people's misery we feel helpless, so we want to find a "rational" explanation for the suffering. Rather than saying that these women were married to men who have violent tempers and behave in inhuman ways, her colleagues set about, with all the analytic tools of their intellectual trade, to figure out how the women "provoked" the abuse.

Since women are usually regarded as more skilled than men at handling interpersonal relationships, when marriages fail the woman is usually blamed. She was too demanding, too cold, let herself go physically, didn't try hard enough, didn't have enough patience with his little failings. When the divorced woman has children, the blame is intensified: "If she had been a good enough wife, she wouldn't have to raise the children alone. She's made her bed; let her lie in it. She brought her misery on herself." Rather than increasing the problems and guilt of single mothers by accusing them of creating their own misery, we must understand how "professionals" have intensified this misery through guilt by perpetuating the belief that a single mother cannot raise normal sons and daughters. The quickest way to make a mother suffer is to tell her that she has hurt her children.

Any time one advocates major changes in a system, one

encounters a substantial number of people who counsel, "Change takes time. You mustn't expect enormous changes overnight." Although that sounds like sage advice, we have to keep in mind that, when it comes to women as therapy patients, the status quo can be horrendous. It is not difficult to imagine what Dr. R. would have said to the bulimic Sylvia, who vomited until her throat bled, if he, rather than Janice, had been her therapist. A therapist who believes that women are masochists can usually convince his patients that he is right, and where does that leave us if we go to him for help? In *Women and Madness,* Phyllis Chesler described an entire "therapy program" that was established to help a group of allegedly paranoid women back to " 'feminine' health." Chesler writes:

> The author's therapeutic technique is as reprehensible as his goal. He decided that his "paranoid" patients needed "strong" male control, both within their marriages and within the hospital. He notes that many of these women's husbands were too "passive and compliant." He therefore "demonstrated to the man his wife's need of him [and helped] him assume a stronger position for her sake." Within the hospital, the psychiatrists were instructed to be firm and authoritarian, to disbelieve and be wary of the women's "inclinations to interpret, react to, and manipulate [their] environment on the basis of their distorted perceptions."

Chesler explains that the women were not, in fact, paranoid, according to the therapist's own report. The patients were responding appropriately to upsetting circumstances in their lives—usually rejection by their husbands. But rather than being helped to regain their sense of self-worth, and rather than being counseled in therapy with their husbands, the women were continually given the message that their mental health depended on their becoming more compliant and relying on other people's perceptions of reality.

What can women in need of help do in view of the sorry

state of so much of clinical psychology and psychiatry? After all, there are probably millions of women in North America who would find some outside assistance useful in understanding the sources of their unhappiness and in learning to redirect their energies. Some will find that talking to a neighbor, friend, or sister over coffee will suffice. Others will find televised programs and books about women's roles and rights helpful. Still others will find their styles of personal development best suited to a consciousness-raising or therapy group. Some women, though, will continue to find the one-to-one experience of intensive work with an outsider to whom one pays a fee the most congenial way to work. Probably, the greater the degree to which social restrictions have been intertwined with problematic family relationships, the more a woman will be likely to benefit from one-to-one, intensive work in therapy. That is, the greater the extent to which a woman has incorporated traditional sex-role expectations from her family, the more help she is likely to need from someone more objective than a family member or a friend.

Women seeking professional assistance need to be well informed about the harm some therapists have done to their patients and to decide what a good therapist might do for them. For example, there are many times when a therapist must be clear in her or his own mind about when a given bit of a woman patient's behavior is a manifestation of a sexist stereotype that she has learned or a manifestation of what would be considered an emotional disturbance *or* a combination of the two. Thus, for example, a patient may be shouldering most of the responsibility for the welfare of her difficult-to-manage child because she has learned that as the mother it is her sole responsibility (or that no one else will share it with her). Or, she may be doing this because, as a child, the only way that she could win any affection from her cold and distant father was to outdo her mother in taking care of him. Or, a woman may have been exposed to some of each of these types of experiences. Patients should take note of the nature of the interpretations of their behavior that the therapist offers. A therapist who focuses exclusively on manifestations of "sickness" within a woman patient is likely to increase the patient's tendency to blame only herself for her unhappiness.

Prospective patients should seek out clinicians who will discuss with them the fact that women are encouraged to misclassify their behavior as masochistic and that this misclassification comes from traditional clinical attitudes and their acceptance by the general public. A good clinician will point out the way that the tendency to attribute all blame to women—not just to women therapy patients—follows this pattern.

Awareness of what helpful therapists can do for their patients should also assist women in choosing a therapist who will do them some good. Ella, who was in the midst of a marital separation, called her therapist at home from time to time, with the therapist's permission. Each time she called, she would say during their next session, "I felt better as soon as you answered the phone. I don't understand why. But I'm ashamed that I was so weak as to call you." The therapist said nothing the first few times Ella made such remarks but then suggested that perhaps Ella was calling him as a way of reminding herself of something about herself; that is, while coping with the immediate stresses in her life, she was working in therapy to identify her strengths and the good things about herself, and so she had come to associate these strengths with the therapist's presence. Calling him, therefore, reminded her of the aspects of herself about which she felt proud. Some therapists might have interpreted her telephoning as masochistic, as a helpless act that placed her in a humiliating, suppliant position with respect to the therapist. But Ella was lucky; her therapist interpreted her telephoning in a way that intensified her sense of being respected by the therapist and of wanting to help herself. Thus, she was able to begin to understand that she owed herself some compassion.

Another patient described a difficult situation involving a man with whom she lived and then asked her therapist, "Do you have any suggestions?" Behind her question was her belief that she was likely to make self-defeating, masochistic decisions. The therapist simply replied, "Is there something wrong with your own ideas?"

The role of "patient" can reinforce the view of females as naïve, powerless children who cannot help but get themselves into unhappy situations. Therefore, the focus in therapy should in most cases be on uncovering, *allowing the patient to look,* rather than on teaching or providing support, although these also have their place in therapy. In this era of deepening understanding of previously ignored aspects of women's distress, therapists face a choice when a woman enters the consulting room. He or she can take a nondirective approach and simply help a patient to endure as she works through feelings of guilt, shame, and inadequacy, some of which are common to people of both sexes, some of which are felt by women in particular and some of which result directly from belonging to an undervalued group. Or, a therapist can help a patient understand her feelings and experiences in a larger context, so that she can see how people who hold traditional beliefs may reinforce her miserable self-image and her image of herself as the sole architect of her misery. The latter choice is directed toward the therapeutic goal of ensuring that the patient becomes increasingly able to distinguish reality from fantasy or from incorrect interpretations.

Most therapists would now readily agree that one must do more than help black people analyze the internal, individual sources of their feelings of inadequacy and shame, that one is obligated to reinforce the sense they may have that their unhappiness begins with an unfair bias in society. Similarly, it does little good for a woman patient who is ashamed because she thinks she causes her own unhappiness if the therapist simply works on the personal origins of that feeling.

No conscientious therapist, of course, would stop at helping the patient understand how her experience is similar to that of other women. The therapist must also help the patient understand what it is about her *particular* experience— her own parents, her own temperament—that has resulted in her internalizing society's views of women as masochistic in her *particular* way.

In order to do this, it is often necessary for the therapist to raise issues that the patient does not mention. A prime example is that of a woman's relationships with other women. Little work throughout the history of personality theory and psychotherapy has been focused on this topic. Woman patients often reflect this societal lack of interest in woman-woman relationships by coming into therapy because of the lack of a boyfriend or because they believe that their masochism led them to destroy a relationship with a man. Often, it does not occur to them that they would not be *so* despondent if they had close women (or even men) friends as well, instead of following the traditional path of placing their entire emotional lives in one man's hands. Women patients should be wary of therapists who spend all their time discussing the patient's relationships with men. People need more than a single support in their lives. If women do not develop other aspects of their lives—varied relationships, work interests, and other activities—they are likely to end up repeatedly feeling alone and despondent, and will likely be called masochistic, as they are driven by their limitations to repeat the same, miserable kind of experience. As discussed in Chapter 2, this is precisely what many therapists would mislabel a masochistic repetition compulsion, because they would focus on the repetition of risk or upsetting experiences rather than on the absence of other, acceptably feminine alternatives for that woman. Even groups of skilled clinicians can reinforce this harmful trend, though. Consider the following typical example:

Six members of a clinical team listened as a psychiatrist described his work with a woman patient who was divorced and had one son living with her. He said that she had dressed in black at their first sessions but that after a few weeks of therapy she seemed happier and dressed in a more attractive way, which the therapist smugly called "seductive." He said, "I think she is treating our sessions as a kind of date, a rehearsal for beginning to go out with men again. This will be hard for her, but I am glad to see that she is starting to take an interest in some of the men she knows." Other team

members of both sexes agreed that this was excellent progress, since she had had a long and painful relationship with a
totally self-centered, impulsive husband who had hurt her
deeply. It was only after about half an hour of discussion that
one team member suggested that it might be harmful—if not
cruel—to encourage her to pour all of her energy yet again
into a relationship with a man. What if this one did not work?
Even if it did work, wouldn't it be unhealthy for her to live
in fear that something might happen to him, which would leave
her again miserably, helplessly alone? Suggestions were then
made about directing the woman toward activities with *friends*
of both sexes, forming close and supportive relationships with
other women, and becoming involved with either paid or unpaid work that would interest her and give her a work-related
identity.

In other words, a therapist sometimes needs to take a
gently directive approach. In the same vein, it is sometimes
appropriate for therapists to inform patients some of what they
learn from research. For example, research on "attribution
theory" has revealed the following remarkably strong pattern, according to researcher Georgina White. When people
are told that a man has failed in an achievement-oriented situation, both males and females tend to attribute his failure to
external factors, such as a difficult exam or that he was up
too late the night before. If the same people are told that a
woman has failed in an achievement-related situation, both
females and males tend to attribute her failure to intrinsic factors, such as that she just isn't very smart. Conversely, people tend to attribute males' success to intrinsic factors (he's
smart) and females' success to extrinsic factors (she was lucky
or it was an easy exam). People of both sexes, from various
socioeconomic backgrounds and in various settings, make these
kinds of attributions with disturbing consistency. This demonstrates the way people locate within women the reasons for
their failures but are less likely to do the same for men.

In most societies, the people who have the largest share
of political and economic power tend to want to maintain the

status quo. Much of men's political and economic power depends on the belief that women are less intelligent and capable than men and on the reality that women have been slow to demand their share of power. When a societal stereotype is broken—a man fails or a woman succeeds at work—a society that wants to remain static must have some way to transform such dissonant events into further *support* for conventional stereotypes and beliefs. The attribution of intelligence and success to men's nature but not to women's, instilled as part of standard child rearing, effects this transformation.

If female patients interpret their own behavior in these ways, good therapists will point out that they have probably learned through many years to do this but that other interpretations are available and are often more apt. A helpful therapist can assist the patient to become aware of how she has learned to misclassify her own behavior and of how quickly, perhaps without realizing it, she makes those classifications, thereby severely restricting her options.

One therapeutic task is, then, to help women to apply appropriate labels, usually less self-blaming ones, to their behavior. The example given earlier, of renaming much of what has been misnamed "dependent" behavior as "relational" behavior, is a prime example of how this can be done. A woman who conceives of herself as helpless, dependent, and needing in some sick way to be involved with other people will not make much progress toward becoming a happy, self-directed woman. But a woman who can understand that her behavior is more appropriately called an interest in and ability to care about and enjoy other people may realize that she is less sick than she thought (perhaps not sick at all) and can be freed to develop even further her interest in and talent for getting along with people.

Societal trends inevitably influence the conduct of both psychological research and psychotherapy. Only during the last fifteen or so years have large numbers of therapists brought to their work the insights of social critics into the socially imposed stresses of being raised as a female. A growing body of writings will, over time, help us begin to understand the consequences of these stresses. In the latest edition of the most widely used handbook of diagnoses for mental disorders, the American Psychiatric Association's *Diagnostic and Statistical Manual—III,* a revolutionary step was taken, a great improvement made over the previous *DSM.* No longer was a patient to be given simply a one-phrase diagnosis, such as "hysterical personality" or "schizophrenic." That alone, the psychiatrists realized, does not tell one nearly enough about the person. So they developed four other "axes," or other kinds of information that must be given along with each diagnostic label. The one most relevant to this book is the axis that involves "psychosocial stressors." In other words, in judging how to try to work with a woman who is diagnosed as a "hysterical personality," it matters a great deal whether she has been subjected to major external sources of stress recently, such as the death of a loved one or the loss of a job. When even as establishment-oriented a body as the American Psychiatric Association declares in its official diagnostic manual that it is crucial to be aware of external sources of stress in the lives of one's patients, then the way is surely paved for therapists to stop identifying the woman herself as the source of all her suffering.

Individual voices are beginning to be raised, suggesting how therapists should treat women. Psychiatrist Teresa Bernardez made a number of suggestions to the 1984 Women's Institute of the American Orthopsychiatric Association, and these can be helpful to women consumers of therapy. A good therapist for women, Bernardez believes, makes sure to explore the patient's passive and submissive behavior. Too often, such behavior has gone uninvestigated in therapy, because it was regarded as healthy feminine behavior. Related to this, according to Bernardez, is the therapist's need to take care not to be quick to interpret women's exercise of emotional or other power as "too powerful" in keeping with the traditional stereotype. Often, Bernardez notes, what may seem like overpowering behavior is a consequence of a woman's actual powerlessness, which is expressed as rage and an attempt to take some *real* power. Many therapists, says Bernardez, fear female power, and this may lead them to try to suppress or pejoratively label it in their women patients.

A good therapist also will point out when a woman is suppressing her anger or bitterness, since silence in the face of that suppression only further discourages the woman from expressing "negative" feelings that need to be vented. If such anger is not acknowledged by the therapist, the woman patient is likely to feel increasingly guilty about her anger. Finally, Bernardez stresses how important it is for the therapist to notice when a woman patient becomes angry because she assumes that her therapist does not *respect* her. Since women have traditionally received so little genuine respect, people of both sexes overlook the importance to women's mental health of knowing that they *are* respected. A good therapist will find opportunities to show that she or he does respect the woman patient, and the patient's knowledge that she is respected will enhance her self-esteem. It will also make her less likely to blame herself for her own misfortunes and to assume that she is a masochist.

Chesler asks in *Women and Madness,* "Are . . . women being punished for rejecting their sex-role stereotype—or for embracing it in too deadly a manner?" With regard to masochism, women have been punished for both. Women who do not behave in selfless, long-suffering ways are punished by being diagnosed as "too masculine" and considered in need of psychotherapy or psychiatric hospitalization to help them learn to accept the feminine role; they are often called "masochistic" because their nontraditional behavior leads many people to reject or mock them, such as women who dress in traditionally masculine ways or who are extremely assertive, enough so that they are rejected for their lack of femininity but not so much that it would not have been considered healthy in a man. But women who accept that role and, consequently, so lose sight of their own needs that they become depressed are also considered masochistic.

The greatest service a therapist can do for a woman patient who mistakenly believes that she has brought all her problems on herself is to begin by according that patient respect, then conscientiously questioning assumptions about what is "normal" or "good" for women, and at all times supporting the woman's work toward strengthening her belief that her life is in her own hands, and she is her only judge.

CHAPTER 10

The Beginning

To those women who say we cannot resist, who say it is too much to ask that we resist . . . I would say: but women have always resisted. As part of their daily efforts to attain self-esteem and survival, women have always fought back.

—SOCIAL SCIENTIST JEAN ANYON

By the time I was 25, I was alcoholic, and had been fired from my 14th job. I was already divorced and going with another jerk. My father made me believe no decent man would look at me.

Through counseling, I learned that I am desirable, smart and interesting—a special lady who deserves a top-notch man. I'm through with the crummy ones and will settle for nothing less than the best. It took four years of hard work, but now I feel very good about myself and I'm going to make it.

—LETTER TO ANN LANDERS

Perhaps this book can help women who have suspected that they are not pain seekers begin to see the health and strength within themselves. Although no single book could cover all of the manifestations of the myth of women's masochism, some of the most salient phenomena that have been mistakenly labeled as signs of women's masochism have been highlighted here.

Now that we have looked in some detail at the way the myth has operated in a variety of areas of women's lives, it seems clear that virtually everything that has been called women's masochism has, in reality, been a manifestation of women's abilities to delay gratification, to put other people's needs ahead of their own, and to try to earn happiness through effort; the scarcity (real or feared) of better alternatives; or their effort to *avoid* pain.

But is there such a thing as genuine masochism? Does anyone really seek pain for its own sake and enjoy pain? The truth is that no one really knows. In my own experience—both professional and otherwise—I have found that every time a person seemed to be masochistic, a little time spent exploring her or his feelings turned up compelling evidence that the behavior was motivated by something else. Furthermore, the definition of "masochism" as "pleasure in pain" is bizarre. I cannot think of any other word that is defined in such a way, since pleasure is, according to *The New Webster's Dictionary of the English Language,* "The feeling produced by the enjoyment or expectation of good; delight; a state of agreeable sensations or emotions" and pain is "Physical ache, discomfort, or distress because of injury, overstrain, or illness; emotional or mental affliction or suffering; grief." Since pleasure involves good feelings and pain involves bad ones, it would seem that "pleasure in pain" makes no sense as a definition. It is as though one defined a word as "tallness in shortness" or "wealth in poverty." Psychologist Sandra Bem suggested to me that it is just possible that a person who as a child had been beaten and then sexually stimulated might transform pain into pleasure instantaneously, and that would be masochism. I am uncomfortable calling even this "masochism," because I believe that the wish to feel good is a basic human motive and that there is no corresponding wish to feel bad. I would prefer to explain Bem's example by calling it the seeking of pleasure through a route that in the past had brought pleasure and happened to involve pain. I will not go so far as to say that no act has ever been committed from a truly masochistic motive, because it is simply impossible to explore the motives behind every conceivable act. As Sandra Bem said, the fact that we cannot explain *why* someone might find pain pleasurable does not prove that they do *not* find it pleasurable. I suggest, though, that unless it is proven that the search for pain *is* a basic human motive, the definition of masochism might be changed to "pain that has been associated with pleasure so that it now gives rise to pleasure or brings pleasure to mind." It is my belief that this kind of definition would help clarify the impossibility of demonstrating irrefutably the existence of a masochistic motive in the traditional sense.

I have been asked why, since my reinterpretation of women's so-called masochism seems intuitively obvious, it has not been proposed before. First of all, in bits and pieces, optimistic and admirable reinterpretations of women's allegedly masochistic behavior *have* been proposed, such as explanations in recent years of why battered wives *really* stay with their husbands. However, to my knowledge, the extent of the damage that results from the mislabeling of women's behavior as masochistic, and the pervasiveness of that practice, have not before been noted, and the reason for this is alarming. It is that the myth of women's masochism has served—in a chillingly effective way—the purpose of masking the real reasons for women's suffering and thereby has helped block the path to change. The people who have a stake in women's continuing subjugation—such as the politically and economically powerful who rely on women's subservience and endurance of misery to contribute to their profits and assent to their continuation in power—have been only too happy to accept and promote the myth. For this reason, the real causes of much of the misery of women have continued largely unabated.

What *are* the real causes of women's unhappiness? The first is their lack of political, economic, and social power, for this lack means that they have very limited resources for improving their own lives. The rarity with which one hears a woman described as masochistic in a relationship of any kind with another woman sheds light on the masochism myth's role in perpetuating men's near monopoly of power. I believe that relationships between women have escaped the label because they have usually been no threat to the status quo. Women have often provided sympathetic ears and shoulders for the sorrow and anger other women feel toward the men who mistreat them. As Total Women are taught to do, they have used other women, rather than men, as sounding boards—or sometimes as emotional dart boards. This has taken a great deal of pressure off the men. Furthermore, in general, women have been called naturally and inevitably masochistic when they have behaved in ways that powerful people want to perpetuate; thus, women who put up with their husbands' or employers' slavelike use of them have supported the system. Without the wife who smilingly entertains the boss and does all the housework and child care so that her husband can give his all to the company, the company would cease to exist. Without underpaid and overworked women employees, most businesses and governments would simply collapse. Since these social arrangements support the status quo but make many women miserable, people are absolved of responsibility for improving women's lives if they believe the women *want* to suffer. It is revealing that lesbians, who have been mistreated and maligned in so many ways, called so many names, have by and large escaped the masochism label. This is partly because that label has not been necessary, since so many other ways have been found to denigrate them. Beyond this, however, although the wielders of power in our society do not want traditional heterosexual women to change, they do want lesbians to change. Many men find it threatening to consider the possibility that not every woman regards a man as the best possible prize. The conservative groups in society would like lesbians to disappear, to be converted to heterosexuality, and—if unwilling to turn from their lesbianism—to give up their children. Thus, for lesbians there was no need for men to invoke masochism as proof that some desired behavior ought to continue because it is natural to women.

Another major cause of women's unhappiness is their poor self-esteem. This is largely an outgrowth of our lack of power, but it also comes in part from the traditional "feminine" stereotype, since the traditional female is not supposed to be particularly strong intellectually, physically, emotionally, or morally, except occasionally in the service of others. It is this stereotype that leads her to endure unhappiness in order to win approval, acceptance, and even her living as mother, daughter, wife, employee, and patient; then that endurance is taken as evidence of her innate masochism. According to the stereotype she must not express even clearly justified anger or protest; but then her failure to protect or defend herself is taken as further evidence of her masochism. The traditional masculine stereotype is a related cause of women's unhappiness, since real men encourage women to be traditionally feminine, and "masculinity" is often interpreted as embodying the right to use and abuse one's physical, economic, and emotional power.

What can be done? We know that change is possible, that unhappy women can improve their lives. A letter in 1984 to Ann Landers illustrates how a woman who might well have been mislabeled masochistic has created a happier, better life for herself:

> I lived with an alcoholic, violent, unemployed slob for longer than I care to admit. Although it was a hard decision to make, I finally decided to dump him when I conquered my fear of being alone.
>
> Today, five years later, I own a small business, have a group of interesting friends and enjoy life. I am single—also celibate. I don't care for one-night stands. . . . I would not choose to be alone, but I did choose not to stay with a man who made me miserable. I'm making the best of my life, being nice to every man, woman and child who passes my way. Perhaps this approach will bring me a partner, but if it doesn't, it certainly is giving me a better life than I had before.

A small yet urgent step on the path to change is to stop misusing the word "masochism," particularly in regard to women. As we have seen, the misuse of the word adds to women's misery by impeding social change that could alleviate women's problems, and continued misuse poisonously erodes women's self-esteem by convincing them that the problems come from within. We can refuse to let it pass when anyone calls a woman masochistic, whether the word itself is used or whether a phrase such as "Why does she do this to herself" or "That's her fear of success" is used. We can insist that alternative explanations for her behavior be considered. Ideally, as part of health classes—in which cholesterol levels and body odor are regularly discussed—children should be taught basic psychological information, such as that females' behavior is often mislabeled in pejorative ways, so that they can be as well armed against attacks on their emotional well-being as they are against attacks on their physical well-being. For older children and adolescents as well as for adults, a massive public education program (which feminists in some areas of North America have already begun) is necessary to increase people's awareness of the difference between genuine erotica, which stimulates sensual and sexual feelings, and pornography, which some may find sexually arousing but which is primarily degrading, antiwoman hate literature and which perpetuates the female masochism myth.

On a larger scale, major political and social changes are required to alleviate women's unhappiness. Steps can be taken in all realms of women's lives to abolish the real causes of our misery. Vastly increased services need to be provided for women victims of violence—of rape, of wife beating, of sexual harassment. Increased availability of high-quality day care and job training would do a great deal to alleviate the stress and misery in the life of the employed woman, as would real sexual equity in the work place, which would increase the recognition and reinforcement of women's competence. Increased dissemination of birth control information, as well as improved, safer methods of birth control and increased availability of safe abortion, would keep young girls and women from forced motherhood and its often accompanying tragedies such as increased poverty, isolation, and likelihood of child abuse. Information of all kinds about women's bodies and women's health needs to be made available, so that women will be in a better position to protect their health and so that they will know where—other than the often unhelpful traditional places—to turn for help. Women consumers of psychotherapeutic services need to be educated to be aware of the pervasiveness of therapists' beliefs in such antiwoman myths as that of masochism, and therapists' training programs and clinical practice need to be revamped so that it is less acceptable to interpret women's motives without reference to what *really* impels women's behavior.

Another major change, which will, no doubt, come slowly but which is fundamental to improving women's lot, is the abolition of sex-role stereotypes. These stereotypes perpetuate the tendency to classify women's behavior as fitting into one of the two basic kinds of myths about women—that they are either cold, rejecting, and castrating, or overemotional, irrational, and emotionally smothering and draining. As long as these myths persist, women as well as men will continue to slip easily into classifying female behavior in one of these two insulting ways. Thanks to the important work of Jean Baker Miller and her colleagues and Carol Gilligan, far superior, health-promoting ways of interpreting women's behavior are available and should be put to regular use.

Abolition of sex-role stereotypes would also allow men to feel male even if they were not more powerful than, or abusive toward, women. It would allow women to feel womanly even while asserting or protecting themselves, expressing anger, exercising power, or doing things for themselves rather than for someone else, all of which can help alleviate women's unhappiness. Furthermore, without the stereotypes, women would not feel pressed to choose between being nurturant and being competent—whether as homemakers or as members of the work force; such a change would likely have the desirable consequences that many feminists have proposed, such as the reconceptualization of power, the redefining of it as not necessarily embodying ruthlessness and abuse. As Jean Baker Miller writes in her paper on "Women and Power," women have often been reluctant to use power (and have therefore been regarded as *wanting* to be powerless and unhappy), because they have been "led by the culture to believe that their own, self-determined action . . . must be destructive." She writes:

> . . . we can consider seriously the proposition that there is enormous validity in women's *not* wanting to use power as it is presently conceived and used. Rather, women may want to be powerful in ways that simultaneously enhance, rather than diminish, the power of others. This is a radical turn—a very different motivation than the concept of power upon which the world has operated.

In a related vein, Phyllis Chesler writes:

> Women whose psychological identities are forged out of concern for their own survival and self-definition, and who withdraw from or avoid any interactions which do not support this formidable endeavor, need not "give up" their capacity for warmth, emotionality, and nurturance. . . . Women need not stop being tender, compassionate, or concerned with the feelings of others. They must start being tender and compassionate with themselves and with other women.

> Abolition of the stereotype of the wife or woman employee who, no matter what, owes unquestioning loyalty to her husband or employer would make it easier for women to turn to other women or to helpful, supportive men when their husbands or employers mistreat them.

My final suggestion for alleviating the unnecessary unhappiness in women's lives is that women celebrate their strengths and their joy. Indeed, the way they have always done this testifies eloquently to the misguidedness of the myth of women's masochism. Two years ago, one of my closest friends learned that her lover of seven years had been having a secret affair with another woman for more than a year. She was

devastated, particularly because a cornerstone of their relationship had been their vow to be completely honest with each
other. Naturally, she went through a prolonged period of feeling
hurt and depressed. According to the myth of women's masochism, she should have delighted in wallowing in her misery. Instead, she sought out a therapist who could help her to
get over the depression, and whenever a holiday came along
or a friend achieved some small success, she took the opportunity to arrange the kinds of loving, joyous celebrations for
which she is well known.

Similar stories can be told about women in all walks of
life. Women left to talk only to infants all day have often
written songs, invented games and toys, and composed riot-
ously funny books and articles about their experiences, showing a kind of spirit despite the limitations of their lives that
men in boring jobs rarely show. Mothers whose husbands were
always "too busy" to help with their toddlers' birthday parties have invited other mothers as well as children to their
parties, trying—sometimes successfully—to turn the responsibility into a little fun for themselves and for others like them.
Women in low-status jobs or at home on welfare have often
formed warm, supportive bonds with other women. Some
wealthy women who were prevented by social expectations
("If a man is financially successful, his wife doesn't have to
work") from taking paid employment have started settlement
houses and massive social welfare programs. Women jilted
by lovers, deserted by husbands, or widowed have sometimes
produced helpful or amusing accounts of their attempts to cope
with their sorrow remarkably soon after their losses. Many
women victims of violence have sought help astoundingly soon,
if one considers the impediments to their seeking help, and
many have found relief and tranquillity in sharing their stories with other women or starting educational programs about
both wife abuse and child sexual abuse in the schools. Women
who have been mistreated by their therapists have kept
changing therapists until they found one who really could help
them. Women whose physical health problems have not been

adequately diagnosed or treated have been inspiringly persistent in their pursuit of further information that might help, in their belief that such information must surely exist. Even the unhappiest of women have usually been responsible for organizing large and joyous celebrations with family and friends at holiday times.

It is deeply moving to realize how much happiness and celebration women have managed to introduce into their lives, in spite of the very real, externally imposed sources of suffering to which they have been subjected. This bodes well for our future. If we can understand how much of women's behavior has been grossly misinterpreted as masochistic and how profound a disservice this has been to women, if we can reinterpret women's reasons for doing things—seeing the health, strength, beauty, and creativity in our motives—we will be able to stop believing that we sought the misery. Then we will be better able to search for the *real* sources of our suffering and begin to cleanse them from our lives.

Notes

viii.   Audre Lorde: Audre Lorde, *Sister Outsider* (Tru-
        mansburg, N.Y.: The Crossing Press, 1984), 58.

CHAPTER 1: WHY DO YOU DO THIS TO YOURSELF?

1. . The powerless: Michele Bograd, "A Feminist Ex-
      amination of the Role of Women as Family Ther-
      apists." Presented to Woman's Institute of Ameri-
      can   Orthopsychiatric   Association   convention,
      Toronto, 1984.
1.   "masochism" is defined: *Random House Dictio-
      nary of the English Language* (New York: Random
      House, 1967).

2. There is nothing essentially: Andrea Blanch, "The Problem of Feminine Masochism," *Cornell Journal of Social Relations* 9 (1) (Spring 1974), 13.

7. "found mounting acceptance": Barbara Ehrenreich and Deirdre English, *For Her Own Good: 150 Years of the Experts' Advice to Women* (Garden City, N.Y.: Anchor, 1979), 271.

7. we wrote a paper: Frances Newman and Paula J. Caplan, "Juvenile Female Prostitution as Gender-Consistent Response to Early Deprivation," *International Journal of Women's Studies* 5 (1982), 128–37.

10. Gilligan: Carol Gilligan, *In a Different Voice: Psychological Theory and Women's Development* (Cambridge, MA.: Harvard University Press, 1982).

11. Miller: Jean Baker Miller, *Toward a New Psychology of Women* (Boston: Beacon, 1976).

11. Allport: Gordon W. Allport, *The Nature of Prejudice* (Garden City, N.Y.: Doubleday, 1958).

12. Farrah Fawcett: Interview on "The Tonight Show," September 27, 1984.

13. "In my opinion": Robert Robertiello, "Masochism and the Female Sexual Role," *The Journal of Sex Research* 6 (1970), 56–58.

13. not a normal, inevitable: Martin Silverman, "Cognitive Development and Female Psychology," *Journal of the American Psychoanalytic Association* 29 (1981), 581–605.

13. 12-volt electrical shocks: W. Gifford-Jones, "The Doctor Game," *The Journal,* Edmonton, Alberta (November 4, 1981), D1.

CHAPTER 2: WHAT THE "EXPERTS" HAVE SAID

17. Eve, the first: Elizabeth A. Waites, "Female Masochism and the Enforced Restriction of Choice,"

Victimology: An International Journal 2 (1977–78), 535.

18. *naturally* masochistic, narcissistic: Helene Deutsch, *The Psychology of Women*, Vol. 1 (New York: Grune & Stratton, 1944).

18. Freud's notion: Sigmund Freud, "The Economic Problem of Masochism." In J. Strachey (Ed. & Trans.), *The Standard Edition of the Complete Psychological Works of Sigmund Freud*, Vol. XIX (London: Hogarth, 1961; original pub. 1924), 159–70.

19. "In coitus, the woman": Marie Bonaparte, cited in J. S. Hyde and B. G. Rosenberg, *Half the Human Experience: The Psychology of Women* (Lexington, MA.: Heath, 1980).

19. It was sex expert: Richard von Krafft-Ebing, *Psychopathia Sexualis: A Medico-forensic Study* (New York: Pioneer, 1950; original pub. 1901).

19. the "Masochian" woman: Clea Elfi Kore, "Decadence and the Feminine: The Case of Leopold von Sacher-Masoch," Ph.D. dissertation (Stanford University, 1983).

20. masochism *is* feminine: Strachey, op. cit., 159–70.

20. "The idea that women": Barbara Ehrenreich and Deirdre English, *For Her Own Good: 150 Years of the Experts' Advice to Women* (Garden City, N.Y.: Anchor, 1979), 273.

20. Ruitenbeek: Hendrik Ruitenbeek, *Psychoanalysis and Female Sexuality* (New Haven: College and University Press, 1966). Cited by Ehrenreich and English, op. cit.

21. Eros and Thanatos: Sigmund Freud, *Beyond the Pleasure Principle* (J. Strachey, Trans.) (New York: Bantam, 1959; original pub., 1920).

21. is instead about other things: e.g., see Leila Lerner (Ed.), *Masochism and the Emergent Ego: Selected*

Papers of Esther Menaker, Ph.D. (New York: Human Sciences, 1979), as Menaker says that the expectation or hope of pleasure keeps people in "masochistic" situations, but she nevertheless calls such motivation masochistic.

22. In a separate paper: Sigmund Freud, "The Economic Problem of Masochism." In Strachey, op. cit., 159–70.

22. In still another paper: Sigmund Freud, " 'A Child is Being Beaten': A Contribution to the Study of the Origin of Sexual Perversions." In Strachey, op. cit., 179–204.

23. Reich: Wilhelm Reich, *Character Analysis,* 3rd ed. (New York: Simon and Schuster, 1972).

23. senses the mounting: ibid., 330.

24. There were also some indications: Alan Parkin, "On Masochistic Enthralment," *International Journal of Psychoanalysis* 61 (1980), 309–10.

26. Shainess: Natalie Shainess, *Sweet Suffering: Woman as Victim* (New York: Bobbs-Merrill, 1984).

26. Lucille: ibid., 7.

27. Anne: ibid., 7.

28. "there is no evidence": Harold P. Blum, "Masochism, the Ego Ideal, and the Psychology of Women." In Harold P. Blum (Ed.), *Female Psychology: Contemporary Psychoanalytic Views* (New York: International Universities, 1977), 187.

28. men who need to regard: Elizabeth A. Waites, "Fixing Women: Devaluation, Idealization, and the Female Fetish," *Journal of the American Psychoanalytic Association* 30 (1982), 435–59.

28. "Negation": Sigmund Freud, "Negation." In Strachey, op. cit., 235–39.

29. "The concept of feminine": Kurt Eissler, "Comments on Penis Envy and Orgasm in Women," *Psychoanalytic Study of the Child,* XXXII (New Haven: Yale University Press, 1977), 73.

30. Sociobiologists: E. O. Wilson, *Sociobiology: The New Synthesis* (Cambridge, MA.: Harvard University Press, 1975).

31. "Whatever is, is right": Alexander Pope, "An Essay on Man." In M. H. Abrams (Gen. Ed.), *The Norton Anthology of English Literature*, Vol. 1 (New York: W. W. Norton, 1962), 1476.

31. essence and totality: Shere Hite, *The Hite Report: A Nationwide Survey of Female Sexuality* (New York: Dell, 1976).

32. "*Receptive aims*": Ruth Moulton, "A Survey and Reevaluation of the Concept of Penis Envy." In J. B. Miller (Ed.), *Psychoanalysis and Women* (New York: Penguin, 1978), 245.

32. "masochism also often proves": Clara Thompson, *On Women* (New York: New American Library, 1964), 133.

32. Bernard: Jessie Bernard, *The Female World* (New York: The Free Press, 1981).

33. Miller: Jean Baker Miller, *Toward a New Psychology of Women* (Boston: Beacon, 1976).

33. Chodorow: Nancy Chodorow, *The Reproduction of Mothering: Psychoanalysis and the Sociology of Gender* (Berkeley: University of California Press, 1978).

33. Newman: Frances Newman and Paula J. Caplan, "Juvenile Female Prostitution as Gender-Consistent Response to Early Deprivation," *International Journal of Women's Studies* 5 (1982), 128–37.

34. "A series of photos": Bonnie Kreps, "The Case Against Pornography," *Homemaker's Magazine* (June 1982), 12.

34. If one were to apply: Newman and Caplan, op. cit., 134.

36. "low comparison level": J. W. Thibaut and H. H. Kelley, *Interpersonal Relations: A Theory of Interdependence* (New York: Wiley, 1978).

36. the father squelches: Deutsch, op. cit.

36. women "have been led": Jean Baker Miller, "Women and Power," No. 82–01 in Work in Progress Series of the Stone Center of Wellesley College, Wellesley, MA., 1982, 4.

36. "It is generally agreed": Kathryn Pauly Morgan, "Women and Moral Madness." Presented to Canadian Society for Women in Philosophy, Montreal, November 1984, and Centre for Women's Studies in Education, Ontario Institute for Studies in Education, Toronto, January 1985, 21.

37. *avoiding pain*: Lynne Dennis, personal communication, 1982.

37. Persephone complex: David McClelland, "The Harlequin Complex." In Robert White (Ed.), *A Study of Lives* (New York: Atherton, 1963), 94–119.

38. "it was surprising": Gertrud Lenzer, "On Masochism: A Contribution to the History of a Phantasy and Its Theory," *Signs* 1 (1975), 278–79.

38. "negative connotations": Mary Jane Herron and William G. Herron, "Meanings of Sadism and Masochism," *Psychological Reports* 50 (1982), 200.

39. relationship of language: Casey Miller and Kate Swift, *Words and Women* (Garden City, N.Y.: Anchor, 1977).

CHAPTER 3: MOTHERS

43. Morgan: Kathryn Pauly Morgan, "Women and Moral Madness." Presented to Canadian Society for Women in Philosophy, Montreal, November 1984, and to Centre for Women's Studies in Education, Ontario Institute for Studies in Education, Toronto, January 1985, 23.

44. professionals give mothers: Barbara Ehrenreich and Deirdre English, *For Her Own Good: 150 Years of*

the Experts' Advice to Women (Garden City, N.Y.: Anchor, 1979), 270.

45. Morgan: Morgan, op. cit. See also P. Susan Penfold and Gillian A. Walker, *Women and the Psychiatric Paradox* (Montreal: Eden Press, 1983), 117–118, for a discussion of this problem.

49. Friedan: Betty Friedan, *The Feminine Mystique* (New York: Dell, 1963).

49. de Beauvoir: Alice Schwarzer, *After the Second Sex: Conversations with Simone de Beauvoir,* Marianne Howarth, Trans. (New York: Pantheon, 1984), 114.

49. Badinter: Elizabeth Badinter, *Mother Love: Myth and Reality* (New York: Macmillan, 1981).

49. Kabatznick: Ronna Kabatznick, "Nurture/Nature," *Ms. Magazine,* August 1984, 76, 78, 102.

50. Hall-McCorquodale: Paula J. Caplan and Ian Hall-McCorquodale, "Mother-blaming in Major Clinical Journals," *American Journal of Orthopsychiatry* (July 1985).

50. "To meet Johnny's mother": Stella Chess, "The 'Blame the Mother' Ideology," *International Journal of Mental Health* 11 (1982), 95.

51. "A nasty woman": Letty Cottin Pogrebin, *Growing Up Free: Raising Your Child in the 80s* (New York: Bantam, 1980), 540.

51. These mothers were rearing: Nancy Chodorow, *The Reproduction of Mothering: Psychoanalysis and the Sociology of Gender* (Berkeley: University of California, 1978), 212.

55. "The mother was nurturant": Ronald E. Smith and Theodore M. Sharpe, "Treatment of a School Phobia with Implosive Therapy," *Journal of Consulting and Clinical Psychology* 35 (1970), 239–40.

55. "Their father, a carpenter": Michael F. Myers, "Homosexuality, Sexual Dysfunction, and Incest in Male Identical Twins," *Canadian Journal of Psychiatry* 27 (1982), 145.

55. "The father, a brick layer": Johannes Nielsen, Sverrir Bjarnason, Ursula Friedrich, Anders Froland, Viggo H. Hansen, and Andreas Sorensen, "Klinefelter's Syndrome in Children," *Journal of Child Psychology and Psychiatry* 11 (1970), 116.

55. Klinefelter's: Nielsen et al., op. cit., 117.

56. school phobia: Smith and Sharpe, op. cit., 240–41.

56. obedient prisoners: John A. Snortum, Thomas E. Hanna, and David H. Mills, "The Relationship of Self-concept and Parent Image to Rule Violation in a Women's Prison," *Journal of Clinical Psychology* 26 (1970), 284–87.

56. fire-setters: R. W. Hill, R. Langevin, D. Paitich, L. Handy, A. Russon, and L. Wilkinson, "Is Arson an Aggressive Act or a Property Offence? A Controlled Study of Psychiatric Referrals," *Canadian Journal of Psychiatry* 27 (1982), 648–54.

57. prisoner-of-war camps: John J. Sigal, "Effects of Paternal Exposure to Prolonged Stress on the Mental Health of the Spouse and Children," *Canadian Psychiatric Association Journal* 21 (1976), 169–72.

57. articles on school phobia: e.g., Alan deSousa and D. A. deSousa, "School Phobia," *Child Psychiatry Quarterly* 13 (1980), 98–103.

59. I never thought I'd be writing: letter to Ann Landers, Toronto *Star* July 23, 1984, C2.

60. four recommendations: Paula J. Caplan and Ian Hall-McCorquodale, "The Scapegoating of Mothers: A Call for Change," *American Journal of Orthopsychiatry* (October 1985).

61. embody respect and high status: Jeri Dawn Wine, Barbara Moses, and Marti Diane Smye, "Female Superiority in Sex Difference Competence Comparisons: A Review of the Literature." In C. Stark-Adamec (Ed.), *Sex Roles: Origins, Influences and Implications for Women* (Montreal: Eden Press Women's Publications, 1980), 176–86.

62. "she responds to their needs": Carole Browner, "Female Altruism Reconsidered: The Virgin Mary as Economic Woman," *American Ethnologist* 9 (1982), 62.

63. "dream of upward mobility": ibid., 67.

63. "Given the difficulties": ibid., 69.

63. "an adaptive mechanism": ibid., 70.

63. Hetherington: E. Mavis Hetherington, Martha Cox, and Roger Cox, "Family Interaction and the Social, Emotional, and Cognitive Development of Children Following Divorce." In V. Vaughn and T. Brazelton (Eds.), *The Family: Setting Priorities* (New York: Science and Medicine, 1979).

64. Greif: Geoffrey Greif (cited in Kabatznick, op. cit., 102).

64. situation has perhaps been worst: see Penfold and Walker, op. cit., 132, for a discussion of mental health professionals' contributions to this problem.

65. A valuable antidote: Joann Ellison Rodgers and Michael F. Cataldo, *Raising Sons: Practical Strategies for Single Mothers* (New York: New American Library, 1984).

66. "My home is not broken": quoted by Carol Kleiman in "My Home Is Not Broken, It Works," *Ms. Magazine,* November 1984, 154.

CHAPTER 4: THE CHILD'S GROWTH
TOWARD "MASOCHISM":
"EXPERT" OPINION AND REALITY

69. I was learning: Rosemary Daniell, *Fatal Flowers: On Sin, Sex, and Suicide in the Deep South* (New York: Avon, 1980), 80.

69. Styron: William Styron, *Sophie's Choice* (New York: Bantam, 1979), 293.

70. "The concept of 'free choice' ": Jeanette Nichols, Darlene R. Pagano, and Margaret Rossoff, "Is Sa-

domasochism Feminist? A Critique of the Samois Position." In Robin Ruth Linden, Darlene R. Pagano, Diana E. H. Russell, and Susan Leigh Star (Eds.), *Against Sadomasochism: A Radical Feminist Critique* (East Palo Alto, CA.: Frog in the Well Press, 1982), 137.

71. "inner space": Erik H. Erikson, "Sex Differences in the Play Configurations of Preadolescents," *American Journal of Orthopsychiatry* 21 (1951), 667–92; *Childhood and Society* (New York: W. W. Norton, 1963); and "Womanhood and the Inner Space." In Jean Strouse (Ed.), *Women and Analysis: Dialogues on Psychoanalytic Views of Femininity* (New York: Dell, 1974), 333–64.

73. In my son's class: Paula J. Caplan, "Erikson's Concept of Inner Space: A Data-Based Re-evaluation," *American Journal of Orthopsychiatry* 49 (1979), 100–108.

73. how things *ought to be*: Christine Pierce, "Natural Law Language and Women." In Vivan Gornick and Barbara K. Moran (Eds.), *Woman in Sexist Society* (New York: New American Library, 1971), 242–58.

73. Blum: Harold P. Blum, "Masochism, the Ego Ideal, and the Psychology of Women." In Harold P. Blum (Ed.), *Female Psychology: Contemporary Psychoanalytic Views* (New York: International Universities, 1977), 188.

74. child becomes angry: Robert Robertiello, "Masochism and the Female Sexual Role," *The Journal of Sex Research* 6 (1970), 56–58.

75. females *constitutionally* suppress: Sigmund Freud, " 'A Child is Being Beaten': A Contribution to the Study of the Origin of Sexual Perversions." In J. Strachey (Ed. & Trans.), *The Standard Edition of the Complete Psychological Works of Sigmund*

Freud, Vol. XVII (London: Hogarth, 1955), 179–204.

75. "penis pity": Paula J. Caplan, *Between Women: Lowering the Barriers* (Toronto: Personal Library Publishers, 1981).

76. "bodily and personal inferiority": Blum, op. cit., 160.

76. Bernstein: Isidor Bernstein, "Masochistic Pathology and Feminine Development, *Journal of the American Psychoanalytic Association* 31 (1983), 467–86.

77. Like the Latinas: Carole Browner, "Female Altruism Reconsidered: The Virgin Mary as Economic Woman," *American Ethnologist* 9 (1982), 61–75.

77. "overwhelming widowed mother": Arthur Valenstein, quoted in Arnold M. Cooper (Chair), Newell Fischer (Reporter), "Masochism: Current Concepts," *Journal of the American Psychoanalytic Association* 29 (1981), 674.

78. "masochism endangers the self": Robert Bak quoted in Martin M. Stein (Reporter), "The Problem of Masochism in the Theory and Technique of Psychoanalysis," *Journal of the American Psychoanalytic Association* 4 (1956), 528.

78. "the narcissistic function": Robert D. Stolorow, "The Narcissistic Function of Masochism (and Sadism)," *International Journal of Psychoanalysis* 56 (1975), 441–48.

CHAPTER 5: WOMEN IN RELATIONSHIPS WITH MEN

81. Weldon: Fay Weldon, *Female Friends* (London: Pan Books, 1977), 47.

81. "She needed pain": John Updike, *The Witches of Eastwick* (New York: Alfred A. Knopf, 1984), 160.

82. 123 single women: Carol Cassell, *Swept Away: Why*

Women Fear Their Own Sexuality (New York: Simon and Schuster, 1984), 111.

85. Reik: Theodor Reik, *Masochism in Modern Man*, Margaret H. Beigel and Gertrud M. Kurth, Trans. (New York: Farrar, Straus, & Giroux, 1941).

86. "Masochism is a search": Jessica Benjamin, "Master and Slave: The Fantasy of Erotic Domination." In Ann Snitow, Christine Stansell, and Sharon Thompson (Eds.), *Powers of Desire: The Politics of Sexuality* (New York: Monthly Review Press, 1983), 286.

86. from Zelda's letters: Nancy Milford, *Zelda: A Biography* (New York: Harper & Row, 1970), 284–85.

86. *Paradise*: ibid., 58.

86. Scott's name: ibid., 102.

86. to them both: ibid., 132.

89. Images of Cleopatra: see P. Susan Penfold and Gillian A. Walker, *Women and the Psychiatric Paradox* (Montreal: Eden Press, 1983), 65–66, for a discussion of images of female archetypes.

90. Count von Sacher-Masoch: Gertrud Lenzer, "On Masochism: A Contribution to the History of a Phantasy and Its Theory," *Signs* 1 (1975), 277–324.

91. "to gain safety": Karen Horney, *New Ways of Psychoanalysis* (New York: W. W. Norton, 1939), cited in Reik, op. cit., p. 74.

91. *Body Politics*: Nancy Henley, *Body Politics: Power, Sex, and Nonverbal Communication* (Englewood Cliffs, N.J.: Prentice-Hall, 1977).

92. *The Mermaid and the Minotaur*: Dorothy Dinnerstein, *The Mermaid and the Minotaur: Sexual Arrangements and Human Malaise* (New York: Harper Colophon, 1974).

93. I went back to my room: Barbara Gordon, *I'm Dancing as Fast as I Can* (New York: Bantam, 1979), 92–93.

94. *The Total Woman*: Marabel Morgan, *The Total Woman* (New York: Simon and Schuster, 1973).

94. *Fascinating Womanhood*: Helen Andelin, *Fascinating Womanhood* (New York: Bantam, 1963).

96. Reik: Reik, op. cit., 116.

98. A neighbor trudged: Marabel Morgan, op. cit., 32–33.

98. drug use among wives: this subject is reviewed in Penfold and Walker, op. cit.

99. Gretchen Grinnell: Gretchen Grinnell, "Women, Depression, and the Folie à Deux." Presented to Women's Institute of American Orthopsychiatric Association, Toronto, 1984.

100. "Self-abnegating": Kathryn Morgan, "Women and Moral Madness." Presented to Canadian Society for Women in Philosophy, Montreal, November 1984, and to Centre for Women's Studies in Education, Ontario Institute for Studies in Education, January 1985, 13–14.

100. "What every woman wants": Ronald B. deSousa, personal communication (1984).

100. Gloria Steinem: Gloria Steinem, *Outrageous Acts and Everyday Rebellions* (New York: Holt, Rinehart and Winston, 1983).

101. A little bitterness: Olive Schreiner, *The Story of an African Farm* (New York: Penguin, 1983), 189–90, 199.

101. "call a girl friend": Marabel Morgan, op. cit., 56.

102. "He doesn't need": ibid., 174.

102. "According to the myth": Rosemary Daniell, *Fatal Flowers: On Sin, Sex, and Suicide in the Deep South* (New York: Avon, 1980), 103.

102. "I couldn't admit": Marabel Morgan, op. cit., 5–6.

102. When your husband asks: ibid., 28.

103. "she becomes really beautiful": ibid., 96–97.

103. the *Playboy* philosophy: Barbara Ehrenreich, *The*

Hearts of Men: American Dreams and the Flight from Commitment (Garden City, N.Y.: Anchor, 1984).

104. "my lover": Daniell, op. cit., 158.
105. in touch with their feelings: Ronnie deSousa, personal communication (1984).
106. *Cinderella Complex*: Colette Dowling, *The Cinderella Complex: Women's Hidden Fear of Independence* (New York: Pocket Books, 1981).
110. I worked while my husband: letter to Ann Landers, Toronto *Star*, May 16, 1984, D24.

CHAPTER 6: WOMEN'S BODIES

113. Lazerson: Judith Lazerson, "The Voices of Bulimia: Experiences in Integrated Psychotherapy," *Psychotherapy: Theory, Research, and Practice*, in press, 28.
114. "At the age of six": Carol Pogash, "Real Live Dolls," *Redbook*, June 1984, 92.
114. "To the Hinkes,": ibid., 92.
114. Today's contest: ibid., 92.
116. not "frumpy" enough: Martin Cohn, "The Top Candidates to Replace Davis," Toronto *Star*, October 9, 1984, A17.
117. Lazerson: Lazerson, op. cit.
117. anxiety about feminine standards: David M. Garner, Paul E. Garfinkel, and M. P. Olmsted, "An Overview of the Socio-cultural Factors in the Development of Anorexia Nervosa." In P. L. Darby, Paul E. Garfinkel, David M. Garner, and D. V. Coscina (Eds.), *Anorexia Nervosa: Recent Developments* (New York: Alan R. Liss, 1983), 65–82; and David M. Garner, Paul E. Garfinkel, D. Schwartz, and M. Thompson, "Cultural Expectations of Thinness in Women," *Psychological Reports* 47 (1980), 483–91.

117. Orbach: Susie Orbach, "Social Dimension in Compulsive Eating Women," *Psychotherapy: Theory, Research, and Practice* 15 (1978), 180.

119. most of whom are women: P. Susan Penfold and Gillian A. Walker wrote in *Women and the Psychiatric Paradox* (Montreal: Eden Press, 1983), p. 27: "Many of the millions of women accused of witchcraft and burnt at the stake . . . were healers and midwives, whose skill was based on empirical knowledge of anatomy, herbology, and what could be described as nursing care. As such, they were often more effective than the physicians whose 'expertise' was drawn from the study of classic Greek and Arab texts."

127. Mendelsohn: Robert Mendelsohn, *Malepractice: How Doctors Manipulate Women* (Chicago: Contemporary Books, 1982).

127. *Doctors' Anti-Breast Cancer Diet*: Sherwood Gorbach, David Zimmerman, and Margo Woods, *The Doctors' Anti-Breast Cancer Diet* (New York: Simon and Schuster, 1984).

128. Flo Kennedy: For example, in Flo Kennedy's lecture to "The Issue is Choice" benefit evening (Toronto, November 1983).

128. "Fetal Rights": Janet Gallagher, Lecture in "Fetal Rights Symposium," National Women's Studies Association convention (Rutgers University, June 1984).

128. Katz-Rothman: Barbara Katz-Rothman, Lecture in "Fetal Rights Symposium," National Women's Studies Association convention (Rutgers University, June 1984).

130. *Ms. Magazine's: Ms. Magazine,* special issue on "Our Bodies" (May 1984).

131. understandable emotional responses: Phyllis Chesler, *Women and Madness* (New York: Avon, 1972).

131. "Change and Creativity": Rachel Josefowitz Sie-

gel, "Change and Creativity in Midlife." In Joan Hamerman Robbins and Rachel Josefowitz Siegel (Eds.), *Women Changing Therapy: New Assessments, Values, and Strategies in Feminist Therapy* (New York: Haworth, 1983, 95–102).

CHAPTER 7: WOMEN AS VICTIMS OF VIOLENCE

133. Any self-respecting John Wayne fan: Andrea Blanch, "The Problem of Feminine Masochism: An Approach Through Theory and Literature," *Cornell Journal of Social Relations* 9 (1) (Spring 1974), 2.

133. "When I first dated": Gloria Steinem, *Outrageous Acts and Everyday Rebellions* (New York: Holt, Rinehart and Winston, 1983), 246.

134. "creatively inspired": ibid., 244.

134. turn her terror: ibid., 247.

134. "attacks the myth": ibid., 248.

135. "If you accept": ibid., 250.

135. As for Chuck: ibid., 252.

136. "I couldn't believe the stuff": quoted in article by Lynda Hurst, "The Public Must Be Re-educated on Pornography," Toronto *Star,* December 11, 1984, F1.

137. "Through romance we learn": Sally Roesch Wagner, "Pornography and the Sexual Revolution." In Robin Ruth Linden, Darlene R. Pagano, Diana E. H. Russell, and Susan Leigh Star (Eds.), *Against Sadomasochism: A Radical Feminist Analysis* (East Palo Alto, CA.: Frog in the Well Press, 1982), 24.

137. Once out of the ivory tower: Susan Cole, "Combatting the Practice of Pornography," *Broadside* 5 (10) (August/September 1984), 6.

138. you found violent hard porn: Anne Cameron, "Exploring the Porn-Again Male," *Broadside* 4 (5) (March 1983), 3.

140. "masochism as a perversion": Theodor Reik, *Mas-*

ochism in Modern Man, Margaret H. Beigel and Gertrud M. Kurth, Trans. (New York: Farrar, Straus, & Giroux, 1941), 214.

140. "the number of women": Andreas Spengler, "Manifest Sadomasochism of Males." In Thomas Weinberg and G. W. Levi Kamel (Eds.), *S & M: Studies in Sadomasochism* (Buffalo: Prometheus, 1983), 57–72.

140. "fulfilling masochistic needs": cited in Elaine Hilberman, "Overview: The 'Wife-Beater's Wife' Reconsidered," *American Journal of Psychiatry* 137 (1980), 1336.

140. Gilman: Irene Gilman, "An Object-relations Approach to the Phenomenon and Treatment of Battered Women," *Psychiatry* 43 (1980), 346–58.

140. Nichols: Beverly B. Nichols, "The Abused Wife Problem," *Social Casework* 57 (1976), 27–32.

141. It could almost be said: Nicole Walton-Allen, "Laypeople's Perceptions of Family Violence: An Examination of Stereotyped Learning," M.A. thesis (Ontario Institute for Studies in Education: Toronto, 1984), 1–2.

141. (Brownmiller): Susan Brownmiller, *Against Our Will: Men, Women, and Rape* (New York: Simon and Schuster, 1975).

141. (Martin): D. Martin, *Battered Wives* (San Francisco: Volcano, 1976).

141. (Davidson): T. Davidson, "Wifebeating: A Recurring Phenomenon Throughout History." In M. Roy (Ed.), *Battered Women* (New York: Van Nostrand Reinhold, 1977), 2–23.

141. Wollstonecraft: Mary Wollstonecraft, *Vindication of the Rights of Women* (Harmondsworth, Middlesex, England: Penguin, 1982; original pub., 1792), 180.

142. (Martin): D. Martin, "Battered Women: Society's Problem." In J. Chapman and M. Gates (Eds.), *The*

Victimization of Women (Beverly Hills: Sage, 1978).

142. Dutton: Donald Dutton, 1983 presentation to Clarke Institute of Psychiatry.

142. "Here's for what you did": Diana E. H. Russell, *Rape in Marriage* (New York: Collier, 1982), 230.

143. "traumatic bonding": Donald Dutton and Susan Lee Painter, "Traumatic Bonding: The Development of Emotional Attachments in Battered Women and Other Relationships of Intermittent Abuse," *Victimology: An International Journal* 6 (1981), 139–55.

143. "The basic fact": Hilberman, op. cit., 1337.

143. Symonds: Alexandra Symonds, "Violence Against Women—the Myth of Masochism," *Journal of American Psychotherapy* 33 (1979), 161–73.

144. "Family therapists": Michele Bograd, "Family Systems Approaches to Wife Battering: A Feminist Critique," *American Journal of Orthopsychiatry* 54 (1984), 562.

144. " 'to trigger' ": Natalie Shainess, "Vulnerability to Violence," *American Journal of Psychotherapy* 33 (1979), 176.

145. it seems grossly unfair: Cannie Stark-Adamec and Robert Adamec, "Aggression by Men Against Women: Adaptation or Aberration?" *International Journal of Women's Studies* 5 (1982), 1–21.

145. the issue is far more complex: Ruth Bleier, *Science and Gender: A Critique of Biology and Its Theories on Women* (Oxford: Pergamon, 1984), 97.

145. *Psychology Today*: R. Stark and J. McEvoy, "Middle-class Violence," *Psychology Today* 4 (November 1970), 52–65.

145. Eva Vincze: Eva Vincze, "Wifebeating: The Private Crime." Presented to National Women's Studies Association convention, Rutgers University, 1984.

146. "these factors point to passivity": Barbara Star,

"Comparing Battered and Non-battered Women," *Victimology: An International Journal* 3 (1978), 42.

146. "believe that any action": ibid.

147. Laura X: Laura X, personal communication (June 1984).

147. Symonds: Symonds, op. cit.

147. when her husband got into financial: quoted in " 'Get Out Before You Kill Him' Prisoner Urges Abused Women," Toronto *Star,* September 1, 1984, L2.

148. Symonds: Symonds, op. cit.

148. if the one who loves you: Richard Gelles, *The Violent Home* (Beverly Hills: Sage, 1972).

148. "It is often assumed": Russell, op. cit., 237.

148. will not let them go: ibid., 228.

148. She gives examples: ibid., 233.

148. brutal pimps: Sgt. Richard Brier of Toronto police morality squad quoted in Toronto *Star* article, "Metro Prostitutes Are as Young as 12," December 9, 1984, A8.

149. Laura X: Laura X, personal communication (June 1984).

149. hold four beliefs: Hilberman, op. cit., 1345.

150. Walton-Allen: Nicole Walton-Allen, personal communication (1984).

151. Vincze: Vincze, op. cit.

151. North Carolina: Erica Rothman and Kit Munson, "Family Violence Treatment Groups." Presented to Women's Institute of American Orthopsychiatric Association convention (Toronto, 1984).

152. surveyed lay people: Nicole Walton-Allen and Paula J. Caplan, "Laypeople's Perceptions of Spouse Abuse," presented to University of Toronto Department of Psychiatry Research Day (1984).

152. "Though provocation . . .": Susan Griffin, "Rape: The All-American Crime." In Mary Vetterling-Braggin, Frederick Elliston, and Jane English (Eds.),

Feminism and Philosophy (Totowa, N.J.: Littlefield Adams & Co., 1977), 316–17.

152. "The fear of rape": ibid., 331.

153. *female* rape victims: James V. P. Check and Neil M. Malamuth, "Sex-role Stereotyping and Reactions to Depictions of Stranger versus Acquaintance Rape," *Journal of Personality and Social Psychology* 45 (1983), 344–56.

153. *A Taste for Pain*: Maria Marcus, *A Taste for Pain: On Masochism and Female Sexuality* (New York: St. Martin's Press, 1981), 46.

153. "needs to overpower women": Signe Hammer, "The Rape Fantasies of Women: Up From Disrepute," *Village Voice,* April 5, 1976, 10.

154. For a woman to fantasize: Molly Haskell, "Rape Fantasy: The 2,000-Year-Old Misunderstanding," *Ms. Magazine,* November 1976, 85.

154. "is based on the assumption": ibid., 92.

154. a pivotal place: ibid., 94.

155. "emphasis is on the prelude": ibid., 85.

155. *Swept Away*: Carol Cassell, *Swept Away: Why Women Fear Their Own Sexuality* (New York: Simon and Schuster, 1984).

155. "a very special kind": Haskell, op. cit., 85.

156. If we come to view: Linda Phelps, "Female Sexual Alienation." In Jo Freeman (Ed.), *Women: A Feminist Perspective*, 2nd ed. (Palo Alto, CA.: Mayfield, 1979), 22.

156. "the account that appears": Haskell, op. cit., 86.

156. Even "pseudo-rape" fantasies: Ti-Grace Atkinson, "Why I'm Against S/M Liberation." In Linden et al., op. cit., 92.

156. Fourteen percent: Russell, op. cit.

157. A male respondent: quoted in ibid., 132, from Shere Hite, *The Hite Report on Male Sexuality* (New York: Ballantine, 1981).

158. "it is very rare": Russell, op. cit., 183.

158. "I would never put myself": ibid., 125.
158. "the seeking of unpleasure": Charles Brenner quoted in Arnold M. Cooper (Chair), Newell Fischer (Reporter) "Masochism: Current Concepts," *Journal of the American Psychoanalytic Association* 29 (1981), 674.
159. Sherman: Julia Sherman, "Commentary," *Signs* 1 (1975), 1007–1009.
159. "It does not seem to be": Thomas S. Weinberg, "Sadism and Masochism: Sociological Perspectives." In Thomas S. Weinberg and G. W. Levi Kamel (Eds.), *S & M: Studies in Sadomasochism* (Buffalo: Prometheus, 1983), 108.
159. "Accidental pain": Paul Gebhard, "Sadomasochism." In Weinberg and Kamel, op. cit., 37.
159. "the suffering of pain": Reik, op. cit., 197.
159. "very desirable and not at all": Robert Robertiello, "Masochism and the Female Sexual Role," *The Journal of Sex Research* 6 (1970), 56.
159. "Among mammals": Havelock Ellis, *Love and Pain* (New York: Random House, 1942), 67. Cited in Linden et al., op. cit., 56.
160. as soon as woman is degraded: Sigmund Freud, "The Most Prevalent Form of Degradation in Erotic Life." In Philip Rieff (Ed.), *Sexuality and the Psychology of Love* (New York: Collier, 1978; original pub., 1912), 62.
161. "[My whip is of]": Juicy Lucy, "If I Ask You to Tie Me Up, Will You Still Want to Love Me?" In SAMOIS (pub. and ed.), *Coming to Power: Writings and Graphics on Lesbian S/M,* 2nd ed. (1982), 35.
161. "Discomfort, stress": Pat Califia, *Sapphistry: The Book of Lesbian Sexuality* (Tallahassee: The Naiad Press, 1983), 128.
161. "The lesbian who self-identifies": ibid., 120.
161. "By saying 'sadist' ": Juicy Lucy, op. cit., 33.

162. In calling "masochistic": Reik, op. cit.
162. "Sadomasochism is defined": Califia, op. cit., 118.
163. "release a great deal": Elizabeth Harris, "Sadomasochism: A Personal Experience." In Linden et al., op. cit., 94.
163. Morgan: Robin Morgan, "The Politics of Sadomasochistic Fantasies." In Linden et al., op. cit., 109–23.
163. "joyful anticipation of children": Reik, op. cit., 64.
164. "to end the pain": Marissa Jonel, "Letter From a Former Masochist." In Linden et al., op. cit., 20.
164. inherently masochistic: Jonel, op. cit., 22.
164. The traditional clinical: e.g., Irving Kaufman, Alice L. Peck, and Consuelo L. Taguiri, "The Family Constellation and Overt Incestuous Relations Between Father and Daughter," *American Journal of Orthopsychiatry* 24 (1954), 266–79, and Eleanor Pavenstedt's discussion at the end of the Kaufman et al., article. For a review of the traditional views, see Sarah Lawton-Speert and Andy Wachtel, *Child Sexual Abuse in the Family: A Review of Trends in the Literature. Child Sexual Abuse Project Working Paper Two.* (Vancouver, B.C.: Social Planning and Research, United Way of the Lower Mainland, April, 1982).
165. Rush: Florence Rush, *The Best Kept Secret: Sexual Abuse of Children* (New York: Prentice-Hall, 1980).
165. Masson: Jeffrey Masson, *The Assault on Truth: Freud's Suppression of the Seduction Theory* (New York: Farrar, Straus, & Giroux, 1984).
166. Barry: Kathleen Barry, *Female Sexual Slavery* (Englewood Cliffs, N.J.: Prentice-Hall, 1979).
166. to allow the degradation: Hilde Hein, "Sadomasochism and the Liberal Tradition." In Linden et al., op. cit., 87.
167. "The fact that": Erich Fromm cited in Linden et al., op. cit., 67.

167. "the worst thing of all": Adrienne Rich, *Twenty-One Love Poems* (Emeryville, CA.: Effie's Press, 1977), VII.
167. Once [Linda] started giving: Steinem, op. cit., 247.
167. *If she really*: ibid., 251.

CHAPTER 8: WOMEN AT WORK

169. For women as a group: Barbara Ehrenreich, *The Hearts of Men: American Dreams and the Flight from Commitment* (Garden City, N.Y.: Anchor, 1984), 175.
169. "head of household": Jan Mears, presentation to Centre for Investigative Journalism seminar (1984).
170. men's conscious and unconscious anger: Anthony Astrachan, "On the Job," *Ms. Magazine,* August 1984, 62–63, 106.
172. Laurie Case: Laurie Case, "Adolescent Girls and Underachievement," M.A. thesis (Toronto: Ontario Institute for Studies in Education, 1984).
176. "motive to avoid success": Matina S. Horner, "Toward an Understanding of Achievement-related Conflicts in Women," *Journal of Social Issues* 28 (1972), 157–75.
178. "self-determined power": Jean Baker Miller, "Women and Power," No. 82-01 in Work in Progress Series of the Stone Center of Wellesley College, Wellesley, MA., 1982, 4.
178. "her sense of identity": ibid.
178. "Hostility toward women": Astrachan, op. cit., 62.
178. If we, in our minds: ibid., 106.
180. "sex-based manipulation": Paula J. Caplan, "Sex-based Manipulation in the Clinical Psychologist's Workplace," *International Journal of Women's Studies* 8 (1985), 175-82.

CHAPTER 9: WOMEN IN THERAPY

189. [After my suicide attempt]: Phyllis Chesler, *Women and Madness* (New York: Avon, 1972), 218.

193. Chesler: ibid.

194. "inner space": Erik H. Erikson, "Womanhood and the Inner Space." In Jean Strouse (Ed.), *Women and Analysis: Dialogues on Psychoanalytic Views of Femininity* (New York: Dell, 1974), 354.

195. Colleagues find her: Harry F. Waters with Lucy Howard, " 'This Morning's' Rising Star," *Newsweek,* May 24, 1984, 83.

196. Wine: Jeri Dawn Wine, Barbara Moses, and Marti Diane Smye, "Female Superiority in Sex Difference Competence Comparisons: A Review of the Literature." In C. Stark-Adamec (Ed.), *Sex Differences: Origins, Influences, and Implications for Women* (Montreal: Eden Press Women's Publications, 1980), 176–86.

197. group of clinical theorists: These include Jean Baker Miller, Irene Stiver, Alexandra Kaplan, Janet Surrey, and Judith Jordan.

197. "relational ability": Janet Surrey, "The Relational Self in Women," No. 82-02 in Work in Progress Series of Stone Center of Wellesley College, Wellesley, MA., 1983.

197. The sense of pleasing herself: Jean Baker Miller, *Toward a New Psychology of Women* (Boston: Beacon, 1976), 110.

198. field of family therapy: Michele Bograd, "A Feminist Examination of the Role of Women as Family Therapists." Presented to Women's Institute of American Orthopsychiatric Association convention, Toronto, 1984.

199. a wife reminds: Michele Bograd, "Family Systems Approaches to Wife Battering: A Feminist Cri-

tique," *American Journal of Orthopsychiatry* 54 (1984), 566.

199. "When the battered": ibid., 565.

200. "the powerless are regarded": Bograd, "A Feminist Examination . . ."

203. "The therapist/counselor": reprinted in P. Susan Penfold and Gillian A. Walker, *Women and the Psychiatric Paradox* (Montreal: Eden Press, 1983), 215–16.

203. sexual relations: Betsy Jean Belote, "Sexual Intimacy Between Female Clients and Male Psychotherapists: Masochistic Sabotage," Ph.D. dissertation (Berkeley: California School of Professional Psychology, 1974)..

208. were all convinced: Alexandra Symonds, "Violence Against Women—The Myth of Masochism," *Journal of American Psychotherapy* 33 (1979), 161.

209. The author's therapeutic: Chesler, op. cit., 71.

216. In the latest edition: American Psychiatric Association, *Diagnostic and Statistical Manual—III* (Washington, D.C.: American Psychiatric Association, 1980).

216. Bernardez: Teresa Bernardez, "Gender-based Countertransference in the Treatment of Women." Presented to Women's Institute of American Orthopsychiatric Association convention, Toronto, 1984.

217. "Are . . . women being punished": Chesler, op. cit., 172.

CHAPTER 10: THE BEGINNING

219. To those women: Jean Anyon, "Interactions of Gender and Class: Accommodation and Resistance by Working-class and Affluent Females to Contra-

dictory Sex Role Ideologies,'' *Journal of Education* 166 (March 1984), 45.

219. By the time I was 25: letter to Ann Landers in Toronto *Star,* June 4, 1984, C3.

220. since pleasure is: *New Webster's Dictionary of the English Language* (Delair, 1981).

220. Sandra Bem: Sandra Bem, personal communication (November 1984).

223. I lived with an alcoholic: letter to Ann Landers in Toronto *Star,* October 17, 1984, D21.

226. "led by the culture": Jean Baker Miller, "Women and Power," No. 82-01 in Work in Progress Series of Stone Center of Wellesley College, Wellesley, MA., 1982, 4.

226. we can consider seriously: Jean Baker Miller, *Toward a New Psychology of Women* (Boston: Beacon, 1976), 184.

226. "Women whose psychological": Phyllis Chesler, *Women and Madness* (New York: Avon, 1972), 301.

Bibliographical References

ALLPORT, GORDON W. *The Nature of Prejudice* (Garden City, N.Y.: Doubleday, 1958).

American Psychiatric Association. *Diagnostic and Statistical Manual—III* (Washington, D.C.: American Psychiatric Association, 1980).

ANDELIN, HELEN. *Fascinating Womanhood* (New York: Bantam, 1963).

ANYON, JEAN. "Interactions of Gender and Class: Accommodation and Resistance by Working-class and Affluent Females to Contradictory Sex Role Ideologies," *Journal of Education* 166 (March 1984), 25–49.

ASTRACHAN, ANTHONY. "On the Job," *Ms. Magazine*, August 1984, 62–63, 106.

ATKINSON, TI-GRACE. "Why I'm Against S/M Liberation." In *Against Sadomasochism: A Radical Feminist Analysis,* Robin Ruth Linden, Darlene R. Pagano, Diana E. H. Russell, and Susan Leigh Star (Eds.) (East Palo Alto, CA: Frog in the Well, 1982), 90–92.

BADINTER, ELIZABETH. *Mother Love: Myth and Reality* (New York: Macmillan, 1981).

BAK, ROBERT. Quoted in Martin M. Stein, (Reporter), "The Problem of Masochism in the Theory and Technique of Psychoanalysis," *Journal of the American Psychoanalytic Association* 4 (1956), 526–38.

BARRY, KATHLEEN. *Female Sexual Slavery* (Englewood Cliffs, N.J.: Prentice-Hall, 1979).

BELOTE, BETSY JEAN. "Sexual Intimacy Between Female Clients and Male Psychotherapists: Masochistic Sabotage," Ph.D. dissertation (Berkeley: California School of Professional Psychology, 1974).

BENJAMIN, JESSICA. "Master and Slave: The Fantasy of Erotic Domination." In Ann Snitow, Christine Stansell, and Sharon Thompson (Eds.), *Powers of Desire: The Politics of Sexuality* (New York: Monthly Review Press, 1983), 280–99.

BERNARD, JESSIE. *The Female World* (New York: The Free Press, 1981).

———. "The Paradox of the Happy Marriage." In Vivian Gornick and Barbara K. Moran (Eds.), *Woman in Sexist Society* (New York: New American Library, 1971), 145–62.

BERNARDEZ, TERESA. "Gender-based Countertransference in the Treatment of Women." Presented to Women's Institute of American Orthopsychiatric Association convention, Toronto, 1984.

BERNSTEIN, ISIDOR. "Masochistic Pathology and Feminine Development," *Journal of the American Psychoanalytic Association* 31 (1983), 467–86.

BLANCH, ANDREA. "The Problem of Feminine Masochism: An Approach Through Theory and Literature," *Cornell Journal of Social Relations* 9 (1) (Spring 1974), 1–15.

BLEIER, RUTH. *Science and Gender: A Critique of Biology and Its Theories on Women* (Oxford: Pergamon, 1984).

BLUM, HAROLD P. "Masochism, the Ego Ideal, and the Psychology of Women." In Harold P. Blum (Ed.), *Female Psychology: Contemporary Psychoanalytic Views* (New York: International Universities, 1977), 157–91.

BOGRAD, MICHELE. "Family Systems Approaches to Wife Battering: A Feminist Critique," *American Journal of Orthopsychiatry* 54 (1984), 558–68.

———. "A Feminist Examination of the Role of Women as Family Therapists." Presented to Women's Institute of American Orthopsychiatric Association convention, Toronto, 1984.

BONAPARTE, MARIE. Cited in J. S. Hyde and B. G. Rosenberg, *Half the Human Experience: The Psychology of Women* (Lexington, MA: Heath, 1980).

BRENNER, CHARLES. "The Masochistic Character: Genesis and Treatment," *Journal of the American Psychoanalytic Association* 7 (1959), 197–226.

———. Quoted in Arnold M. Cooper (Chair), Newell Fischer (Reporter), "Masochism: Current Concepts," *Journal of the American Psychoanalytic Association* 29 (1981), 673–88.

BRIER, SGT. RICHARD. Quoted in "Metro Prostitutes Are as Young as 12," Toronto *Star,* December 9, 1984, A8.

BROVERMAN, D. M.; KLAIBER, E. L.; KOBAYASHI, Y.; and VOGEL, W. "Roles of Activation and Inhibition in Sex Differences in Cognitive Abilities," *Psychological Review* 75 (1968), 23–30.

BROWNER, CAROLE. "Female Altruism Reconsidered: The Virgin Mary as Economic Woman," *American Ethnologist* 9 (1982), 61–75.

BROWNMILLER, SUSAN. *Against Our Will: Men, Women, and Rape* (New York: Simon and Schuster, 1975).

CALIFIA, PAT. *Sapphistry: The Book of Lesbian Sexuality* (Tallahassee: The Naiad Press, 1983).

CAMERON, ANNE. "Exploring the Porn-Again Male," *Broadside* 4 (5) (March 1983), 3.

CAPLAN, PAULA J. *Between Women: Lowering the Barriers* (Toronto: Personal Library, 1981).

———. "Erikson's Concept of Inner Space: A Data-based Re-evaluation," *American Journal of Orthopsychiatry* 49 (1979), 100–108.

———. "Sex-based Manipulation in the Clinical Psychologist's Workplace," *International Journal of Women's Studies* 8 (1985), 175–82.

CAPLAN, PAULA J., and HALL-MCCORQUODALE, IAN. "Mother-blaming in Major Clinical Journals," *American Journal of Orthopsychiatry* (July 1985).

———. "The Scapegoating of Mothers: A Call for Change," *American Journal of Orthopsychiatry* (October 1985).

CASE, LAURIE. "Female Adolescents and Underachievement," M.A. thesis (Toronto: Ontario Institute for Studies in Education, 1984).

CASSELL, CAROL. *Swept Away: Why Women Fear Their Own Sexuality* (New York: Simon and Schuster, 1984).

CHECK, JAMES V. P., and MALAMUTH, NEIL M. "Sex-Role Stereotyping and Reactions to Depictions of Stranger versus Acquaintance Rape," *Journal of Personality and Social Psychology* 45 (1983), 344–56.

CHESLER, PHYLLIS. *Women and Madness* (New York: Avon, 1972).

CHESS, STELLA. "The 'Blame the Mother' Ideology," *International Journal of Mental Health* 11 (1982), 95–107.

CHODOROW, NANCY. *The Reproduction of Mothering: Psychoanalysis and the Sociology of Gender* (Berkeley: University of California Press, 1978).

COHN, MARTIN. "The Top Candidates to Replace Davis," Toronto *Star,* October 9, 1984, A17.

COLE, SUSAN. "Combatting the Practice of Pornography," *Broadside* 5 (10) (August/September 1984), 6.

DANIELL, ROSEMARY. *Fatal Flowers: On Sin, Sex, and Suicide in the Deep South* (New York: Avon, 1980).

DAVIDSON, T. "Wifebeating: A Recurring Phenomenon Throughout History." In M. Roy (Ed.), *Battered Women* (New York: Van Nostrand Reinhold, 1977), 2–23.

DENNIS, LYNNE. Personal communication, 1982.

DESOUSA, ALAN, and DESOUSA, D. A. "School Phobia," *Child Psychiatry Quarterly* 13 (1980), 98–103.

DESOUSA, RONALD B. Personal communication, 1984.

DEUTSCH, HELENE. *The Psychology of Women,* Vol. 1 (New York: Grune and Stratton, 1944).

DINNERSTEIN, DOROTHY. *The Mermaid and the Minotaur: Sexual Arrangements and Human Malaise* (New York: Harper Colophon, 1974).

DOWLING, COLETTE. *The Cinderella Complex: Women's Hidden Fear of Independence* (New York: Pocket Books, 1981).

DUTTON, DONALD. Lecture to Clarke Institute of Psychiatry, 1983.

DUTTON, DONALD, and PAINTER, SUSAN LEE. "Traumatic bonding: The Development of Emotional Attachments in Battered Women and Other Relationships of Intermittent Abuse," *Victimology: An International Journal* 6 (1981), 139–55.

EHRENREICH, BARBARA. *The Hearts of Men: American Dreams and the Flight from Commitment* (Garden City, N.Y.: Anchor, 1984).

EHRENREICH, BARBARA, and ENGLISH, DEIRDRE. *For Her Own Good: 150 Years of the Experts' Advice to Women* (Garden City, N.Y.: Anchor, 1979).

EISSLER, KURT. "Comments on Penis Envy and Orgasm in

Women," *Psychoanalytic Study of the Child* XXXII (New Haven: Yale University Press, 1977), 29–83.

ELLIS, HAVELOCK. *Love and Pain* (New York: Random House, 1942), 67, cited in Robin Ruth Linden, Darlene R. Pagano, Diana E. H. Russell, and Susan Leigh Star (Eds.), *Against Sadomasochism: A Radical Feminist Analysis* (East Palo Alto, CA: Frog in the Well, 1982), 56.

ERIKSON, ERIK H. *Childhood and Society* (New York: W. W. Norton, 1963).

———. "Sex Differences in the Play Configurations of Preadolescents," *American Journal of Orthopsychiatry* 21 (1951), 667–92.

———. "Womanhood and the Inner Space." In Jean Strouse (Ed.), *Women and Analysis: Dialogues on Psychoanalytic Views of Femininity* (New York: Dell, 1974), 333–64.

FAWCETT, FARRAH. "The Tonight Show" interview, September 27, 1984.

FREUD, SIGMUND. *Beyond the Pleasure Principle* (J. Strachey, Trans.) (New York: Bantam, 1959; original pub. 1920).

———. " 'A Child is Being Beaten': A Contribution to the Study of the Origin of Sexual Perversions." In J. Strachey (Ed.& Trans.), *The Standard Edition of the Complete Psychological Works of Sigmund Freud,* Vol. XVII (London: Hogarth, 1955), 179–204.

———. "The Economic Problem of Masochism." In J. Strachey (Ed. & Trans.), *The Standard Edition of the Complete Psychological Works of Sigmund Freud,* Vol. XIX (London: Hogarth, 1961; original pub. 1924), 159–70.

———. "The Most Prevalent Form of Degradation in Erotic Life." In Philip Rieff (Ed.), *Sexuality and the Psychology of Love* (New York: Collier, 1978; original pub. 1912), 58–70.

———. "Negation." In J. Strachey (Ed. & Trans.), *The*

Standard Edition of the Complete Psychological Works of Sigmund Freud, Vol. XIX (1961; original pub. 1925) 235–39.

FRIEDAN, BETTY. *The Feminine Mystique* (New York: Dell, 1963).

GALLAGHER, JANET. Fetal Rights Symposium presentation, National Women's Studies Association convention, Rutgers University, 1984.

GARNER, DAVID M.; GARFINKEL, PAUL E.; and OLMSTED, M. P. "An Overview of the Socio-cultural Factors in the Development of Anorexia Nervosa." In P. L. Darby, P. E. Garfinkel, David M. Garner, and D. V. Coscina (Eds.). *Anorexia Nervosa: Recent Developments* (New York: Alan R. Liss, 1983), 65–82.

GARNER, DAVID M.; GARFINKEL, PAUL E.; SCHWARTZ, D.; and THOMPSON, M. "Cultural Expectations of Thinness in Women," *Psychological Reports* 47 (1980), 483–91.

GEBHARD, PAUL. "Sadomasochism." In Thomas Weinberg and G. W. Levi Kamel (Eds.), *S & M: An Introduction to the Study of Sadomasochism* (Buffalo: Prometheus, 1983), 36–39.

GELLES, RICHARD. *The Violent Home* (Beverly Hills: Sage, 1972). " 'Get Out Before You Kill Him' Prisoner Urges Abused Women," Toronto *Star,* September 1, 1984, L2.

GIFFORD-JONES, W. "The Doctor Game," *The Journal* (Edmonton, Alberta), November 4, 1981, D1.

GILLIGAN, CAROL. *In a Different Voice: Psychological Theory and Women's Development* (Cambridge, MA: Harvard University Press, 1982).

GILMAN, IRENE. "An Object-relations Approach to the Phenomenon and Treatment of Battered Women," *Psychiatry* 43 (1980), 346–58.

GORBACH, SHERWOOD; ZIMMERMAN, DAVID; and WOODS, MARGO. *The Doctors' Anti-Breast-Cancer Diet* (New York: Simon and Schuster, 1984).

GORDON, BARBARA. *I'm Dancing as Fast as I Can* (New York: Bantam, 1979).

GREIF, GEOFFREY. Quoted in Ronna Kabatznick, "Nurture/Nature," *Ms. Magazine* (August 1984).

GRIFFIN, SUSAN. "Rape: The All-American Crime." In Mary Vetterling-Braggin, Frederick Elliston, and Jane English (Eds.), *Feminism and Philosophy* (Totowa, N.J.: Littlefield Adams & Co., 1977), 313–32.

GRINNELL, GRETCHEN. "Women, Depression, and the Folie à Deux." Presented to Women's Institute of American Orthopsychiatric Association convention, Toronto, 1984.

HALES, DIANE. "When Love Isn't Enough," *McCall's,* September 1984, 10–14.

HAMMER, SIGNE. "The Rape Fantasies of Women: Up From Disrepute," *Village Voice*, April 5, 1976, 10–12.

"The Hard Facts: Woman Today," *Second Century: Radcliffe News* (January 1984), 23.

HARRIS, ELIZABETH. "Sadomasochism: A Personal Experience." In Robin Ruth Linden, Darlene R. Pagano, Diana E.H. Russell, and Susan Leigh Star (Eds.), *Against Sadomasochism: A Radical Feminist Analysis* (East Palo Alto, CA.: Frog in the Well Press, 1982), 93–95.

HASKELL, MOLLY. "Rape Fantasy: The 2,000-Year-Old Misunderstanding," *Ms. Magazine,* November 1976, 84–96.

HEIN, HILDE. "Sadomasochism and the Liberal Tradition." In Robin Ruth Linden, Darlene R. Pagano, Diane E. H. Russell, and Susan Leigh Star (Eds.), *Against Sadomasochism: A Radical Feminist Analysis* (East Palo Alto, CA: Frog in the Well Press, 1982), 83–89.

HENLEY, NANCY. *Body Politics: Power, Sex, and Nonverbal Communication* (Englewood Cliffs, N.J.: Prentice-Hall, 1977).

HERRON, MARY JANE, and HERRON, WILLIAM G. "Meanings of Sadism and Masochism," *Psychological Reports* 50 (1982), 199–202.

HETHERINGTON, E. MAVIS; COX, MARTHA; and COX, ROGER. "Family Interaction and the Social, Emotional, and Cognitive Development of Children Following Divorce." In V. Vaughn and T. Brazelton (Eds.), *The Family: Setting Priorities* (New York: Science and Medicine, 1979).

HILBERMAN, ELAINE. "Overview: The 'Wife-beater's Wife' Reconsidered," *American Journal of Psychiatry* 137 (1980), 1336–47.

HILL, R. W.; LANGEVIN, R.; PAITICH, D.; HANDY, L.; RUSSON, A.; and WILKINSON, L. "Is Arson an Aggressive Act or a Property Offence? A Controlled Study of Psychiatric Referrals," *Canadian Journal of Psychiatry* 27 (1982), 648–54.

HITE, SHERE. *The Hite Report: A Nationwide Study of Female Sexuality* (New York: Dell, 1976).

———. *The Hite Report on Male Sexuality* (New York: Ballantine, 1981).

HORNER, MATINA S. "Toward an Understanding of Achievement-related Conflicts in Women," *Journal of Social Issues* 28 (1972), 157–75.

HORNEY, KAREN. *New Ways of Psychoanalysis* (New York: W. W. Norton, 1939). (Cited in Reik, p. 74.)

HURST, LYNDA. "The Public Must Be Re-educated on Pornography," Toronto *Star,* December 11, 1984, F1.

JONEL, MARISSA. "Letter from a Former Masochist." In Robin Ruth Linden, Darlene R. Pagano, Diana E. H. Russell, and Susan Leigh Star (Eds.), *Against Sadomasochism: A Radical Feminist Analysis* (East Palo Alto, CA.: Frog in the Well Press, 1982), 16–22.

KABATZNICK, RONNA. "Nurture/Nature," *Ms. Magazine,* August 1984, 76, 78, 102.

KATZ-ROTHMAN, BARBARA. Fetal Rights Symposium presentation, National Women's Studies Association convention. Rutgers University, 1984.

KAUFMAN, IRVING; PECK, ALICE L.; and TAGUIRI, CONSUELO L.

"The Family Constellation and Overt Incestuous Relations Between Father and Daughter," *American Journal of Orthopsychiatry* 24 (1954), 266–79.

KENNEDY, FLO. Lecture to "The Issue Is Choice" benefit evening, Toronto, November 1983.

KLEIMAN, CAROL. "My Home Is Not Broken, It Works," *Ms. Magazine*, November 1984, 154.

KORE, CLEA ELFI. "Decadence and the Feminine: The Case of Leopold von Sacher-Masoch," Ph.D. dissertation (Stanford University, 1983).

KRAFFT-EBING, RICHARD VON. *Psychopathia Sexualis: A Medico-forensic Study* (New York: Pioneer, 1950; original pub. 1901).

KREPS, BONNIE. "The Case Against Pornography," *Homemaker's Magazine,* June 1982, 7–22.

LANDERS, ANN. letters to. In Toronto *Star,* May 16, 1984, D24; June 4, 1984, C3; July 23, 1984, C2; and October 17, 1984, D21.

LAURA X. Personal communication. June 1984.

LAWTON-SPEERT, SARAH, and WACHTEL, ANDY. *Child Sexual Abuse in the Family: A Review of Trends in the Literature. Child Sexual Abuse Project Working Paper Two* (Vancouver, B.C.: Social Planning and Research, United Way of the Lower Mainland, April 1982).

LAZERSON, JUDITH. "Voices of Bulimia: Experiences in Integrated Psychotherapy," *Psychotherapy: Theory, Research, and Practice,* in press.

LENZER, GERTRUD. "On Masochism: A Contribution to the History of a Phantasy and Its Theory," *Signs* 1 (1975), 277–324.

LERNER, LEILA (Ed.). *Masochism and the Emergent Ego: Selected Papers of Esther Menaker, Ph.D.* (New York: Human Sciences, 1979).

LINDEN, ROBIN RUTH; PAGANO, DARLENE R.; RUSSELL, DIANA E. H.; and STAR, SUSAN LEIGH (Eds.). *Against Sadomas-*

ochism: A Radical Feminist Analysis (East Palo Alto, CA: Frog in the Well Press, 1982).

LORDE, AUDRE. *Sister Outsider* (Trumansburg, N.Y.: The Crossing Press, 1984).

LUCY, JUICY. "If I Ask You to Tie Me Up, Will You Still Want to Love Me?" In SAMOIS (pub. and ed.), *Coming to Power: Writings and Graphics on Lesbian S/M*, 2nd ed. (1982).

MARCUS, MARIA. *A Taste for Pain: On Masochism and Female Sexuality* (New York: St. Martin's Press, 1981).

MARTIN, D. *Battered Wives* (San Francisco: Volcano, 1976).

———. "Battered Women: Society's Problem." In J. Chapman and M. Gates (Eds.), *The Victimization of Women* (Beverly Hills: Sage, 1978).

MASSON, JEFFREY. *The Assault on Truth: Freud's Suppression of the Seduction Theory* (New York: Farrar, Straus, & Giroux, 1984).

MCCLELLAND, DAVID. "The Harlequin Complex." In Robert White (Ed.), *A Study of Lives* (New York: Atherton, 1963), 94–119.

MEARS, JAN. Seminar on Women for Centre for Investigative Journalism, Toronto, November 24, 1984.

MENDELSOHN, ROBERT. *Malepractice: How Doctors Manipulate Women* (Chicago: Contemporary Books, 1982).

MILFORD, NANCY. *Zelda: A Biography* (New York: Harper & Row, 1970).

MILLER, CASEY, and SWIFT, KATE. *Words and Women* (Garden City, N.Y.: Anchor, 1977).

MILLER, JEAN BAKER. *Toward a New Psychology of Women* (Boston: Beacon, 1976).

———. "Women and Power," No. 82-01 in Work in Progress Series of the Stone Center of Wellesley College, Wellesley, MA., 1982.

MORGAN, KATHRYN PAULY. "Women and Moral Madness." Presented to Canadian Society for Women in Philosophy, Montreal, November 1984, and to Centre for Women's Studies in Education, Ontario Institute for Studies in Education, Toronto, January 1985.

MORGAN, MARABEL. *The Total Woman* (New York: Simon and Schuster, 1973).

MORGAN, ROBIN. "The Politics of Sadomasochistic Fantasies." In Robin Ruth Linden, Darlene R. Pagano, Diana E. H. Russell, and Susan Leigh Star (Eds.). *Against Sadomasochism: A Radical Feminist Analysis* (East Palo Alto, CA.: Frog in the Well Press, 1982), 109–23.

MOULTON, RUTH. "A Survey and Reevaluation of the Concept of Penis Envy." In J. B. Miller (Ed.), *Psychoanalysis and Women* (New York: Penguin, 1978), 240–58.

Ms. Magazine Issue on "Our Bodies," May 1984.

MUSSEN, PAUL HENRY; CONGER, JOHN JANEWAY; and KAGAN, JEROME. *Child Development and Personality* (New York: Harper & Row, 1963).

MYERS, MICHAEL F. "Homosexuality, Sexual Dysfunction, and Incest in Male Identical Twins," *Canadian Journal of Psychiatry* 27 (1982), 144–47.

New Webster's Dictionary of the English Language (Delair, 1981).

NEWMAN, FRANCES, and CAPLAN, PAULA J. "Juvenile Female Prostitution as Gender-Consistent Response to Early Deprivation," *International Journal of Women's Studies* 5 (1982), 128–37.

NICHOLS, BEVERLY B. "The Abused Wife Problem," *Social Casework* 57 (1976), 27–32.

NICHOLS, JEANETTE; PAGANO, DARLENE; and ROSOFF, MARGARET. "Is Sadomasochism Feminist? A Critique of the Samois Position." In Robin Ruth Linden, Darlene R. Pagano, Diana E. H. Russell, and Susan Leigh Star (Eds.), *Against Sadomasochism: A Radical Feminist Analysis* (East Palo Alto, CA.: Frog in the Well Press, 1982), 137–46.

NIELSEN, JOHANNES; BJARNASON, SVERRIR; FRIEDRICH, UR-
SULA; FROLAND, ANDERS; HANSEN, VIGGO H.; and SO-
RENSEN, ANDREAS. "Klinefelter's Syndrome in Children," *Journal of Child Psychology and Psychiatry* 11
(1970), 109–19.

ORBACH, SUSIE. "Social Dimension in Compulsive Eating
Women," *Psychotherapy: Theory, Research, and Practice* 15 (1978), 180.

Oxford English Dictionary, A Supplement to the, Vol. II.
R. W. Burchfield (Ed.) (Oxford: Clarendon, 1976).

PARKIN, ALAN. "On Masochistic Enthralment: A Contribution to the Study of Moral Masochism," *International
Journal of Psychoanalysis* 61 (1980), 307–14.

PAVENSTEDT, ELEANOR. Discussion at end of Irving Kaufman, Alice L. Peck, and Consuelo L. Taguiri, "The
Family Constellation and Overt Incestuous Relations Between Father and Daughter," *American Journal of Orthopsychiatry* 24 (1954), 266–79.

PENFOLD, P. SUSAN, and WALKER, GILLIAN A. *Women and the
Psychiatric Paradox* (Montreal: Eden Press, 1983).

PHELPS, LINDA. "Female Sexual Alienation." In Jo Freeman
(Ed.), *Women: A Feminist Perspective,* 2nd ed. (Palo
Alto, CA.: Mayfield, 1979), 18–26.

PIERCE, CHRISTINE. "Natural Law Language and Women."
In Vivian Gornick and Barbara K. Moran (Eds.), *Woman
in Sexist Society* (New York: New American Library,
1971), 242–58.

POGASH, CAROL. "Real Live Dolls," *Redbook,* June 1984, 91–
93.

POGREBIN, LETTY COTTIN. *Growing Up Free: Raising Your
Child in the 80s* (New York: Bantam, 1980).

POPE, ALEXANDER. "An Essay on Man." In M. H. Abrams
(Gen. Ed.), *The Norton Anthology of English Literature,*
Vol. 1 (New York: W. W. Norton, 1962), 1469–76.

Random House Dictionary of the English Language: The Un-abridged Edition (New York: Random House, 1967).

REICH, WILHELM. *Character Analysis,* 3rd ed. (New York: Simon and Schuster, 1972).

REIK, THEODOR. *Masochism in Modern Man,* Margaret H. Beigel and Gertrud M. Kurth (Trans.) (New York: Farrar, Straus, & Co, 1941).

RICH, ADRIENNE. *Twenty-One Love Poems* (Emeryville, CA.: Effie's Press, 1977).

ROBERTIELLO, ROBERT. "Masochism and the Female Sexual Role," *The Journal of Sex Research* 6 (1970), 56–58.

RODGERS, JOANN ELLISON, and CATALDO, MICHAEL F. *Raising Sons: Practical Strategies for Single Mothers* (New York: New American Library, 1984).

ROTHMAN, ERICA, and MUNSON, KIT. "Family Violence Treatment Groups." Presented to Women's Institute of American Orthopsychiatric Association convention, Toronto, 1984.

RUITENBEEK, HENDRIK. *Psychoanalysis and Female Sexuality* (New Haven: College and University Press, 1966).

RUSH, FLORENCE. *The Best Kept Secret: Sexual Abuse of Children* (New York: Prentice-Hall, 1980).

RUSSELL, DIANA E. H. *Rape in Marriage* (New York: Collier, 1982).

SAMOIS (Pub. and ed.). *Coming to Power: Writings and Graphics on Lesbian S/M,* 2nd ed. (1982).

SCHREINER, OLIVE. *The Story of an African Farm* (New York: Penguin, 1983).

SCHWARZER, ALICE. *After the Second Sex: Conversations with Simone de Beauvoir* (Marianne Howarth, Trans.) (New York: Pantheon, 1984).

SHAINESS, NATALIE. *Sweet Suffering: Woman as Victim* (New York: Bobbs-Merrill, 1984).

———. "Vulnerability to Violence: Masochism as Process," *American Journal of Psychotherapy* 33 (1979), 174–89.

SHERMAN, JULIA. "Commentary," *Signs* 1 (1975), 1007–1009.

SIEGEL, RACHEL JOSEFOWITZ. "Change and Creativity at Midlife." In Joan Hamerman Robbins and Rachel Josefowitz Siegel (Eds.), *Women Changing Therapy: New Assessments, Values, and Strategies in Feminist Therapy* (New York: Haworth, 1983), 95–102.

SIGAL, JOHN J. "Effects of Paternal Exposure to Prolonged Stress on the Mental Health of the Spouse and Children," *Canadian Psychiatric Association Journal* 21 (1976), 169–72.

SILVERMAN, MARTIN. "Cognitive Development and Female Psychology," *Journal of the American Psychoanalytic Association* 29 (1981), 581–605.

SMITH, RONALD E., and SHARPE, THEODORE M. "Treatment of a School Phobia with Implosive Therapy," *Journal of Consulting and Clinical Psychology* 35 (1970), 239–42.

SNORTUM, JOHN A.; HANNA, THOMAS E.; and MILLS, DAVID H. "The Relationship of Self-concept and Parent Image to Rule Violation in a Women's Prison," *Journal of Clinical Psychology* 26 (1970), 284–87.

SPENGLER, ANDREAS. "Manifest Sadomasochism of Males." In Thomas Weinberg and G. W. Levi Kamel (Eds.), *S & M: Studies in Sadomasochism* (Buffalo: Prometheus, 1983), 57–72.

STAR, BARBARA. "Comparing Battered and Non-battered Women," *Victimology: An International Journal* 3 (1978), 32–44.

STARK, R., and MCEVOY, J. "Middle-class Violence," *Psychology Today* 4 (November 1970), 52–65.

STARK-ADAMEC, CANNIE, and ADAMEC, ROBERT. "Aggression By Men Against Women: Adaptation or Aberration?" *International Journal of Women's Studies* 5 (1982), 1–21.

STEIN, MARTIN M. (Reporter of panel). "The Problem of Masochism in the Theory and Technique of Psychoanalysis," *Journal of the American Psychoanalytic Association* 4 (1956), 526–38.

STEINEM, GLORIA. *Outrageous Acts and Everyday Rebellions* (New York: Holt, Rinehart and Winston, 1983).

STOLOROW, ROBERT D. "The Narcissistic Function of Masochism (and Sadism)," *International Journal of Psychoanalysis* 56 (1975), 441–48.

STYRON, WILLIAM. *Sophie's Choice* (New York: Bantam, 1979).

SURREY, JANET. "The Relational Self in Women," No. 82-02 in Work in Progress Series of Stone Center of Wellesley College, Wellesley, MA., 1983.

SYMONDS, ALEXANDRA. "Violence Against Women—The Myth of Masochism," *Journal of American Psychotherapy* 33 (1979), 161–73.

THIBAUT, J. W., and KELLEY, H. H. *Interpersonal Relations: A Theory of Interdependence* (New York: Wiley, 1978).

THOMPSON, CLARA. *On Women* (New York: New American Library, 1964).

UPDIKE, JOHN. *The Witches of Eastwick* (New York: Alfred A. Knopf, 1984).

VALENSTEIN, ARTHUR. Quoted in Arnold M. Cooper (Chair), Newell Fischer (Reporter), "Masochism: Current Concepts," *Journal of the American Psychoanalytic Association* 29 (1981), 673–88.

VINCZE, EVA. "Wifebeating: The Private Crime." Presented to National Women's Studies Association convention, Rutgers University, 1984.

WAGNER, SALLY ROESCH. "Pornography and the Sexual Revolution: The Backlash of Sadomasochism." In Robin Ruth Linden, Darlene R. Pagano, Diana E. H. Russell, and Susan Leigh Star (Eds.), *Against Sadomasochism: A Radical Feminist Analysis* (East Palo Alto, CA.: Frog in the Well Press, 1982), 23–44.

WAITES, ELIZABETH A. "Female Masochism and the Enforced Restriction of Choice," *Victimology: An International Journal* 2 (1977–78), 535–44.

———. "Fixing Women: Devaluation, Idealization, and the Female Fetish," *Journal of the American Psychoanalytic Association* 30 (1982), 435–59.

WALTON-ALLEN, NICOLE. "Laypeople's Perceptions of Family Violence: An Examination of Stereotyped Learning," M.A. thesis (Ontario Institute for Studies in Education, Toronto, 1984).

———. Personal communication, 1984.

WALTON-ALLEN, NICOLE, and CAPLAN, PAULA J. "Laypeople's Perceptions of Spouse Abuse." Presented to University of Toronto Psychiatry Research Day, 1984.

WATERS, HARRY F., with LUCY HOWARD. " 'This Morning's' Rising Star," *Newsweek,* May 24, 1984, 83.

WEINBERG, THOMAS S. "Sadism and Masochism: Sociological Perspectives." In Thomas Weinberg and G. W. Levi Kamel (Eds.), *S & M: An Introduction to the Study of Sadomasochism* (Buffalo: Prometheus, 1983), 99–112.

WELDON, FAY. *Female Friends* (London: Pan Books, 1977).

WILSON, E. O. *Sociobiology: The New Synthesis* (Cambridge, MA.: Harvard University Press, 1975).

WINE, JERI DAWN; MOSES, BARBARA; and SMYE, MARTI DIANE. "Female Superiority in Sex Difference Competence Comparisons: A Review of the Literature." In Cannie Stark-Adamec (Ed.), *Sex Roles: Origins, Influences, and Implications for Women* (Montreal: Eden Press Women's Publications, 1980), 176–86.

WOLLSTONECRAFT, MARY. *Vindication of the Rights of Women* (Harmondsworth, Middlesex, England: Penguin, 1982; original pub. 1792).

YEGER, TRUDI, and MIEZITIS, SOLVEIGA. "Pupil Sex as It Relates to the Pupil-teacher Dependency Relationship," In press in Paula J. Caplan (Ed.), *Sex Roles II: Feminist Psychology in Transition* (Montreal: Eden Press).

Index